The Making of

The Making
of
South East Asia

by

G. CŒDÈS

Director of the Ecole française d'Extrême-Orient,
Member of the Institut de France,
Corresponding F.B.A.

Translated *by*

H. M. WRIGHT

University of California Press
Berkeley and Los Angeles · 1969

Translated from the French
LES PEUPLES DE LA PÉNINSULE INDOCHINOISE
© Dunod, Paris, 1962

University of California Press
Berkeley and Los Angeles, California

English translation
©H. M. Wright, 1966

Third printing, 1969
Library of Congress Catalogue
Card Number: 66–4402

Printed in the United States of America

Introduction

DURING THE PAST FIFTEEN YEARS a number of general works on the history of South East Asia and of more specialized histories of Indochina have appeared.[1] In most of them, the first fifteen centuries are dismissed in a few chapters, or even a few pages, as a sort of preamble to the following five centuries, which are treated from a European rather than from an Asian point of view – let alone from the standpoint of an individual Asian country. Moreover only a few pages are devoted to the origins and prehistory of the peoples of Indochina and Indonesia and to the nature of their contacts with the two great Asian civilizations – the Indian and the Chinese.

By way of contrast, my history of 'The Hinduized States of Indochina and Indonesia' (*Les États Hindouisés d'Indochine et d'Indonésie*)[2] ends with the taking of Malacca by the Portuguese in 1511, and deliberately ignores later events. I know of no work in which a balance is struck between the account given of the events prior to this date and the account of those that followed.

It is this lack which the following pages attempt to remedy. The area covered is restricted to the Indochinese peninsula, to the exclusion of the Malay Peninsula and Indonesia. The relations between Indonesia and Indochina were never as close or as historically important as the relations the Indochinese States had with each other, and the two areas followed separate paths of development because of the greater impact of Islam on Indonesia, and because Europeans arrived and started colonizing there earlier than on the continent. As for the Malay Peninsula, its early history – of which, incidentally, little is known – is closely linked with that of Indonesia, with which it is to some extent related geographically.

So here only Indochina, in the sense of the Indochinese peninsula (the 'India beyond the Ganges' of the ancient world), will come into question – a 'crossroads'[3] where the most diverse racial groups came into contact with each other and mixed with each other, and where since ancient times the two main civilizations of Asia have confronted each other. In Indochina these civilizations were transformed, in varying degrees, through contact with the indigenous societies, and the civilizations resulting from this contact reacted upon each other and were subsequently enriched or changed by later influences from abroad, such as Buddhism from Ceylon, and European civilization.

These Indochinese civilizations display great variety, but have a number of features in common. There is a 'unity in diversity' – to quote an old Indonesian saying inscribed by a Vietnamese writer at the beginning of his *Histoire de l'Asie du Sud-Est* ('History of South East Asia')[4] – which, in the linguistic field for instance, can be seen in a certain 'family resemblance' acquired by languages which were originally of different stock; or, in the legal sphere, in the survival over the centuries of certain general trends which have withstood the changes brought about by foreign influences.

The birth and development of the Indochinese civilizations can only be understood if seen in the light of certain geographical facts, certain prehistorical and ethnological data, and certain historical events such as wars, conquests, internal revolutions, and the repercussions of large-scale upheavals in neighbouring countries. It was Ch'in Shih-huang-ti's policy of commercial expansion which gave rise to Chinese colonization of the Red River delta, and it was the Mongol conquests which brought about the consummation of the decline of Indian cultural influence and the ruin of the old Indianized kingdoms. On the other hand, and whatever some people may say, the course of political and cultural history has been influenced or directed into certain channels by forceful personalities such as Aniruddha of Burma, Jayavarman VII of Cambodia, and Rama Khamheng of Thailand. Hence a large part of the present work consists of the kind of history known as *histoire événementielle* or the 'history of events'.

I am fully aware that history of this kind, with its enumeration of kings, wars, and changes of frontier, and its descriptions of customs at Court and among the ruling classes, is no more than a skeleton that lacks both body and soul, since it gives no account of the social environment, of popular customs and beliefs, of economic trends and social changes, or of the hidden forces which threw up the powerful personalities. But unfortunately we are not yet in a position, it seems to me, to fill in the picture in this way with any degree of accuracy, because we do not yet know enough about Indochina's past. Research in this field has been conducted for less than a century by a very small number of people, and they can scarcely be blamed for having followed the example of the Renaissance philologists and humanists in making the collection and publication of both textual and archaeological source material their first task, and proceeding from there to use the material for establishing a valid chronological framework. Only now can the possibility be envisaged of using the material for other purposes – namely, for providing sociological and economic data with which to fill in the framework and present a more complete picture.[5]

I thought it might facilitate the task of future research workers if I were to sift out the information at present available about the main events and historical personages which stand out like landmarks in the national histories of the Indochinese States, and try to introduce some order into it, straightening out the confused tangle of events and clarifying some of the obscurities, while at the same time highlighting the discussion with a few ideas concerning the institutions, religions, arts, and other cultural aspects in so far as these are known. This book, which is intended for the general public rather than for specialists, may therefore be regarded as a sort of outline sketch indicating the lines on which a future balanced history of Indochina might be planned.

I hope I may be excused for having included in it material taken from my book *Les États Hindouisés d'Indochine et d'Indonésie* and from several of my earlier works. But if some of the material is the same, the treatment is different. There is a much fuller discussion here of the geographical framework, and of the origins of the people of Indochina and their location during prehistoric times, than in my book on the Indianized States, and I have continued my account here well beyond the taking of Malacca. I have also included the history of Viet-nam, which had no place in a work devoted to the Indianized countries, and about which I have no specialized knowledge. Another difference in treatment is in the manner of giving an account of events. Instead of taking the history of Indochina as a whole and cutting it into horizontal slices, each corresponding to a given historical period within which the history of the various States was treated synchronically,

Introduction

I have used a diachronic method here, except when recounting the events of the thirteenth century. Because every country experienced the same profound break in continuity at that time, these events have been treated synchronically in a chapter which comes in the middle of the other chapters, each of which gives a continuous narrative of events in one country only. To remedy the lack of balance deplored above between the amount of space given by recent publications to the seven centuries prior to the thirteenth century and the amount devoted to the six centuries after it, I have given a very much abridged account of events during the later period, these being in any case better known to the general public than the events of the earlier period. In particular, I have reduced to a strict minimum all mention of the role of the West in South East Asia, since this had far more important repercussions on European affairs than on the political and cultural history of the Indochinese States, at least as far as the period prior to the beginning of colonization in the nineteenth century is concerned. Lastly, I have laid stress on the most characteristic period in the history of each country, or the one in which its civilization reached its highest point, and I have endeavoured to trace as accurately as possible the influences undergone or exerted by each country.

Perhaps it would have been wiser 'to content oneself once more with the publication and translation of texts . . . but, if only for educational purposes, the task of writing syntheses – general histories consisting of a chronicle of events seasoned with a certain amount of critical comment and arranged in some sort of logical order – is one that must not be shirked.' (Gaudefroy-Demombynes.)

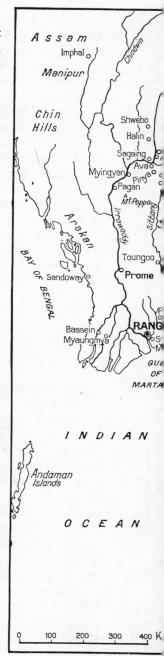

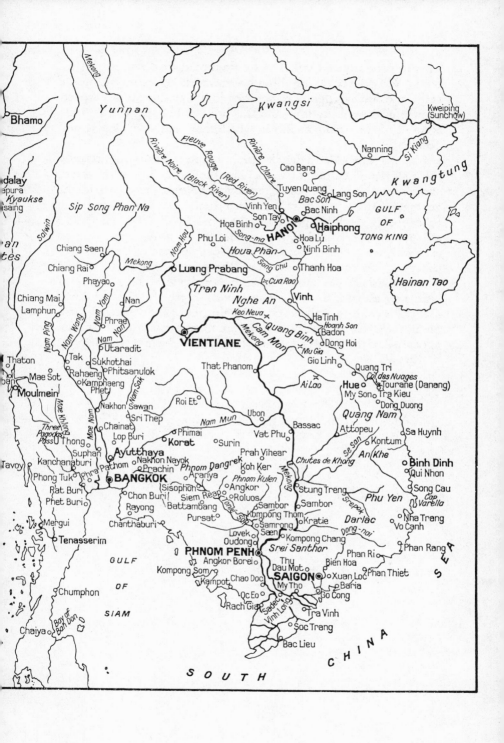

This is precisely the task I have attempted to carry out in this book. We do not, in my opinion, have enough documentation yet to warrant an attempt to describe in full all the various aspects of each of the civilizations, but this book at least provides a brief account of the circumstances in which they arose, developed, and declined.

I have not included a detailed bibliography of works concerning the history and culture of Indochina. Bibliographies of this kind, some more and some less comprehensive, will be found in the general works on these subjects mentioned below in note 1 (the fullest being the bibliography in the work by D. G. E. Hall), and also in the specialized bibliographies.[6] The notes appended to each chapter refer to works dealing with points of detail, or to others which have appeared since the general works mentioned were published. To some extent they provide a bibliography of works specializing in the subjects with which the chapter deals. General works on each of the five countries of Indochina (Burma, Siam, Laos, Cambodia, Viet-nam) are mentioned in the first note appended to the three chapters of Part III and the first two chapters of Part V.

Translator's Note

THE INTRODUCTION concludes with explanations of a number of points concerning spelling, transcriptions, etc., which do not entirely apply to the translation. It explains that, since the book is intended for the general public rather than for specialists, a simplified spelling of proper names was adopted. In the translation the spelling has been still further simplified. All diacritical signs have been omitted in the transcription of Sanskrit and Vietnamese names and words. The only diacritical signs employed are those retained in the simplified version of the Wade-Giles romanization of Chinese which has here been substituted for the French form of romanization. The spelling of Vietnamese words and names used in the French text was based on that used by M. Lê Thành Khôi in his book *Le Viêt-nam*. This, except for the omission of diacritical signs, has been followed in the translation, and so has the spelling of words and names in the other Indochinese languages.

Geographical names follow current English usage, including the retention of French names for some Indochinese geographical features (such as the Col des Nuages). Vientiane is written Vieng Chan, as in the French text, in passages referring to its early history.

In the French text words of Indian origin are written in their romanized Sanskrit form wherever this can be reconstructed with reasonable certainty, so as to preserve some uniformity with the early history of other areas in which the Indian written form of the word is the only one known. The local pronunciation is written in brackets after the first appearance of the word. (Thus Sukhodaya, not Sukhothai, is used throughout to refer to the first Siamese kingdom.) This practice has been followed in the translation.

Contents

Contents

Illustrations

PART ONE

---

*The Pattern of Settlement
in Indochina*

I

The Geographical Framework

THE PRELIMINARY TASKS for a study of the Indochinese civilizations consist firstly in getting to know something about the geographical framework, and secondly in surveying the prehistoric and ethnological data likely to throw light on the social environment which gave rise to them.

In dealing with the first of these tasks it is unnecessary to undertake a description of the physical geography of Indochina, for this can be found in the relevant geographical textbooks.[1] But, disregarding the present pattern of settlement, we should have a look at the map and try to discover which regions were most favourable for human habitation, or rather which regions offered the best choice from which man could select one where he would be able to deploy the means and techniques at his disposal for supplying his basic needs. Next, we must find out why some regions lent themselves better than others for the development of a centralized State based on the organized exploitation of the area by the peoples settled there. Lastly, we must investigate the natural lines of communication which could serve as channels for external influences and internal culture contacts.

Indochina lies within the tropical zone,[2] where countries are proverbially endowed with natural riches and fertile soil, although the riches and the fertility are perhaps more illusory than real. The only way of ensuring a supply of cereals abundant enough to provide the staple diet of an expanding population is to practise irrigated rice cultivation. Once a population of sedentary agriculturalists becomes established, it can evolve a social organization which enables it to cultivate every inch of the soil and obtain complete control over the natural environment, thus turning a naturally insalubrious terrain into a healthy one. For example, the Red River delta was well placed geographically for settlement by a people from outside the tropical zone who were familiar with the agricultural techniques suitable for this area, and it became the cradle of a race of peasants[3] and then the centre from which they thrust southwards in a dynamic process of expansion.

THE SOIL

Generally speaking, the Indochinese peninsula has soil of rather poor quality, and the only areas suitable for agriculture – which in this particular instance means wet rice cultivation – are the deltas of the main rivers (the Red River, the Mekong, the Menam, the Salween, and the Irrawaddy) and the plains bordering their middle reaches, the coastal plains on the China Sea, and the Tonle Sap basin. Of these, the Tonle Sap basin, being a self-contained territorial unit with the required natural features, was best fitted to become the area of settlement for a homogeneous population of sedentary agriculturalists and to give rise to a civilization based on a centralized State.[4]

The mountainous regions and the high plateaux were too dry to permit of anything but slash-and-burn cultivation, and this entails a form of semi-nomadism which is incompatible with the founding of a centralized State and the development of a civilization capable of reaching the higher stages. As for the famous 'red soil' areas so much coveted in modern times, the soil there does not have the fertility that was required for the development of the early civilizations and is only suitable for the cultivation of recently imported crops such as tea, coffee, cotton, and rubber (hevea), so these areas need not be taken into account when considering the possibilities open to the first settlers.

In these circumstances, one would not expect to find large-scale settlement such as would lead to the rise of civilized States in any areas except the deltas and the other favourable regions. But the first settlers, or at least the first of whom traces have been found, seem for the most part to have preferred to inhabit the caves and natural shelters provided by limestone formations rather than the plains and the deltas, which, before they had been drained and brought under cultivation, must have been extremely unhealthy. These earliest inhabitants relied on hunting and fishing to supply their needs, and found plentiful supplies of game and above all of fish. For while the soil of Indochina is poor except in the areas mentioned, both its salt and its fresh waters provide an inexhaustible supply of food. The Tonle Sap or Great Lake of Cambodia is full of fish, not to mention the shellfish which prehistoric peoples found so easy to collect and to which they were so addicted; and the supply of fish from the sea is amply attested by the accounts of the ancient geographers, who mention the ichthyophagous peoples of the 'India beyond the Ganges', and by the account of the Franciscan monk Odoric de Pordonone, who visited Champa in 1320, and who relates how all the many fish inhabiting the in-shore waters of the China Sea came once a year 'to pay their respects to the king of this country'.

CLIMATE

Indochina enjoys a tropical climate in which a hot, dry season alternates with a rainy one. This type of climate with its sharply contrasted and on the whole fairly regular seasons is due to the phenomenon of the monsoon, the mechanism of which is so well known that there is no need to describe it here. There is a great difference between the climate of the tropical south and that of the subtropical north. The contrast is in part due to the difference in latitude, but also to the difference in altitude between the low-lying lands in the south and the mountainous regions in the north. Throughout the whole of the northern part of the peninsula one has the impression of being as it were on the shores of an ocean from which from time to time a flood-tide comes in from the north, bringing positively wintry weather. This creates very different conditions, affecting food, clothing, and types of dwelling, from those in the south.

3

HABITABILITY

Indochina participates in the general unhealthiness of all tropical climates. If, in spite of this, prosperous States have been successfully founded there, this is due to the climatic improvements brought about by cultivation of the soil. So close is the connection between healthy climatic conditions and the presence of man, that in the case of a region which archaeological evidence proves to have been once inhabited but which is now deserted and uninhabitable, the question arises as to whether the people who inhabited it were forced to leave because the region was unhealthy, or whether on the contrary the region became unhealthy because historical events caused the inhabitants to abandon it. In a country with a naturally unhealthy climate, it is those regions where the quality of the soil has induced men to settle there that are the first to be made healthy through cultivation of the soil, and that then become centres for population expansion. The quality of their soil, through man's intervention, makes it possible for these regions to become fit for human habitation, and it is these two factors in conjunction that give rise to the kind of stable society that will eventually attain a high degree of social organization.

What all this amounts to is that the mountains and plateaux, where there are quite a number of traces of early inhabitation, were either destined to remain the habitat of social groups which had neither the will nor the opportunity to descend upon the plains and the deltas, or else to become the refuge of social groups which were pushed back there by developing societies of sedentary agriculturalists. Both types of social group were able to support themselves there by hunting, gathering, or slash-and-burn cultivation. By contrast, the plains and the deltas are for the most part suitable for wet rice cultivation, which gives two harvests per annum; and in some places this is combined with the cultivation of dry crops, for which the lower river valleys, annually enriched by fertilizing silt, offer a choice terrain.

Thus it was the plains and the deltas of Indochina that were destined to become the areas of settlement for agriculturalists who were then able to proliferate owing to the climatic improvement brought about by cultivation of the soil. The cultivation of the soil entailed drainage and irrigation, both of which are in the nature of public works carried out by, and in the interests of, the

4

community as a whole, and this led to a form of centralized social organization which was the initial step towards a centralized State.

The east coast of the peninsula, along which a north-to-south marine current runs, is much exposed to winds. It is a somewhat forbidding coast, being muddy in the Gulf of Tongking and at the mouth of the Mekong, and rocky in between. The modern ports of Haiphong and Saigon are inland ports; sheltered bays, such as the bay of Tourane (Danang), are few; and the only deep-water anchorages are those in the bays of Along and Camranh – but this is of no importance except for modern shipping. Even in ancient times, however, the China Sea coast of Indochina is not likely to have been a normal means of access for the importation of foreign influences. Its roadsteads and havens mainly served as ports of call for coastal shipping used by merchants in the coastwise trade.

By contrast, the western coast of Indochina on the Gulf of Siam offered easy access to boats coming from various parts of the Malay Peninsula that lies on the opposite side of the gulf, and the narrowness of this peninsula enabled merchants to 'break bulk' – that is, to trans-ship merchandise coming from India and the West, which could be easily done by unloading on the western coast and then reloading on the eastern coast for transportation to Indochina.

As for that part of the western coast of Indochina lying on the Gulf of Bengal, it has a number of good havens, the possession of which has been a never-ending subject of dispute between the States controlling the lower valley of the Menam on the one hand, and those controlling the lower valley of the Irrawaddy on the other.

While access to Indochina is in some places difficult by sea routes, the same cannot be said of land routes, for its land frontiers are not so much natural as historically determined – except in the west, where the Arakan mountains constitute a barrier between Assam and the valleys of the Irrawaddy and the Chindwin which is easier to go round, either to the north or to the south, than to cross.

In the north, the frontier between Indochina and China could scarcely be less impregnable, and it has always been difficult to defend, whether from Viet-nam or from Laos and Burma. The Red River valley is the natural means of access to Yunnan, and this accounts for the French settlement in Tongking. From the other side of the frontier, Chinese expansion in the Red River delta was facilitated by the ease of communications between the Red River and the West River valleys, for the Lang-son and Cao-bang rivers are tributaries of the Si Kiang or West River, which flows through Kwangsi and enters the sea below Canton.

Again, the valley of the Irrawaddy has always been a natural line of communication between Yunnan and the Burmese plain, and was the traditional route for Chinese troops invading Burma. There are a number of possible routes across the region occupied by the Shan States, which is traversed by the Salween, and during the last war the main supply route to China was constructed in the northern part of this region, after the Japanese had cut off communications by sea and by the Red River route.

INTERNAL COMMUNICATIONS

In eastern Indochina there are a number of what might be described as natural frontiers, and these make communications difficult between the regions separated by them. To the east, the mountain range that used to be known as the Annamite Chain, and to the west another mountain range which is a continuation of the mountain system of the Shan States that extends as far as the Malay Peninsula, make communication difficult between the valley of the Mekong and the China Sea coast on the one hand, and between the valley of the Menam and the Gulf of Bengal coast on the other. The more easterly of these ranges has passes lying at an altitude of over 3,000 feet at the head of the valleys of the Black River, the Song Ma and the Song Ca, in the northern part of the range. Farther south communications are less difficult. The Tran-ninh plateau can be reached via Cua Rao, and from the Nghe-an plain on the Mekong the Cam-mon plateau can be crossed via the Ha-trai and Keo Nua passes, at an altitude of 2,164 feet, or, a little farther south, via the Mu Gia pass, at an altitude of 1,370 feet. Lastly, the Ai Lao pass, the gateway to Laos, at an altitude of 1,344 feet, provides an easy means of communication between Quang-tri and the reach of the Mekong north of the Kemmarat rapids. All these passes have played an important role in the history of the relations between the Vietnamese, the Khmers, the Chams, and the Laotians.

The mountain spurs which divide the China Sea coastal strip into a number of coastal plains can be crossed either by passes or by corniches, which rise to a height of 393 feet at Hoanh-son, the gateway of Annam, 1,541 feet at the Col des Nuages, and 1,312 feet at Cape Varella. But none of the plains on this jagged coastline provided sufficient space for large-scale settlement and the growth of a homogeneous social group capable of founding a centralized State strong enough to overcome particularist tendencies.

It is true that the Chams succeeded in achieving a civilization of some brilliance, but from the very beginning of their history in the second century A.D. they were under constant pressure from the Vietnamese who, under Chinese suzerainty, were firmly established in the deltas of the Red River and the Song Ma, and who embarked upon a dynamic process of expansion, using their base there as a sort of springboard for successive leaps which took in one after another of the coastal plains.

The natural barrier formed by the eastern mountain chain is characterized by a marked contrast in the environmental conditions on either side of it. Along the coast the natural environment favoured the development of small social groups that could not easily be unified, while difficulty of access to the plains and the deltas kept the inhabitants of the mountains and plateaux from participating in cultural developments there.

On the western side of the peninsula the central massif of Den Lao, between the Salween and the Mekong, divides into three mountain chains running in a general north-south direction. The farthest west of the chains is the largest and the longest. It continues into the Malay Peninsula, of which it forms the dorsal spine. It can be crossed without much difficulty via the Me Sot pass which links the Burmese port of Moulmein with the Siamese town of Rahaeng, and via the Three Pagodas pass which links the Burmese port of Tavoy with the Siamese town of Kanchanaburi on the Mae Khlong. Between the ribs of the fan formed by the three chains running south from the Den Lao massif, the valleys of the four rivers which conjoin to form the

7

Menam all provide comparatively easy access from their upper and middle reaches to the central plain and the delta.

In the centre of the peninsula the Mekong today is a political frontier; but it is in no way a natural frontier. On the contrary, it is not only primarily a link, despite its poor navigability, between the north and the south, but also between the territories on either side of it, which in the past have always formed part of a single civilization. In addition to the lines of communication afforded by the Mekong, the passes of the Dangrek mountains (in particular the Dangkor or Tako passes) made communication possible between the Korat plateau and the basin of the Great Lake, and from the latter there was easy access westwards to the plain of the Menam via the Aranya gap and the Prachin river.

The fact that Indochina is divided internally into separate geographical areas, and the obstacles to and means of communication between these areas, were important factors determining the pattern of settlement and the general course of events in the peninsula as a whole.

The question has been raised as to whether the geographic configuration outlined above was the same in prehistoric times. It is a question which does not, of course, apply to the mountain formations, because the main orographical features were in existence long before the date of the earliest traces of human habitation. But the plains and, above all, the deltas are another matter. Some people have advanced the theory that the deltas were formed in historical times, basing their conjectures on the progressive extension of the shoreline in the Gulf of Tongking, which is thought to have gained six miles between 1830 and 1930. But it is futile to make calculations based on the retreat of the sea in an area which has been profoundly changed by the incessant labours of man in search of more land to cultivate. Indeed, between 1470 and 1830 a gain of only six or seven miles is recorded – that is, just under two miles every hundred years. In the Mekong delta the increased amount of land due to the silt deposits brought down by the river varies greatly at different points of the shore, and the Ca-mau point, which some people regard as being of recent formation, was certainly marked on the very earliest European maps of Indochina.

I do not of course mean to imply that the coasts of the peninsula had exactly the same outline in prehistoric times as they have today. It is known for a fact that the shoreline on the coast of the China Sea has moved farther out to sea, that lagoons have filled in and dunes have shifted, that the silt from the Mekong and the Red River has added several dozen miles to the shores, and that several former ports on the Burmese Gulf, such as Pegu, have become silted up. But it is true to say that, at the time when the first signs of human habitation appeared, the geographic configuration of Indochina was, if not identical with, at least very similar to what it is today, and that the great deltas, which were important areas of early settlement, were for the main part already in existence.

2

Prehistory

NOW THAT I have indicated what choices lay open to the first settlers of Indochina in the way of natural environment and soil, and have discussed the potentialities of each of the various geographical areas and their internal and external lines of communication, the time has come to introduce man upon the scene that has been set and to enter upon discussion of the peopling of Indochina.

There are here four avenues of approach. First, the prehistoric remains left by man can be studied. Second, the migrational movements leading to the earliest settlements can be reconstructed, although the results will be largely hypothetical. Third, the present geographical distribution of the various languages spoken can be examined, as well as what little is known of their history; at the present stage of research language is the only criterion for distinguishing the various ethnic groups that share the soil of the peninsula between them. Fourth, a study can be made of the social organization of the backward peoples among the present inhabitants of the peninsula in the hope that it may throw light on that of the early inhabitants.

THE PREHISTORIC CULTURES

It is very difficult to make a general survey of Indochinese prehistory, because research work on it is at unequal stages of advance in the various countries concerned. In those countries which until recently formed French Indochina, research by specialists has reached an advanced stage,[1] while in others it has only just begun;[2] one hesitates to synthesize the disparate results.[3] Moreover, the study of Indochinese prehistory has long suffered from the fact that not enough attention has been paid to the archaeological stratigraphy, either because the layers were in a condition that made such study impossible – sometimes because they had been disturbed by digging for guano or phosphates – or because excavations were carried out by fieldworkers who were insufficiently trained in the observation of stratigraphy, which is of primary importance in prehistoric archaeology. Although what follows mostly concerns Viet-nam and Laos, and to a lesser extent Cambodia, while Siam and Burma are scarcely mentioned, an impression will nevertheless be obtained – and this is the important point – of the great diversity of cultures and also of the wide variation in the physical characteristics of the human remains. Indeed diversity is the only hard fact that emerges, for any attempt to relate a particular culture to a particular ethnic group too often enters the realm of pure speculation. In many sites, a layer displaying a fairly homogeneous culture contains human remains of very diverse human types.

In Europe the terms palaeolithic and neolithic indicate two epochs marked respectively by the exclusive use of artifacts of chipped stone and by the predominant use of polished stone tools. In Indochina, however, these terms cannot be employed to distinguish between two distinct periods with an absolute chronology, but only to describe two types of culture which cannot yet be dated with any certainty, and which may or may not be contemporary with similar types in Europe.

It was for long thought that there was no true palaeolithic culture in Indochina, but now it is generally agreed that it did exist in a more or less pure form, and that man-made tools appeared in the peninsula at the end of the Lower Pleistocene. The gradual improvement in techniques during the course of time, perhaps up to the end of the Pleistocene era, probably took place without any outside influence.

The oldest example of this early industry is that found in Burma, and is called Anyathian. It is characterized by pebbles chipped into the form of choppers, similar to the tools found at the Sohan sites in north-west India. The same industry has been discovered at Fing Noi in Siam and at Phu Loi in Upper Laos, where human remains were found at the same level as the artifacts. These remains are unfortunately so fragmentary that it is difficult to attribute them with any degree of certainty to any known type of man or hominid. Such comparisons as could be made seem to indicate, however, a possible relationship with the *Pithecanthropus sinensis* discovered near Peking, who indeed had the same industry, or a very similar one. There is nothing surprising about this, for the region seems to have been inhabited since the Quaternary by a human type, possibly proto-Australoid, who, to judge from the geographical distribution, may have been an intermediate type between Pithecanthropus of Java and Pithecanthropus of north China. Probably these proto-Australoids were the earliest human inhabitants of South East Asia, who later mixed with other groups of early man from the north and the west.

The period characterized by (protoneolithic) tools polished only on the cutting-edge marks, by its stratigraphy, the transition between the palaeolithic and later industries. There is in fact a mixture of two cultures; a surviving palaeolithic and another which had acquired the technique of polishing from elsewhere. Such late palaeolithic finds have been discovered in the Vietnamese provinces of Hoa-binh, Ninh-binh, and Ha-nam, in the provinces of Than-hoa and Quang-binh farther south, and in Siam, as well as at the Luang Prabang site in Laos mentioned above. As the first discoveries were made in the province of Hoa-binh, where there is a particularly large number of sites, the name 'Hoabinhian' was given to this culture, and has been retained. The advantage of this purely geographical term is that it does not prejudge either the dating or the type of artifact. The Hoabhinian industry in its earliest stages is in some ways reminiscent of the Magdalenian, and is comparable with the later palaeolithic of Ceylon. The shape of the tools follows the natural form of the pebbles from which they are made, and they give the appearance of being clumsy first attempts. Usually the pebbles are worked on one side only, which indicates a relationship between the Hoabhinian and the earliest industries of South East Asia. No pottery is found, nor any trace of agriculture or of the domestication of animals, except perhaps of the dog.

When this industry was in the middle of its development, the protoneoliths, polished only at the cutting edge, which are characteristic of its latest period (which is indistinguishable from the 'Bacsonian'; see below) made their appearance. In northern Viet-nam the intermediate layer containing protoneoliths has another layer on top containing palaeoliths only, while in Laos the layer containing protoneoliths has remains of a fully neolithic culture immediately on top of it. It appears therefore that in northern Viet-nam the protoneolith was introduced into a culture using palaeolithic artifacts, whereas in Laos the one culture simply succeeded the other. In both cases, the protoneolith seems to have been an introduction and not to have been developed locally from earlier forms. It is interesting to note that even in prehistoric times the autochthonous peoples of Indochina seem to have been lacking in creative genius and showed little aptitude for making progress without stimulus from outside.

Human remains, in particular some fairly well preserved skulls, have been found in association with Hoabhinian artifacts. In Laos a skull has been discovered at Tham Pong, in the Phu Loi massif, which J. Fromaget regards as being a sort of 'prototype combining the characteristics of the earliest Europoids (such as Ainus, Polynesians, and later Indonesians), the Papuan negroids, and the Veddo-Australoids. His ancestors must have had their habitat somewhere in the south of China on the borders of Yunnan and Tibet, whence they must have spread towards the east and the south throughout the whole of South East Asia, in all parts of which remains of their culture have been found.' In Viet-nam, particularly at Lang Nao, other skulls belonging to the same cultural layer have been found, some of which have Melanesian, and others Indonesian affinities, which shows that they are more differentiated in type than the skull found at Tham Pong.

Just as the lower – that is, the earlier – layer of the Hoabinhian culture is related to the upper palaeolithic, so its upper level is related to the lower neolithic. This upper level of the Hoabinhian bears the name of Bacsonian, after Bac-son, where, in the limestone massif of that province, there are sites containing layers belonging to this culture. The characteristic tool of the Bacsonian culture is the 'short axe', made by splitting a bifacial tool and polishing it at the cutting edge on one side only. In northern Viet-nam this protoneolith is always found along with palaeolithic artifacts, though not in Laos, and sometimes with artifacts made of bone or shell. Little pottery has been found in Bac-son, but more in Than-hoa. It is of the primitive type with patterns on the body made by impressions of basketwork. A few pestles suggest that there may have been some rudimentary form of agriculture. As I have already said, the Bacsonian culture seems to have been introduced from outside into the midst of a culture which had scarcely yet emerged from the palaeolithic stage.

A study of the numerous skulls or fragments of skulls found in Bac-son indicates that several racial types coexisted in northern Viet-nam at that time, for, as well as Australoid skulls, there are other remains of individuals similar in type to the present inhabitants of Melanesia – Papuans, or Melanesians in the proper sense of the word – and to Indonesians. The lower levels contain proto-Melanesians and a proto-Australian skull; above them were Indonesians, who must have been latecomers and inhabited the area alongside the former. Other finds made in Bac-son, particularly at Pho-binh-gia, confirm the coexistence of Indonesian and Melanesian types in the same area. What was the probable place of origin of these newcomers? They seem to have come from the southern regions of China lying between Kwangsi and Assam. They already have certain Mongoloid characteristics which were to become more pronounced, but true Mongoloids did not appear in China until the neolithic period, and only reached Indochina at a much later period, well within historical times. Be that as it may, the introduction of the Bacsonian culture, which may have occurred during the fourth millenium, marks a turning point in the prehistory of South East Asia.

In what was, as we have seen, a hostile natural environment for human habitation, the early Hoabinhian and Bacsonian settlers chose to inhabit the caves and rock shelters that abound in the limestone formations of northern Viet-nam and the country immediately to the south. These were, in fact, the only areas where a troglodyte existence was possible; and among the sites at their disposal, the early inhabitants chose those in the vicinity of volcanic rocks, or near streams that bore down the pebbles they required for the manufacture of their tools. They have left no traces below an altitude of fifty feet, which is precisely the altitude above which the Vietnamese dislike to settle. Contrary to what happened in Europe, where prehistoric remains are often found in sites still inhabited today, the Indochinese troglodytes settled in areas which are seldom inhabited by the indigenous peoples of the present day. The reason for this is simple: the early settlers had not yet become true agriculturalists, but were mainly hunters, whose cooking sites revealed the bones of mammals, the remains of deer, and large quantities of mollusc shells; whereas nowadays the inhabitants of these regions are primarily agriculturalists, and the land they seek is the fertile land of the delta, which lies below the fifty feet mark.

The Bacsonian layers of the Da-but site in Than-hoa – which is exceptional in being situated in the plain – contain burials of individuals of the Melanesian type. The burials show how varied were the funerary rites practised by these peoples. Some of the dead were buried with their axe and pendants by their side; others had had the flesh removed and had probably been tied into a crouching position; others again were partially cremated, and in one case the bones had been collected together and arranged to simulate a crouching position. Sometimes the bones and objects were painted with red ochre. Another feature of the Bacsonian layers is the number of bone utensils they contain, a feature found elsewhere in Indochina towards the end of the Hoabinhian.

In contradistinction to the Hoabinhian-Bacsonian culture, in which artifacts made from a coarse-grained volcanic rock predominate, the neolithic cultures had a preference for tools made out of very fine-grained stone that could be highly polished. The earliest neolithic, which cannot be earlier than the second millennium, used an oval axe with a rounded butt, specimens of which have been found in Burma and in the north of Cambodia. But the typical neolithic tool in Indochina is the shouldered axe, which may have been made there, or may only have been brought there from southern China or north-east India, where many examples have been found. The potter's wheel was unknown, and a rather coarse carboniferous clay with grains of quartz in it was used for making the neolithic pottery. Specimens found include bowls, pots with wide mouths and pots with legs, decorated with incised patterns or with designs in relief for which few affinities can be found. A point should be noted here, to which I shall return when discussing migrations – namely, that the area where the shouldered axe is found is merely an enclave within the much wider area characterized by the rectangular axe, which is found in Japan,

Korea, the valley of the Yellow River, and throughout Indonesia, and which is the typical neolithic tool of this whole area.

In general, the neolithic peoples do not seem to have been troglodytes. The finds show marked differences in different areas, and the human remains belong to several different racial types. In northern Viet-nam neolithic sites are on the whole rare; they contain skulls belonging to the Indonesian type. Along the coast of the China Sea the industry is of a rather crude kind, although it tends to be less crude the farther west the sites are, while the pottery is particularly skilful; the skeletons and skulls belong to a race of pygmies similar to the negritos of the Andaman Islands and to certain Papuans of Melanesia. In Laos, the workmanship both in stone and in pottery is of a remarkably high standard. Lastly, in Cambodia the culture of the large neolithic site at Samrong Saen, at the head of the Great Lake,[4] includes a great variety of artifacts, made with care and having a certain elegance, and many specimens of richly decorated pottery in all manner of shapes. This site appears to be contemporary with the beginning of the bronze age, because several bronze objects have been found along with numerous ornaments such as bracelets, rings, pendants, and beads. The bronze is an alloy of copper (95 per cent) and tin which indicates a fairly advanced knowledge of metallurgical technique. It would appear that the technique was of foreign origin, and was introduced into the midst of a rather late form of neolithic industry. The skulls found at Samrong Saen are similar in type to those of the present inhabitants of the region.

The question arises as to whether the whole Indochinese neolithic characterized by the shouldered axe was not contemporary with the bronze age, or rather as to whether social groups which had arrived at this stage of neolithic culture may not have continued to exist alongside other groups which had advanced to the metal-using stage. There would be nothing unusual in this, since even today Indochina contains peoples at an advanced stage of civilization such as the Vietnamese and the Cambodians, along with peoples improperly called 'primitive', who have scarcely advanced at all since prehistoric times.

With the coming of the bronze age, prehistoric times give way to proto-historic times, for while it is true that there are no written documents dating from this period, we know that it was contemporary with the Chinese dynasties that reigned during the last centuries B.C.

The largest number, and the most interesting, of the Indochinese bronzes come from northern Viet-nam, where there seems to have been no permanent form of settlement before the third century B.C. The oldest bronzes belong to the Huai style (fifth to third century) and may have been cast outside Indochina and then brought there. Much the most important site is that of Dong-son, on the right bank of the Song Ma in the province of Than-hoa.[5] This very picturesque site must have been inhabited since very early times, or at any rate well before the occupation of the area by the Chinese discussed in Chapter 3, because remains of houses built on piles have been found there. But it is the burials along the river bank that yielded the richest store of bronze objects. These burials are very different from the brick-vaulted Chinese tombs of northern Viet-nam. They are merely trenches in which the dead have been placed in a lying position. In them were found bronze objects, some fragments of iron weapons and tools, and a number of ornaments, some of them of jade – all in association with axes of polished stone and tools made of schist suggesting an earlier cultural stage than the bronze objects. These last include drums, weapons, agricultural tools, containers of various shapes, and ornaments, and seem to have been the products of an indigenous industry in which Chinese influence can be traced. A few of the bronzes are of Chinese provenance.

The Dong-son culture is found in the north to the west of the river Day, in the south down to Quang-binh, and as far as Port Courbet to the east. It has 'basket' pottery reminiscent of the neolithic pottery found in Viet-nam. Very little use was made of iron. But by far the most characteristic feature of this culture was the bronze drum shaped like an upturned cooking pot.[6] Specimens in all sizes have been found. The area of distribution of the oldest type extends from China to Indonesia; numerous specimens of a later type are still in use among the Muongs in the central region of northern Viet-nam; and a third type, most commonly found among the T'ais, was until recently still being cast by Karen craftsmen in Burma. Because so many of the oldest type of drum have been found in northern Viet-nam, and because the decoration on them is similar to that on several pieces excavated at Dong-son, the supposition is that they originated there, or at least that the Dong-son region was the centre of diffusion.[7]

The decoration and the scenes with human figures engraved on the most elaborate of these drums have led to several attempts to connect them with other cultures. They are thought to have been used in funerary rites, which would fit in well with the use still made of them by the Muongs, who hang the family drum above the corpse of the head of the family during the fairly long period when the corpse is displayed, and sound it when offerings of food are made to the deceased. The scenes with human figures have been interpreted in the light of the funeral rites of several Indonesian peoples, in particular, those of the Dyaks of Borneo.[8] The decoration has been found to have affinities with Melanesian art, and with Oceanic art in general.[9] Western affinities have also been suggested, in particular with the Hallstadt culture which, during the first millennium B.C., was brought to the Far East by the nomads of the steppes.[10] But all the motifs which appear on the Dong-son drums are also found in Chinese art of the fourth to third centuries B.C.[11] This does not necessarily mean that the affinities with either Oceanic or Western motifs are to be discounted entirely; but it is reasonable to suppose that fourth-century China probably had the most immediate influence on the style of decoration of the Dong-son drums, just as it had on the technique of bronze-casting. It was the Chinese who taught the Dongsonians how to work metals, with the result that musical instruments and household utensils which had previously been made from perishable materials were transformed into richly decorated bronzes. Analysis of the Dong-son bronzes shows that the formula used was much closer to that of Chinese bronze than was the bronze of Samrong Saen with its 95 per cent of copper. Dong-son bronze has only 55 per cent of copper, along with 15 to 16 per cent of tin, 17 to 19 per cent of lead, and traces of gold and of silver.

Were the Dongsonians Indonesians? It is tempting to suppose that they were, and to regard them as latecomers in the later stages of the Indonesian migration from the continent to the islands, and the ancestors of the backward peoples of Indonesian type who inhabit the Vietnamese mountains. Sometime in the fourth or third century B.C. the Chinese techniques of metal-working (chiefly in bronze) and of making pottery of superior grade were superimposed upon their ancient neolithic culture.

It is also tempting to suppose that it was Indonesians who were responsible for the installation of certain constructions of unknown date which are still in use today – so that it is impossible to carry out the kind of excavations that might provide information about their origin. I refer to the dry-stonework tanks found in the basalt massif of Gio-linh (Quang-tri province), which provide a regionally integrated irrigation system.[12] A typical installation consists of an upper terrace with an upper tank below it which stores water coming off the mountain; below that again is a service tank, fed by water from the upper tank, where the villagers come to draw water, wash clothes, and perform ablutions; at the bottom is an overflow tank – a large artificial lake with gently sloping sides, nowadays filled with stagnant water; from this conduits carry water to the paddy-fields. These constructions are similar to systems found in Assam, Bali, and the island of Nias. They are used nowadays by the Vietnamese, who, however, did not inhabit this region before the sixteenth century A.D., and to whose ways and techniques works of this kind are completely foreign. Given the resemblance between these installations and similar ones found among various Indonesian peoples, it seems probable that they were constructed by Indonesians who were drawn to this region because of the fertility of the soil in the basalt mountain region of Gio-linh and the plentiful water supply at the foot of the mountains. The people who now inhabit the mountains of the hinterland are perhaps in part descended from the builders of the tanks, their ancestors having been pushed back into the mountains by the Vietnamese.

In several parts of Indochina there are important remains of megalithic cultures dating from the bronze age and the beginning of the iron age in proto-historic times. The erection of these megaliths was probably contemporaneous with the beginnings of a higher stage of civilization in areas more accessible to foreign influences.

The oldest megaliths are undoubtedly the menhirs or standing stones in the province of Hua Phan in Laos.[13] These menhirs are flat, pointed slabs of schist, grouped together in fields, or making an avenue along a path from which often a fine view can be obtained. Trenches with stone covers are often found along with them, clearly intended for burials judging from the human teeth and fragments of cremated bone found in them. The objects buried along with these remains belong to the bronze age.

Of later date, because they have been carved with iron tools and are found in association with iron objects, are the jars of Tran-ninh,[14] large monolithic urns firmly fixed in the ground and usually arranged in groups. They are in all sizes, the largest big enough to hold up to ten men in a standing position. Almost all of them have a very thick base which gives them great stability. By the side of the main field, which is named Ban Ang, there rises a small limestone hill which contains a natural cave with an air vent at the top. On the floor of this cave are a large number of earthenware jars which have been distorted by heat and blackened by smoke, some of which are partly calcined. Obviously this cave was a kind of cremation oven as well as being a columbarium where the ashes were preserved in earthenware containers. Examination of the large jars has revealed human teeth and bones bearing traces of calcination and embedded in a carboniferous kind of mud, which leads to the inference that they too served as funerary urns. The dead must have been cremated in the near-by cave and the ashes of ordinary mortals preserved there in humble earthenware jars, while the remains of chiefs were placed in the monolithic jars.

In some fields the jars are accompanied by groups of stones lying flat on the ground and half buried. They look like covering stones, but do not seem to have been used for this purpose. They are circular disks which lie at the foot of the jars, and are often decorated on one side, either with a design representing a pile of disks of ever decreasing diameter, or with a human or an animal figure; but the decorated side is usually face downward and buried in the ground. The objects that have been dug up from around and underneath these 'covers' are similar to those found beside the jars: polished stone tools, ceramic ware, glass beads, bronze objects, iron utensils. So without any doubt these disks were in some way connected with funeral rites, even if we do not know what their exact function was.

The fragmentary nature of the human remains makes it impossible to identify the racial characteristics of the megalith-builders of Laos. The country is now inhabited by T'ais, but they were comparative latecomers to this area, and they explain the size of the jars by saying that they were made by a race of giants who were the ancestors of the Khas, the present aboriginal inhabitants of the mountains.

One of the most curious of the Indochinese megalithic monuments, and undoubtedly the most recent, is the chamber-tomb at Xuan-loc, fifty miles to the north-east of Saigon.[15] It is a kind of huge sarcophagus made of six granite slabs buried under about ten feet of earth, and around it are buried a dozen pillars, which may have been placed round the stone chamber in order to support a framework of the kind found over the tombs of some mountain tribes. Excavation of this monument revealed nothing about its date or its builders. It is, however, similar to tombs found in the Malay Peninsula and in Indonesia, and even in India there are genuine megalithic chambers surrounded by standing stones. The Xuan-loc burial chamber can only have been constructed with iron tools, and this leads to the supposition that it is of fairly late date, perhaps as late as the beginning of the Christian era. It may well have been the work of the people who inhabited the southern delta area of Viet-nam.

This brief survey of the chief prehistoric sites of Indochina, very lacking in details about the western part of the peninsula, shows that from the earliest times it was inhabited by a variety of peoples, some of whom were related to the negritos and the Veddas, some to the Australians and the Melanesian Papuans, and others again to the Indonesians. The Mongoloid strain, which is only found at the Samrong Saen site of comparatively late date, seems to be of much later origin. In the very earliest times, Indochina already fulfils its historical role as the meeting place of highly diverse ethnic groups with cultures at widely varying stages of advance, some of whom met without intermixing, while others succeeded earlier arrivals without entirely eliminating them, so that in the twentieth century social groups still survive whose material culture and social organization can perhaps throw light on the life of those prehistoric peoples of whom otherwise we know nothing except what can be inferred from the archaeological remains of their industries.

Where did the various ethnic groups come from? Most of them are related to the present inhabitants of Indonesia and the Pacific Islands. Was the Indochinese peninsula merely a temporary stopping place for them, or was it the final goal of their migrations? It should be possible to trace the general direction and the particular stages of these migrations, and this is the problem that must now be examined.

MIGRATIONS

If one sets aside the human remains belonging to the palaeolithic period proper as being too incomplete and fragmentary to allow for any definite classifications, the earliest human type found in Indochina is almost certainly the specimen from Tham Pong in the mountain massif of Phu Loi. He appears to be a sort of proto-type combining the physical characteristics of the Australians, the Melanesian Papuans, the Indonesians, and the Polynesians. He must therefore belong to a period prior to the migrations which led to the peopling of the Pacific Islands from the direction of the continent and which brought about racial differentiations of a common human type. It is true that the diffusion of certain types of artifact found in Indochina does not necessarily correspond with large movements of population, for it is a well-known fact that techniques move more rapidly from one place to another than people. The same is true of languages, the study of which supplies the basis for migration theories. It is however impossible to deny that migrational movements took place, since some of them continued to take place during historical times.

According to the views generally accepted,[16] there were three successive waves of migration which resulted in the peopling of the Pacific Islands, firstly by the Australians, then by the Melanesians, and lastly (a much later wave) by the Indonesians and Polynesians. All these migrational movements originated in South East Asia, and their general direction was towards the south and the south-east. Perhaps it was the call of the sea that acted as stimulus.

All the migrants had to do was to follow the course of the rivers which have their source in China and on the Tibetan borders, and which flow through valleys that sometimes lie very close together, and then debouch into Indochina as if through the neck of a bottle. There has been a southwards population drift from the very earliest times, and this accounts for the present distribution of ethnic groups in the peninsula.

The presence in Indochina of proto-Australoids, to whom the

earliest industries may be ascribed, belongs to much too distant a past for there to be the least chance of finding any traces of their physical or cultural characteristics even among the most backward of the peninsula's present inhabitants. The Melanesians, to whom the Bacsonian culture has been attributed,[17] have not left any direct descendants, except perhaps in the limestone mountains of Quangbinh, where a few individuals of pygmoid type have been noted. But it would be interesting to carry out research among the peoples now inhabiting the former habitat of the Melanesians (of whom there seem to have been quite large numbers until neolithic times) to see whether any traces of them can be found in the physical characteristics of the present inhabitants and also in the vocabulary of some of the dialects spoken by them. As for the Melanesian culture, it is difficult to distinguish its traits from those of the Indonesian culture which came under its influence. The two cultures in combination succeeded the Australoid culture.

With regard to the neolithic period, when the Indonesians were predominant, it must first of all be pointed out that the distinction usually made between Austro-Asiatic peoples, who never left the continent, and Austronesians, who peopled the islands, is primarily based on linguistic data, and it would be rash to infer anything whatsoever about their racial affinities. Having said this, I shall now proceed to list what are generally accepted to have been the successive waves of migration in South East Asia during neolithic times.[18]

1. A branch of the human race possessing the culture characterized by the ellipsoidal axe migrated from either China or Japan, passed through Formosa, the Philippines, the Celebes, the Moluccas, etc., towards New Guinea and Melanesia, and introduced neolithic culture into Australia, but did not touch Indochina.

2. From some undetermined centre peoples speaking Austro-Asiatic languages, and possibly of Mongoloid race, possessing a culture characterized by the shouldered axe, spread over Indochina, the south coast of China, Formosa, the Philippines, North Celebes, Japan, the north-east of Korea, and part of eastern India.

3. During the first half, or towards the middle, of the second millennium B.C. a migration of primitive Austronesian peoples possessing a culture very similar to the late Chinese neolithic

culture known as Yang Shao, and characterized by the rectangular axe, started from China and moved in the direction of Indochina. It is to this wave of migration that have been ascribed a number of cultural traits found in Indochina and belonging to different periods and different cultural stages, such as basket pottery or that made by coil techniques, bone utensils, rings made of stone or of shell and used both as ornaments and as money, necklaces made of glass beads or small glass tubes, houses built on piles, the cultivation of rice and of millet, the domestication of the pig and the ox, the construction of megaliths, headhunting, the most primitive form of the outrigger canoe, and perhaps also the making of garments of bark-cloth.

4. A people of mixed Austronesian and Austro-Asiatic stock, possessing a culture that combined features of the rectangular axe and the shouldered axe cultures, established settlements in Indochina.

5. Before this mixed group became firmly established, a group of primitive Austronesians advanced southwards and settled among the peoples inhabiting the southern part of the Malay Peninsula, who were still at the palaeolithic stage or just at the beginning of the neolithic.

6. A branch of these primitive Austronesians who had acquired skill in navigation continued their advance, starting from the Malay Peninsula. Some of them went in the direction of Indonesia and the islands farther east, where they mixed with the peoples there belonging to the ellipsoidal axe culture; others in the direction of Borneo, the Philippines, Formosa, and Japan.

The stratigraphy of excavations carried out in Japan, where the shouldered axes characteristic of the Austro-Asiatic culture were found at a deeper level than the rectangular axes belonging to the Austronesian culture, accounts for the placing of the Austro-Asiatic migration at an earlier period than that of the Austronesians. But in Indochina the two types of axe are usually found together, or in conditions which make it impossible to distinguish the layers, so things may have been different there. I must confess that it is awkward to find a migration of Mongoloid peoples preceding a migration of Austronesians or Indonesians. Again, there is no way of explaining how it is that Austronesians with their rectangular axe reappear with their culture untouched in Malaysia and Indonesia after intermixing in, or on the borders of,

Indochina with the Austro-Asiatic inventors of the shouldered axe, except by supposing that some Austronesians migrated towards the south and passed through a region inhabited by Austro-Asiatics without intermixing with them or being culturally influenced by them. This is not a very satisfactory hypothesis, and it ought to be possible to find another.

It has indeed been argued that in Indochina, where the shouldered axe is found much more frequently than the rectangular axe, the shouldered axe culture, instead of having been submerged under a migrational wave of the rectangular axe culture, is more likely to have been a later intrusion. It looks as though the shouldered axe area had originally been settled by Austronesians who were then broken up by invading Austro-Asiatics of Mongoloid type. This argument is supported by three kinds of evidence. We have seen that there is reason to suppose that the characteristic tool of the Bacsonian culture – the proto-neolith polished at the cutting edge only, which in northern Viet-nam is found in an intervening layer between layers of the pebbles chipped on one side typical of the Hoabinhian culture, and in Laos in a layer which succeeds the layers of pebbles – was introduced by a migration of Melanesians intermixed with Indonesians. This migration, which preceded and was a prelude to the neolithic, might be regarded as the vanguard of the great migration of Austronesians belonging to the rectangular axe culture. Next, an examination of linguistic evidence shows that in Indochina the T'ai languages, at one time confined to the south of China, display distinct affinities with the Indonesian languages, which means that the two groups must be regarded as being, if not of common parentage, at least closely related through territorial propinquity and cultural exchanges. Now these two inter-related groups of languages flank, as it were, the Mon-Khmer group of languages spoken by the Austro-Asiatic peoples of Indochina. If, as I am inclined to believe, the Austro-Asiatic language group and culture was an intrusion into territory occupied by Austronesians, it becomes understandable how this intrusion, whatever its cause, would have the effect of separating geographically two language groups that had formerly belonged to the same area, and that traces of this former state of affairs would be preserved in correspondences between them. Thirdly, it has been pertinently remarked[19] that while in Indochina the shouldered axe area coincides with territory inhabited by Mon-Khmer speaking peoples, in India it coincides with the habitat of the Munda tribes of Chota Nagpur (western Bengal) – the only Indian tribes with a language showing some relationship with the Mon-Khmer group. It may in fact have been the disturbance caused by the arrival in Indochina of Austro-Asiatics belonging to the shouldered axe culture that made some of the Austronesians – namely, the Indonesians – set off for the islands.[20]

Whatever the truth of the matter may be, one thing is certain, and that is that in prehistoric times communications by sea existed, not only between the peninsula and the islands, but also between India and the whole of South East Asia. Evidence for this lies in the large quantity of glass beads of Indian origin found in the neolithic layers in Indochina and in Indonesia, and also in the wide distribution of similar types of fundamental beliefs and important rites throughout the monsoon area of Asia. It looks as though pre-Aryan India had to some extent shared a common culture with Indochina and Indonesia. This culture was characterized by the following traits:[21] on the ideological plane, cosmological dualism and institutions based on the importance of woman and even on matriarchal principles; on the plane of material culture, probably irrigated rice cultivation entailing a certain degree of social organization, the domestication of the ox and the buffalo, a rudimentary use of metals, skill in navigation, shrines built on high places, the use of jars and dolmens for burial of the dead. Some of these traits derived from the early Austronesian culture and from the 'bow-and-arrow' culture which resulted from its intermixture with the ancient ellipsoidal axe culture.[22]

The cultural unity which we may assume to have existed in the various countries of the continent and islands of South East Asia is above all reflected in the widespread use of isolating languages with a marked faculty for word-derivation by means of prefixes, suffixes, and infixes. So let us now proceed to examine the distribution of the languages of Indochina.

LANGUAGES

Perhaps the best way of obtaining some idea of how varied and how complex is the pattern of settlement in Indochina is to look at a linguistic map, especially if the map includes the extensions of the various linguistic territories into neighbouring countries. First come the national languages of the various States which have arisen during the course of history. These are, running from west to east: Burmese (in the lower valleys of the Irrawaddy and the Sittang), Mon (in Lower Burma), Siamese (in the lower valley of the Menam and on the eastern coast of the Malay Peninsula), Laotian (on the Korat plateau and in the middle Mekong valley), Cambodian (in the basin of the Great Lake and the lower Mekong valley), Vietnamese (in the Red River and the Mekong deltas and the coastal plains between the mountains and the China Sea), and Cham (in the Phan-rang and Phan-ri regions in southern Vietnam).

These national languages are the most important ones, both for historical reasons and because of the number of people who speak them. Around them gravitate their related dialects, which are spoken by backward peoples who have been less influenced by the languages of the higher civilizations of India and China.

Since the first centuries of the Christian era the linguistic map of Indochina has undergone many profound changes before finally presenting the appearance that has just been described. Only ten centuries ago, and taking only the languages used in inscriptions into account, one finds that over a large part of the area where Burmese is now spoken, Pyu, another language of the same family, was in use; that Mon was spoken in part of the lower Menam valley as well as in the Burmese deltas; that Siamese and Laotian were non-existent, although T'ai was almost certainly in use by then in the upper valleys of the Menam and the Mekong; that Khmer covered a much wider area than that of present-day Cambodia, and was spoken in the Mekong delta, the whole of the Korat plateau, and in part of the lower Menam valley; that Cham was in use all along the coast, from the mouth of the Dong-nai to the Col des Nuages; and finally, that Vietnamese was only just beginning to be spoken south of the mountain spur of Hoanh-son. Thus it can be seen that, since the tenth century, the Mon, Khmer, and Cham linguistic areas have appreciably diminished owing to the descent towards the south of the Burmese down the Irrawaddy valley, the Siamese down the Menam valley, the Laotians down the Mekong valley, and the Vietnamese along the coast.

The spoken languages of Indochina belong to several linguistic families which to a greater or lesser degree extend beyond the frontiers of the peninsula. Burmese, and the Bodo, Naga, Kuki-chin (and Karen?) dialects, together with Tibetan and the Kachin and Lolo dialects, form the Tibeto-Burman family. Khmer and its related dialects (the most important of which are Stieng, Mnong, and Bahnar), and Mon, along with a number of dialects spoken in the mountains of Upper Laos and Burma (Wa, Palaung, Rieng) and the Khasi dialect spoken in Assam, together make up the Mon-Khmer family, which in turn is related to the Munda languages of India. Siamese and Laotian, along with the Shan language of Burma and the Ahom language spoken in ancient Assam are the most important of the T'ai family of languages, which has dialects covering a vast area including the mountain regions of northern Viet-nam and part of the Chinese provinces of Yunnan, Kwangsi, and Kweichow. Cham and the Rhadé and Jarai dialects belong to the Indonesian family.

Several attempts have been made to establish genetic links between some of the large families of languages that have been mentioned, which might go some way towards proving that the languages of Indochina and the neighbouring countries had a common origin in the more or less distant past. Thus Vietnamese, the Mon-Khmer spoken languages, and Munda have been grouped together in one family to which the name 'Austro-Asiatic' was given, and this family in turn was placed in a still larger group which included all the Malayo-Polynesian languages and which was termed 'Austrian'.[23] Another theory groups Chinese and the T'ai and Tibeto-Burman languages into one single 'Indo-Chinese' family,[24] and an effort has been made to establish a relationship between these 'Indo-Chinese' languages and the Malayo-Polynesian languages.[25] Lastly, evidence for a relationship between the T'ai and the Indonesian languages was sought, and the undeniable similarities between T'ai and Chinese was explained as due to a prolonged period of Chinese influence.[26]

With regard to Vietnamese, which has a tonal system very similar to that of the T'ai languages, but a vocabulary of largely Mon-Khmer origin, discussion has centred on whether it should be regarded as a T'ai[27] or a Mon-Khmer[28] language. The point to be decided was whether it was more likely that a Mon-Khmer language without tones had adopted the T'ai tonal system, or whether a T'ai language had borrowed a large part of its vocabulary from the Mon-Khmer group. In either case, the theory arrived at was that of a 'mixed' language. But it has now been observed that tones may arise in Chinese and in T'ai as a result of phonetic changes,[29] and the same may have been true of the Mon-Khmer spoken languages, which were originally toneless; so that the presence of tones in Vietnamese no longer prevents it from being regarded as belonging to the Mon-Khmer family, with which it has the major part of its basic vocabulary in common. Indeed it may now be assumed to be a Mon-Khmer language in which a tonal system similar to that of the T'ai languages has arisen. But granted that this is so, the question still arises as to whether the appearance of tones was a spontaneous phenomenon due to phonetic changes in the language itself, or whether it was the result of contact with the tonal system of T'ai or even of Chinese. The second hypothesis has been ruled out by those who maintain that a language is only affected by another as far as its vocabulary is concerned.[30] But it is a hypothesis that cannot be dismissed so easily nowadays, and all that is required to make it acceptable is that there should have been a prolonged period of contact, amounting perhaps to a symbiosis, between a people speaking a non-tonal Mon-Khmer language and a people speaking a tonal one, with some degree of bi-lingualism on the part of the native Mon-Khmer speaking people using a tonal language as their second language, or on the part of the immigrant group of tonal speech acquiring the use of a non-tonal language, or on the part of both. We shall learn in the next chapter what light is thrown by history on the problem of knowing which ethnic group the people who spoke the Mon-Khmer dialect that had become tonal belonged to, and which group the people belonged to whose dialect imposed its tones on the Mon-Khmer dialect that was later to become Vietnamese; and we shall see whether the circumstances were favourable for enabling contact between them to lead to contagion of the language. For while the ancestry of the Mons, the Khmers, the Chams, and the mountain people related to them stretches far back into the neolithic past, that of the Vietnamese does not go back any earlier than the bronze age, and the Tibeto-Burmans and the T'ais do not appear in Indochina until much later, after the beginning of the Christian era.

Although the languages of Indochina are so many and so varied, displaying different characteristics according to which linguistic family they belong to (for instance, being tonal or non-tonal, with or without mechanisms for the derivation of words, having Chinese or Indian loan-words, following a different word-order), there is nevertheless a certain family resemblance between them. It is as if their individuality had become blurred through co-existence and culture contacts.[31] Cham, for example, has a much more rudimentary mechanism for derivation than the other Indonesian languages, and its structure has become so similar to that of the Mon-Khmer languages that some writers have classed it as belonging to that family. T'ai, which is strictly monosyllabic in China and in Viet-nam, has lost this feature in Siam and Laos because of the many words borrowed from polysyllabic languages. The Tibeto-Burman group, which in Tibet has retained voiced initial occlusives, has lost them in Burma through a sort of phonetic conformism with the other Indochinese languages. There is even a curious parallelism between the tonal and the non-tonal languages of Indochina as to the influence voiced or voiceless initials have on the rest of the syllable. Probably this levelling process affecting the languages spoken in the peninsula is due both to reciprocal influence and to the presence of a common substratum.

The linguistic picture I have just outlined gives some indication of where the peoples of Indochina originally came from and of migrational trends in ancient times, although we must remember that language does not always coincide with race, and that languages sometimes spread faster and further than the people who speak them.

An attempt may now be made to form a picture of the geographical distribution of the ethno-linguistic groups whose origins we have been investigating at the time when they were about to enter the cultural orbits of the two great Asian civilizations – that is, during the last centuries B.C. I suggest that their distribution may have been as follows:

Given the fact of a population drift towards the south, the ethnic groups settled farthest south are likely to have been those that had been longest in possession of their habitat. There are therefore good reasons for supposing that at the time when Indian cultural influence was first introduced, the southern and central areas of the peninsula (that is, an area corresponding roughly to the area covered by former Cochin-china, and by Cambodia, the

Mekong valley, and Viet-nam as far north as Than-hoa) were inhabited by peoples who had come with the two great waves of migration – the Austronesian and the Austro-Asiatic. But it is not always possible to draw a clear distinction between their respective domains. The distribution of languages would seem to indicate, however, that the descendants of the Austro-Asiatics – the Khmers and the groups speaking Mon-Khmer languages – occupied the territory to the west of the mountains, and the descendants of the Austronesians – the Chams and other groups speaking Indonesian languages – the territory to the east, probably as far south as the Mekong delta. Farther north, a people who were a cross between, or an admixture of, these southern racial strains and a Mongoloid strain of T'ai origin, began to spread over the region of the Red River delta and to swarm southwards. These were the pre-Vietnamese, who later differentiated into the Vietnamese in the low-lying areas, and the Muongs in the mountain regions. The Menam valley and Lower Burma were peopled by the Mons, linguistically related to the Khmers; and the lower valleys of the Irrawaddy and the Sittang by the advance guard of the Tibeto-Burman peoples, of which the Pyus were the most important group.

SOCIAL ORGANIZATION

There is very little direct information about the societies of South East Asia before they entered into contact with India and China. Theoretically it should be possible to gain some information about them by studying the backward groups that still exist in the Indo-chinese peninsula. But the results of such a study must be handled with the greatest care. In Indonesia the Dutch have conducted research of this kind with a certain amount of success, and some of their findings can be confidently applied when making a hypo-thetical reconstruction of ancient Indonesian society. But remote Indonesian islands which have never been in touch with foreign civilizations such as the Indian and the Chinese offer a much better field for investigation than Indochina, where it is rare to find peoples who have never been in contact with more civilized neighbours. Now the method of using present-day findings to reconstruct ancient forms of social organization depends upon the assumption that, at some time in the distant past, the social groups studied solved all the problems involved in adapting to their environment and satisfying their basic needs, and on the further assumption that there has not since been any alteration of the environment or technological innovation to make them change their way of life and their social organization. The method operates, in short, in a sphere of conjectures based on these assumptions rather than in a sphere of facts conveyed by the study of documents. I shall, therefore, refrain from attempting to give a picture of the social organization of the Indochinese peoples before their contact with China and India, and shall confine myself to quoting some opinions of a very general nature which seem to have some pertinence.

The difference that exists between the social organization of the plains-dwellers and that of the peoples inhabiting the mountain areas has been explained as being due 'less to racial differences than to there having been a different pattern of development in areas remote from civilization. . . . The deltas offered the best opportunities, provided that man took full advantage of them, for the development of powerful States, which gained in might as more and more land was brought under cultivation, for as the area of cultivated land increased, the social groups involved became welded into vigorous societies of agriculturalists. Thus the fertility of the soil combined with foreign cultural influences produced the civilizations of the Indochinese plains, and these offered a more and more marked contrast to the way of life of the mountain peoples.'[32]

It is these mountain peoples one would have to study in order to form some idea of what society in Indochina was like before contact was made with the higher civilizations. All of them are agriculturalists whose entire social and religious life centres upon the cultivation of rice, but they fall into two distinct types of social group which are in sharp contrast in almost every respect.[33]

The first type has no form of political organization at all. Except in areas where strong foreign influence has been brought to bear, the group never extends beyond the village, and each village is an independent unit. Religion is an individual or family affair in which the community plays no part. This type is further subdivided into two sub-types distinguished by a difference in language and, to a certain extent, in kinship relations. In one, consisting of the Chams and related tribes who speak languages belonging to the Indonesian family, a matriarchal system prevails, name and property being inherited through the maternal line; in the other, consisting of the Bahnar, the Sedang, the Mnong, and other tribes whose languages belong to the Mon-Khmer group, the family is usually patriarchal, although it is matriarchal in tribes such as the Koho, Chau Sre, Chau Ma, etc., who have perhaps been influenced by neighbouring tribes.

The second type of social group has a hierarchical organization of the feudal variety, in which each district is a ritual unit governed by a hereditary lord or is in the possession of a particular family. The family is patriarchal, name, office, and property being transmitted from father to son. Religion is an affair of the territorial group, not of the individual, and the ceremonies which inaugurate the main seasonal activities are carried out once and for all for the whole district by its lord. This is the type to which the Muong, the T'ai, the Lolo, the Man, and indeed all the peoples speaking a tonal language belong. It is found in northern Viet-nam, but no farther south than the province of Tran-ninh, which covers the hinterland of the provinces of Nghe-an and Ha-tinh; and in Laos, where it extends farther south as a result of the descent of the T'ais down the valleys of the Mekong and the Menam in comparatively recent times.

When the Chinese conquered the Red River delta in the second century B.C., and when, a little later, Indian merchants began to establish themselves in south Indochina, they met with 'barbarians' whose beliefs and social organization had something in common with those of their own Chinese or Indian early ancestors; and this goes some way towards explaining why they were so rapidly and so easily able to impose their own civilizations, for these civilizations were simply a later, more advanced stage of a common cultural basis.

PART TWO

The Founding of the First Indochinese States

SO FAR DISCUSSION has centred on the origins and the probable geographical distribution at the end of the first millennium B.C. of the various ethnic groups that encountered each other and settled together in the Indochinese peninsula. Now the time has come to introduce the two great protagonists whose arrival upon the scene was to determine the destiny of the major part of these peoples. China will be treated first, because, according to the sources at our disposal, China's presence was felt in Indochina several centuries earlier than that of India. The Chinese dynastic annals provide the main source of information, to which must be added travel accounts and encyclopaedias, as well as the supplementary documentation supplied by archaeological finds. We have to rely on the same sources of information about the spread of Indian culture in Indochina, although a few additional items are to be found scattered among certain literary texts of India and of classical antiquity. Epigraphy, which becomes the major source of information from the sixth century onwards, only provides a minute number of inscriptions for the period prior to this date.

I

The Chinese Conquest of the Red River Delta and the Birth of Viet-nam

IN 221 B.C. an event occurred in China which was decisive for the future of that country and which had profound repercussions throughout the whole of South East Asia: the kingdom of Ch'in triumphed over its rivals, thus bringing to an end the anarchic period of the Warring States. Thirty-five years earlier, in 256 B.C., the imperial domain of the Chou had been annexed by Ch'in, and now the king of Ch'in was able to unite the whole of China under his rule and found the first fully centralized empire in its history.

The emperor, Ch'in Shih-huang-ti, had already in 221 planned an expedition against the country of the Yüeh (Sino-Vietnamese pronunciation: *Viet*), the principalities of which lay along the coasts of Chekiang, Fukien, and Kwangtung. The motives that lay behind this expedition were perhaps economic rather than political.[1] The area south of the Yangtze was still far from being completely sinicized, but the coastal regions forming the kingdom of Yüeh had for long been the theatre of commercial exchanges between northern China and the 'barbarians of the south'. The latter, in exchange for silk, supplied the Court with luxury articles and commodities which were in great demand there: ivory, rhinoceros horn, tortoise-shell, pearls, peacock and kingfisher feathers, spices, and aromatic woods. The Chinese had apparently obtained command of certain routes and of certain ports in the Yüeh kingdom from the end of the fourth century B.C. Nor were they unaware of the economic importance of the deltas of the West River and the Red River.

The expedition decided upon in 221 did not actually take place until three years later. When it had reached the western part of the Yüeh kingdom, the indigenous Hsi Ou tribes (*Tay Au*) retreated into the wastelands, leaving the countryside deserted in face of the advancing Chinese; and at the request of Chao T'o (*Trieu Da*), reinforcements had to be sent. These were composed for the most part of men who were regarded in China as undesirable elements. They subsequently founded military colonies in the conquered territories.

After crossing the passes leading to the valley of the West River, the expedition reached the fertile plain of Canton. In 214 B.C. three forts were established, which became the chief towns (Canton, Hsün-chou, and Nan-ning) of the commanderies of Nan-hai, Kuei-lin, and Hsiang. The Red River delta, which lay beyond the immediate objectives of the expedition, retained its independence for several years longer. It was ruled over at that time by feudal lords called by the Chinese the Lo princes (*Lac*), the territory being subdivided into fiefs governed by hereditary chiefs in a feudal organization of the kind still found among mountain peoples today, as described in the preceding chapter.

The death of Ch'in Shih-huang-ti brought civil war to China. His son only reigned for two years (209–207), after which military leaders fought with each other for the throne. One of them, Liu Pang, was finally victorious and founded the Han dynasty (202 B.C.–A.D. 220). The governor of the conquered territories of the Yüeh kingdom took advantage of the situation and attempted to become independent, but, exhausted by the climate, he had to give up the attempt before he had brought it to a successful conclusion. In 209 he called in the support of Chao T'o, who succeeded him after his death. Chao T'o had all the officials who retained their allegiance to Ch'in executed, and replaced them with his own followers. In 207 he assumed the title of King of Nan-yüeh (*Nam Viet*). The kingdom was formed from the three commanderies of Nan-hai, Kuei-lin, and Hsiang. He was already firmly established there when the Han dynasty was founded in 202, and in the pacification of the empire that followed, he was recognized by the new dynasty in 196 in exchange for acceptance of its suzerainty. But when the Empress Lü, widow of the first Han emperor, forbade him to trade in iron, he broke off relations with her for economic reasons, and in 183 assumed the title of emperor. An expedition was sent against him by the Empress which ended in disaster, and Chao T'o then made his southern neighbours recognize his rule. These neighbours were the Lo of Hsi Ou (*Tay au lac*), the feudal lords of the Red River delta and the coastal plains lying immediately south of it. He divided their territory into two commanderies: Chiao-chih (*Giao-chi*), which included the delta, and Chiu-chen (*Cuu-chan*), consisting of the lower parts of the present provinces of Thanh-hoa, Nghe-an, and Ha-tinh. In 179 the Han Court dispatched an embassy to him, after which he relinquished the title of emperor which he had usurped and once more took that of King of Nan-yüeh.

From this account of historical events it can be seen that Nan-yüeh or the Yüeh (*Viet*) of the South, which gave its name to Viet-nam, was the southernmost of a number of coastal principalities, and that the area where Viet-nam was to arise – that is, the Red River delta – was originally inhabited by tribes bearing the name of Lo (*Lac*), who were probably intermixed with the people of Yüeh long before the Chinese conquest and the founding of the kingdom of Nan-yüeh.

Lo appears to be the earliest ethnic term used to designate the group of peoples who were later to form the nucleus of the Vietnamese. It regularly forms part of the various names by which they were known to the Chinese: *Lo*-yüeh under the Chou dynasty, Hsi Ou-*lo* or simply Ou-*lo* under the Ch'in. If anything certain were known as to which ethno-linguistic groups the Lo and the Yüeh belonged, the problem of the origins of the Vietnamese people would *ipso facto* find its solution. But on this point one can only make conjectures. Following upon what has already been said about the probable origins of the Vietnamese language, one might, however, formulate the following hypothesis.

According to Chinese texts based on sources of information dating from the Chinese conquest and the founding of the kingdom of Nan-yüeh, the early inhabitants of the Red River delta wore no clothes, blackened their teeth, chewed betel, tilled the fields with hoes of polished stone, and used poisoned arrows, thus evincing the traits characteristic of the Mon-Khmer and Indonesian peoples of southern Indochina speaking non-tonal languages. But they had a hierarchical social organization of a feudal type completely foreign to the southern peoples, yet identical with that of the T'ais and other ethno-linguistic groups of southern China speaking tonal languages. It is thus possible to distinguish two components in the pre-Chinese culture of northern Viet-nam, belonging to two contrasting types of culture, of which Vietnamese legends concerning the earliest times seem to have retained a memory. Were the southern cultural elements contributed by the Lo, and the northern by the Yüeh? This seems very likely. The important point, however, is that the presence of the two components of their culture relates the ancient inhabitants of this region both to Mon-Khmer and to T'ai speaking peoples.

This fusion of cultures resulting from the encounter and subsequent symbiosis between two ethnic groups of different origin may have occurred long before the Chinese conquest, and is probably what is expressed by the name Lo-yüeh, the 'Yüeh of Lo', which was one of several applied to the early inhabitants of northern Viet-nam. There was in addition some degree of admixture of other foreign elements, including immigrant Hok-lo who came by sea from Fukien.[2] The incorporation of the region within the kingdom of Nan-yüeh around 180 B.C. must have reinforced the Yüeh element, and must also have strengthened Chinese influence. But Chinese influence was mainly felt in the plain, and considerably less so in the valleys of the midland regions. For this reason, the whole area which, long before the rise of Viet-nam, had had its bronze age and had given rise to the Dongsonian culture, became divided into two parts, the one to be inhabited by the Vietnamese, who became progressively more and more sinicized, and the other by the Muongs, who were less affected by Chinese cultural influence, and with whom most of the incoming T'ais, whose culture was not very different from theirs, became fused.[3]

After this digression on the probabilities of the ethnic origins of the Vietnamese, let us return to the historical events which followed upon the founding of the kingdom of Nan-yüeh.

The Lo princes remained in Chiao-chih as vassals of the kings of the Chao (*Trieu*) dynasty founded by Chao T'o (*Trieu Da*). But when this dynasty broke its ties of vassalage to China in 112, the Han emperor Wu-ti proceeded to occupy the country. In 111 B.C.

Nan-yüeh was incorporated into the empire and formed the *chou* (province) of Chiao (*Giao*), consisting of nine commanderies, six of which corresponded to the geographical area comprising the present Chinese provinces of Kwangtung and Kwangsi and the island of Hainan, while the other three corresponded to what had formerly been Ou-lo – that is to say, the two commanderies of Chiao-chih and Chiu-chen – with the addition of that of Jih-nan (*Nhat-nam*), stretching from Hoanh-son to the Col des Nuages.

After the Han had conquered Nan-yüeh, they did not bring it under the imperial administration, and did not in any way alter the institutions they found there. The commanderies were more or less treated as colonies, where a Chinese minority lived amidst the indigenous peoples. The main result of the conquest was the opening of the sea route to the south for Chinese trade, which plied between the ports of Kwangtung and of northern Viet-nam. The two legates of Yüeh at Chiao-chih and Chiu-chen, who had submitted without offering any resistance, were confirmed in office. As for the native feudal lords, only one of them attempted to become independent, and he was very soon eliminated by an Ou-lo general even before the arrival of the Chinese. The others rallied to their new masters. The whole native feudal organization continued as before under the authority of the Chinese prefect, the largest fiefs receiving the title of sub-prefectures, although they continued to be governed by their hereditary lords.

It was not until the beginning of the first century A.D. that the Chinese governors began to change their policy towards the subject peoples. One of the prefects of Chiao-chih – a man named Hsi Kuang (*Tich Quang*) – who governed between A.D. 1 and 25, 'changed the people through rites and justice', or in other words, endeavoured to sinicize them more thoroughly than before. The number of Chinese settlers of all sorts – fugitives, exiles, deported criminals – was continually on the increase, and they helped to spread the Chinese language and Chinese customs. In addition, a new type of settler, very different from the undesirables who had previously arrived, began to come to the Red River delta during the early years of the first century A.D. The prefect Hsi Kuang had refused to recognize the usurper Wang Mang who, from 9 to 25, substituted his rule for that of the Han emperors, and many scholar-official families who remained faithful to the dynasty came to seek refuge with him.

Most of the tombs of Chinese officials and settlers discovered in northern Viet-nam date from this period.[4] They are constructed entirely of brick, and are found in considerable numbers in regions where there were hillocks that met the exigencies of geomancy. Some consist of a single vault, some of several, and some present quite a complicated lay-out. One of them, in the province of Bac-minh, contains no less than twelve tiled chambers on six alignments. The vaults have cradle-vaulting, and the bricks are large in size and are often decorated or painted. When they were opened, some of the tombs still contained numerous pieces of pottery, as well as bronzes, fragments of weapons, and strings of cash coins, many of which date, as might be expected, from the reign of the usurper Wang Mang, and others from the Later Han period (25–220). Most of the bronzes seem to have been imported from China, and consist of mirrors, bowls, and spherical wine cups. The pottery objects – jars, cups, vases of all kinds – are in many different shapes. In several tombs excavations brought to light miniature models of houses, granaries, wells, and small stoves, such as have been found in tombs in China of the same period. But miniature versions of the bronze drums of the Dongson burials are never found.

The new type of Chinese settler must have encouraged and assisted the prefect Hsi Kuang in his efforts to sinicize the country. He initiated a number of measures of varying importance. He founded schools. He taught the natives the use of the plough – that is, of the metal plough, which they had never used before. But he also wanted them to conform to Chinese marriage rites and to wear footwear and headgear. In addition, he formed a militia armed and trained in Chinese fashion, and a body of subordinate officials of all kinds, both recruited from the native population; and this had a disintegrating effect on the old feudal order. At first the feudal lords did not oppose Hsi Kuang's efforts, but as soon as they realized that their authority was threatened by the setting up of a permanent Chinese administration they did not hesitate to show their hostility. A violent conflict broke out shortly after the departure of Hsi Kuang, and his successor, Su Ting (*To Dinh*), who took up office in 34, soon found himself openly opposed by a whole section of the local aristocracy.

The main instigators of the rebellion against the Chinese administration which took place in the year 40 centred round two women, the sisters Cheng (*Trung*), who, on account of their royal birth, had acquired an ascendancy over the Lo feudal lords and indeed over the people as a whole. Following upon an initial success on the part of the older sister, who managed to gain possession of the capital, Lien-liu (*Lien-lau*), the rebellion spread to sixty-five native fiefs. Chiao-chih and the surrounding territories became independent, and the inhabitants raised their liberator, Cheng Tse (*Trung Trac*), to be queen. Since various other rebellions were at that time keeping the imperial armies occupied, China had to wait nearly two years before being able to undertake an expedition to repress this one. In January of the year 42 one of the best generals of the time, the seventy-year-old Ma Yüan (*Ma Vien*), was put in command of the expedition.[5] As circumstances prevented him going by sea, he had to take his forces by the land route. He encountered no resistance on his way, since, outside of her own fief of Mi-ling (*Me-linh*), 'queen' Cheng Tse's authority was of the most precarious kind; and as soon as news came of the approach of a Chinese army, enthusiasm for her reign rapidly dwindled. Ma Yüan, with 20,000 men, penetrated as far as the delta, and then turned inland and marched against the rebellious fiefs of Mi-ling and Hsi-yü (*Tay-vu*). But when approaching the latter, the size of the enemy force compelled him to retreat into the hills of Tien-du. A bloody but decisive battle at Lang-po (*Lang-bac*) in May 43 ended in the rout of the indigenous armies. Ma Yüan ordered one of his lieutenants to pursue them, who after several months succeeded in catching up with Cheng Tse, probably in the region of Son-tay, and in taking her prisoner. Ma Yüan had meanwhile succeeded in surprising the younger sister, Cheng Ni (*Trung Nhi*), who held the country east of the delta, in the south of the present province of Hai-duong.

Ma Yüan followed up his victory by organizing a permanent administration in the delta area. The Lo feudal lords had their privileges removed, and their titles disappeared from this time on. Many of the lords had already perished, and the rest took refuge in the highland regions, where they continued to survive as petty chiefs of districts or villages, probably under the authority of Chinese officials. They came more and more under Chinese influence, and were forced to intermarry with Chinese settlers. It was from this aristocracy of mixed racial origin from which sprang later 'nationalists' such as Ly Bon and Ly Phat-tu, who, despite being of partially Chinese descent, fought against Chinese rule.

After having crushed the last rebels in the south and achieved the submission of Chiu-chen, Ma Yüan returned to Chiao-chih, where he stayed for several months in order to put the final touches to his reforms before returning to the capital of the empire, where he was given a triumphal reception.

The conquest and reforms of Ma Yüan are memorable events in the history of Viet-nam, into which now poured large numbers of Chinese immigrants, evidence for which is provided by the many tombs dating from the Later Han dynasty. The country, which until then had been administered as a protectorate, became simply a province of the empire. With varying degrees of intelligence and tact, its governors in sequence applied the policy of assimilation laid down by the Chinese Court.

One of the best of these governors, of whom special mention must be made, was Shih Hsieh (*Si Nhiep*), who administered the country from 187 to 226. He had been sent to Chiao-chih in the capacity of prefect, and took over during a very troubled period, when in China the power of the Han was being called into question and in the delta area the leaders of the separatist movement hoped to gain the upper hand. It was he who first organized Chinese studies there, and his reputation as a good governor survives to this day. The use of the Chinese language had been introduced by Chao T'o, the founder of Nan-yüeh, and himself a highly cultivated man. We have seen how, at a later date, former officials had come to enlarge the Chinese colony at Chiao-chih. In the second century two native Vietnamese went to China and obtained their degree in the literary examinations, and their example aroused the emulation of their compatriots. Thus the efforts of Shih Hsieh to stimulate Chinese studies fell on well-prepared ground. From then on, over a period of nearly two thousand years, Chinese remained the only learned and official language of Viet-nam, and left indelible traces on its language, literature, and institutions, and indeed the whole of its intellectual life.

Shih Hsieh, upon whom the Ch'en dynasty (sixth century) conferred the posthumous title of Shih Wang, 'Prince Shih' (hence the Sino-Vietnamese name of Si Vuong used at the shrines where his memory is honoured), is reputed to have welcomed the first Buddhist missionaries, who were authorized to propagate their doctrine and to build monasteries – an authorization that was also extended at the same time to the followers of Taoism and Confucianism, who had arrived earlier. Formal documentation on the introduction of Buddhism does not, however, appear until a century later, when monks from India – the Sogdian K'ang-seng-hui, the Indo-Scythian Kalyanaruchi, and the Indian Marajivika – arrived; and it was not until 580, after the arrival of the Indian Vinitaruchi, that the school of Dhyana Buddhism became established in Viet-nam, where Buddhism was to have a chequered career, with a particularly brilliant period from the eleventh to the fourteenth century.[6]

Not all the Chinese governors displayed the same qualities as Shih Hsieh, so that a Vietnamese author[7] could write: 'The Chinese governors were not always models of integrity; they were more concerned with their own well-being than with the happiness of the people. Wicked, ambitious, and avaricious, they only sought to further their own interests on the road to power and to enrich themselves at the expense of the people. History has preserved the memory of their exactions, their injustice, and their cruelty. Hence, during the long period of Chinese domination, the country several times rose violently against Chinese rule.' Yet it is only apparently paradoxical to maintain, as Henri Maspero did,[8] that the Chinese seizure of power was later to serve the cause of independence: 'If Annam, after gaining its independence, was able for centuries to resist Chinese aggression, while all the neighbouring States – Yeh-lang, Tien, Nan Chao – gradually succumbed, it was because it was the only one to have been subjected to government by a permanent Chinese administration, and this, by breaking the power of particularist institutions and local groups, and by introducing Chinese ideas and social organization, gave it a cohesion and a formal structure which its neighbours lacked.'

The history of the Chinese occupation, which lasted for nearly ten centuries, was dominated by two problems: internal opposition from members of the native population who were attached to their traditional institutions and hostile to foreign rule; and the external threat presented by Champa's attempts at expansion towards the north, which the Chinese governors had to take measures against.

The first rebellion was instigated, not by a native, but by governor Shih Hsieh's own son, Shih Hui (*Si Huy*), who was

47

inclined to regard the country as a fief belonging to the family, and who, on his father's death in 226, tried to force his way into succeeding him. The new governor, Lü Tai (*Lu Dai*) obtained his surrender by promising that his life would be spared, but later he had him executed.

A second rebellion broke out in 248 at Chiu-chen, led by a woman who had gathered some thousand followers round her. She was finally driven to commit suicide after Chinese troops had taken victorious action against her.

These risings and others that followed between 263 and 280 must have had an adverse effect on the maritime trade in luxury goods, which seems to have been less brisk than before. We shall see later how the founding in 192 of the Cham kingdom to the south of the southernmost of the Chinese commanderies gave rise, from the third century onwards, to a series of conflicts between the governors of the commanderies and these turbulent neighbours.

The second half of the sixth century (more exactly, from 541 to 603) saw the revolt of three native chiefs, each bearing the family name of Ly, which has given rise to the belief that has long been held that a local dynasty, 'the former Ly', reigned during that period.[9] From 541 to 547 Ly Bi (or Ly Bon) succeeded in having his authority recognized in the Red River delta and as far south as the frontier of Champa, but he finally had to seek refuge with his neighbours the Lao, who put him to death. In 589–90 Ly Xuan gained mastery over the whole region for a short time. After this the administration was reorganized to bring it into line with the rest of the empire, and the capital of Chiao-chih was removed from Long-bien to Tong-binh, the site of present-day Hanoi. Lastly, during the closing years of the sixth century Ly Phat-tu succeeded in occupying the delta for a fairly brief period, until he was eliminated in 603 by General Liu Fang (*Luu Phuong*), who two years later had to lead a campaign against Champa.

In 622 the T'ang dynasty that was reigning in China reorganized the administrative boundaries of the region and created the general government of Chiao, which in 679 became the general protectorate of An-nan (*An-nam*), which means 'the pacified south'. Its area corresponded approximately to that later covered by Tongking together with the coastal plains as far south as Hoanh-son. The lowlands came directly under the Chinese administration in the same way as the other provinces of the empire. The mountainous regions were in some places made into Chinese prefectures and in others into special districts left under the rule of native chiefs. The plains were divided into seven departments. It is estimated that at this period the delta had a population of 95,000 to 100,000.[10]

The introduction of Chinese civilization into the north-east of the peninsula, whence it spread in the course of time all along the east coast, was thus a direct result of the policy of assimilation or integration put into practice by the Chinese after their conquests. As I have said elsewhere,[11] 'the extreme centralization of the Chinese administrative system, of which no part could function in isolation from the whole, the very concept of a world centred on the Empire of the Middle, which exists 'under Heaven', and beyond which all is barbarism and confusion, and the extent to which the individual was integrated into the community, meant that Chinese civilization was unlikely to spread except as a result of conquest and annexation of territory.'

An important fact has recently come to light[12] – namely, that Chinese influence reached Viet-nam exclusively by land, with trade playing very little part. We have seen that originally, before the conquest, trade in luxury goods destined for the Court had been carried on in the South Seas and had continued for several centuries with alternating periods of activity and depression. From the sixth century, the population of the larger Chinese towns provided a new type of customer, whose demands for rare products from the west such as incense, perfumes, dyes, and medicaments, for use in religious establishments, channelled the trade into new directions. In addition, from the beginning of the T'ang dynasty new kinds of dealer appeared – Arabs and Persians. The Chinese merchants did not themselves take an active part in navigation. Those concerned with the trade were big financiers who were content to operate in the ports as shipowners and sleeping partners, leaving the transport of merchandise to their underlings, or, preferably, to foreign navigators. These navigators, who, even if they were Chinese, were lower-class Chinese, could scarcely have played much part, if any, in the propagation of Chinese culture. It was only as a result of military conquest, followed by Chinese immigration and the sinicization of the indigenous people, that Chinese civilization took root.

The spread of Indian cultural influence is a very different story.

2

The Introduction of Indian Culture into Indochina

WHILE THE EVENTS leading to the sinicization of the north-east of the peninsula are known to us through reliable sources and can be dated with accuracy, the same cannot be said of the process of Indianization, for it is only from the results that emerged that we can infer how the process began and how it developed. Nor was Indian culture ever introduced for political purposes, as was the case with the sinicization of Viet-nam, which was conquered by China and then administered for several centuries as a province of the empire; whereas none of the Indochinese States of Indian type was ever a dependency of an Indian metropolitan power.

It would be impossible to try to establish a precise date for the beginning of a process which probably goes fairly far back into the past, for two-way relations between India and Indochina both by sea and by land apparently began in quite early times. In the case of Viet-nam we know the dates of the various stages of Chinese conquest and colonization; but all we can say about the process of Indianization is that no archaeological remains showing a trace of Indian origin or influence date from earlier than the second century A.D., nor does the earliest mention of place-names in the peninsula with an Indian sound to them, or of institutions on the Indian pattern; and the earliest Sanskrit inscription found in Indochina – the stele of Vo Canh, which will be mentioned later –

dates from the end of the second century or the beginning of the third.

The beginning of the Christian era was a particularly active period for the spread of Indian cultural influence, and various theories have been put forward, mainly by Dutch scholars, to account for this. All these theories suffer from the common failing of attempting to explain everything according to one single principle, but each would seem to contain some part of the truth. Thus according to one hypothesis, Indian culture was spread by high-caste Indians who ventured forth to seek their fortune in the lands of gold and spices[1] – an idea which cannot be rejected out of hand, but which remains no more than a hypothesis so long as no precise facts are found to confirm it. Another theory has laid great stress on the stimulus to commercial expansion provided at the beginning of the Christian era by the extension of the Chinese market after China's conquest of the countries south of the Yangtze, by the advances in navigation, and by the propagation of Buddhism – a religion without any prejudices against non-Indian peoples or against overseas voyages.[2] But objections have been raised to this theory on the grounds that it would have been difficult for Indian merchants, confined to their godowns on the coast, to have prolonged or close enough contact with the indigenous societies and their chiefs to exercise any very great cultural influence.[3] Again, the bearers of Indian culture are thought to have been Indian literati who visited South East Asia and introduced manuals of ritual and technical treatises there; or, more important still, natives who returned to their own countries after spending some time in India.[4] Undoubtedly people of this kind played an important role at later stages of Indianization, but they can hardly have provided the initial stimulus, because their travels presuppose already existing and continuous relations between India and the countries of the East. An international network of trading relationships had indeed existed since early times, in which the Indians were not the only people involved. But perhaps they were more skilful in establishing contacts with the natives, and these contacts, even if they were only sporadic, may have favoured the subsequent spread of cultural influence. There is an interesting hypothesis[5] along these lines, according to which native chiefs who wanted to increase their prestige and consolidate their power called in Brahmans in order to make use of their magical powers, the fame of which had been spread abroad by merchants; and that it was these Brahmans who introduced Indian religious rites.

Whoever the propagators of Indian culture may have been, the fact that it was characterized by its having a way of life laid down by a specific philosophical and religious doctrine led to its being adopted *en bloc* by the native chiefs who were attracted by it. The adoption of Hinduism brought with it the adoption of the Indian way of life, just as the adoption of the Indian way of life brought about the adoption of Hinduism. Under Indian influence, native chiefs did not have a ready-made administration forced upon them, but were merely presented with a technique of administration which could be adapted to varying conditions in countries overseas.

The mixed marriages which emigrant Indians were forced into (since it is unlikely that Indian women ever accompanied them overseas), constitute another factor that must have promoted the Indianization of the peoples of South East Asia. It has been argued that such marriages could not have taken place.[6] It is, however, known for certain that they were customary at that time in the petty kingdoms of the Malay Peninsula, for a Chinese text of the fifth century says in so many words that, in one of those kingdoms, 'there are over a thousand Brahmans from India; the people practise their doctrine and give their daughters to them in marriage, so that many Brahmans stay there'.[7]

In order to understand how it was that Indian culture spread with such ease and such rapidity in Indochina and throughout South East Asia in general, it must be remembered that it contained within it many pre-Aryan elements and many survivals of a basic culture common to all the monsoon area of Asia. The Indochinese do not seem to have reacted towards Indian influence as if they were being confronted with an alien culture, and they 'may not always have been aware of changing their religion when adopting that of India'.[8]

It is not easy to find out which part of India the Indians who came to Indochina came from, because apart from three Tamil texts of comparatively late date, no early documents survive except those in Sanskrit, the scholarly language in common use in all parts of India. The oversimplified view according to which they came exclusively from southern India via the Coromandel ports can only be accepted with reservations. Examination of the sources at our disposal (Indian sources concerning navigation, accounts of Chinese and Mediterranean travellers and geographers, and topographic, palaeographic, and archaeological evidence) does indeed show that the south of India, and in particular the region of Kanchi (Conjeveram), played a preponderant part in the Indianization of Indochina, but also indicates that all the other regions of India, including the Dekkan, the Ganges valley, and even North West India and the Iranian frontier, contributed in varying degrees towards the spread of Indian culture.

In addition to the great maritime ports of India – Tamralipti (Tamluk, at the mouth of the Ganges), Kamara, Podouke (Pondicherry) and Sopatma on the east coast, and Bharukaccha (Broach), Surparaka, and Muchiri (Cranganore) on the west – which are known to have had relations with Indochina and Indonesia, it must be remembered that there were also various centres of Indian culture external to India proper which acted as relay stations between it and countries overseas. Centres of this kind existed in the Malay Peninsula, and we have seen how thousands of Indians settled there and married native wives. The narrowness of this peninsula made it possible for merchandise from India to be unshipped on the west coast and transported across it by land, and then re-shipped to the ports on the Gulf of Siam, which were easier of access than those on the Bay of Bengal or the coast of the China Sea. In this way the long and perilous voyage through the straits was avoided.

The political outcome of the spread of Indian influence in Indochina was that a number of States on the Indian pattern were founded, the chief of which were:

Champa, on the east coast of the peninsula, between the mountain spur of Hoanh-son and the Mekong delta;

Fu-nan, in the Mekong delta, later succeeded by the kingdom of Kambuja, which included the basin of the Great Lake as well as the Mekong delta in its territory;

Dvaravati, in the southern part of the Menam valley;

Shrikshetra, in the lower valley of the Irrawaddy.

Very little is known about how these kingdoms came into being, but one may assume either that Indians imposed their form of political organization on an indigenous society, or that an indigenous society which had been affected by Indian cultural influence created a political organization on the Indian pattern. Chinese accounts and epigraphic material both point to the latter hypothesis as being the more likely one. That being so, either of two things may have happened. Either an Indian became the ruler of an indigenous society, or a native chief may have called upon the help of a Brahman in order to set up for himself a monarchy of the Indian type. In the first case, it would have been only to be expected that the Indian should have contracted a marriage with a woman of the country, preferably a daughter of the local chief, in order to establish his prestige and secure his succession. A marriage of this kind took place at the founding of the kingdom of Fu-nan. But the alternative procedure may have been the manner in which the other Indian-type kingdoms of Indochina were founded, since Indonesia supplies many instances of this kind.

When a kingdom of the Indian type was established, several local groups, each with its own tutelary deity or god of the soil, were brought together under the authority of a single ruler, who may have been either an Indian or an Indianized native. Usually this was accompanied by the inauguration of a cult devoted to an Indian god closely associated with the person of the king, and symbolizing the unity of the kingdom, the place of worship being a natural or an artificial mountain. This custom, found in conjunction with the founding of a new kingdom or a new dynasty, is well attested for all the Indianized kingdoms of Indochina. It reconciled the native custom of worshipping supernatural beings on high places with the Indian conception of kingship, and provided some sort of national god, closely associated with the monarchy, for the peoples brought under a single ruler. It is a typical example of the way Indian culture, as it spread through Indochina, was able to appropriate and assimilate foreign cults and beliefs, and one which illustrates how Indian and native elements each played a part in forming the early Indochinese civilizations, each reacting upon the other.

With regard to this last point, there are two opposing views about which it might be useful to say a word or two, since they touch upon the very heart of the problem of the penetration of Indian cultural influence in Indochina. Those who view the problem from the sociological standpoint,[9] and who sometimes lack an adequate knowledge of Indian civilization and of the textual source material, are primarily interested in ethnological data and folk traditions, and maintain that the indigenous cultures retained their own characteristic features after contact with Indian civilization. The Indianists,[10] on the other hand, basing their views mainly on archaeological and epigraphic evidence, see the early civilizations of Indochina and Indonesia as branches springing directly from the main trunk of Indian civilization. In other words, the sociologists declare that these early civilizations were the result of changes brought about in local cultures by having Indian culture grafted upon them, whereas the Indianists see them as resulting from the adaptation of Indian culture to new conditions overseas. The former envisage the process as one of development of the indigenous cultures in response to an Indian 'stimulus', and regard the fundamental nature of each indigenous group – its 'local genius' – as having been the determinative factor in its particular kind of response. This way of seeing things has been fiercely attacked,[11] and its opponents are of the opinion that India supplied much more than a graft, maintaining that it was the whole plant that was exported, and that according to the nature of the ground where it flourished, the same plant bore fruits of varying flavour.

The syncretism typical of Indian thought is what chiefly characterized Brahmanism and enabled it, despite its lack of centralized organization and of a programme of action, to give spiritual unity to India; and it was this, together with the tolerance of Shivaism, that enabled Indian culture to assimilate, as we have seen, the most diverse foreign elements when it was transplanted overseas. In this respect, the Indianization of Indochina does not differ essentially from that of the Dravidian countries in India itself. As has been well said by de la Vallée Poussin,[12] it is no more than 'the extension overseas of the process of Brahmanization which started long before the time of Buddha, and which, from its area of origin in North West India, has spread and still continues to spread in Bengal and the south'. I should be inclined to go farther and to add that perhaps the only difference between the Aryanization of Bengal and the Dravidian countries and that of South East Asia is that the first, being a process which took place over an inland area, occurred so to speak by osmosis, whereas this was not the case when the same process took place overseas. It is questionable whether there is a greater variety of cultures in the Indianized countries overseas than is found among the various ethnic groups of India itself; and if it is permissible to use the term 'Indian civilization' to cover a wide variety of cultures, there is nothing to prevent one including within it those of South East Asia.

I am aware that these views have been contested,[13] and that the idea of an 'Indian superstructure' superimposed upon an 'indigenous substratum' is one which has been declared to be 'untenable'. I willingly admit that these expressions which I used ten years ago may lead to misunderstandings.[14] When I spoke of a superstructure, or referred in a more general way to Indian civilization in Cambodia or some other Indianized kingdom, what I had in mind was of course the civilization revealed by inscriptions and archaeological evidence. This civilization was that of an *élite*, and only included certain special spheres, such as religion, art, philosophy, and literature, as well as the concept of the State and of the monarchy. The social structure as a whole, the mode of life and the beliefs of the common people, and economic conditions – these belong to another sphere about which very little is known. But there is reason to suppose that more searching study of epigraphic material, especially of inscriptions in the native languages – hitherto used almost exclusively for exploring the history of events and the history of art – will reveal a great many facts about the 'indigenous substratum' which will bear out the view that Indian influence penetrated more deeply than sociologists realize. When this has been done, only then will it be appropriate to attempt to solve the problem as to whether the indigenous societies retained the essential part of their original features, or whether they became integrated into a society fundamentally Indian in type. In Cambodia for instance the former division of society into classes following hereditary occupations and designated by the same word (*varna*) as that used for Indian castes, and the existence of an administrative system officered by a bureaucracy whose functions were designated by Indian words, greatly facilitated the integration of Khmer society into a society modelled on the Indian pattern.

3

The Spread of Indian Cultural
Influence in the Peninsula

I. IN THE SOUTH: FU-NAN

IT WAS IN the first century A.D. that a kingdom was founded in the
lower valley of the Mekong which so far is only known by the
Chinese name of Fu-nan[1] – probably a transcription of the word
bnam, common to most of the Mon-Khmer dialects, meaning
'mountain'. This is the word which is translated into Sanskrit in
the dynastic title *Shailaraja* or *Parvatabhupala*, 'king of the mountain', where it apparently refers to one of those mountains upon
which, as has been mentioned above, the founder of a State or a
dynasty instituted the cult of a sort of god or national guardian
spirit which transcended the particularist cults of local gods.

Fu-nan came into being as the result of one of those mixed
marriages already referred to. Legend has it that an Indian Brahman named Kaundinya (the name of a well-known clan in North
West India) arrived in the country and married Soma, the daughter
of the King of the Naga – that is, of the local native chief. This is
similar to the marriage to which the Pallava kings of Kanchi
traced their ancestry. Opinions are divided as to the remoter
origins of this legendary theme, which is sometimes thought to
have come from the West, and sometimes from the maritime
regions of South East Asia. However that may be, Kaundinya and
Soma were regarded as the founding ancestors of the line of kings
that ruled over Fu-nan.

It may be assumed that the kingdom was founded sometime during the first century A.D., because by the second century historical personages are mentioned in the Chinese sources. The most outstanding of them was a military leader called Fan Man or Fan Shih-man,[2] who was raised to the throne by popular acclaim. A Chinese text says: 'He attacked and conquered the neighbouring kingdoms; all gave allegiance to him. He himself took the title of Great King of Fu-nan. Then he had great ships built, and, after crossing the wide seas, he attacked more than ten kingdoms . . .'

From this it can be seen that from the beginning Fu-nan was organized after the manner of an Indian kingdom, governed by a maharaja with surrounding vassal kingdoms. It is difficult to make any accurate assessment of the extent of the conquests of Fan Shih-man. His suzerainty may have extended eastwards as far as the region of Nha-trang, where the stele of Vo Canh was erected by one of his descendants, upon which he is mentioned under the Sanskrit form of his name, Shri Mara;[3] southwards to the northern part of the Malay Peninsula, the probable objective of the maritime expeditions he undertook for the purpose of ensuring command of the maritime trade routes and the land transport routes; and westwards as far as Lower Burma, where he may have met his death, for he is said to have disappeared during an expedition against the Chin-lin or 'Golden Frontier', which may correspond either to Suvannabhumi, the 'gold land' of Pali texts, or to Suvarnakudya, the 'gold wall' of Sanskrit texts (in Lower Burma).

His successor, Fan Chan, entered into relations with India and China, and this step, which was undertaken with commercial considerations in view rather than with any political ambitions, confers some importance on his reign. This was the period of the Three Kingdoms in China, and in south China (the kingdom of Wu), where the land routes for trade with the west were cut off by the kingdom of Wei, endeavours were made to procure the luxury goods required there by the sea routes.[4] Now Fu-nan occupied a key position with regard to the maritime trade routes, and was inevitably a port of call both for the navigators who went through the Straits of Malacca and for those – probably more numerous – who made the transit over one of the isthmuses of the Malay Peninsula. Fu-nan may even have been the terminus of voyages from the Eastern Mediterranean, if it is the case that the Kattigara mentioned by Ptolemy was situated on the western coast of Indochina on the Gulf of Siam.

The embassy sent by Fan Chan to India shortly after 225 arrived at the mouth of the Ganges and went up river to the capital of a Murunda prince. It brought back a present of four horses from the country of the Indo-Scythians.

The embassy sent to China in 243 presented products of the country to the emperor, and also some musicians, for whom an institute was established the following year, near Nanking. The Chinese mission which came to Fu-nan sometime between 245 and 250 found a usurper, Fan Hsün, on the throne, and encountered at his Court an envoy of the Murunda. This first Chinese mission recorded an interesting account of Fu-nan which mentions walled cities, palaces, and dwelling-houses. The people, it says, were 'all ugly, black, and frizzy-haired, and went about naked and barefoot', and it describes them as practising agriculture and as being 'fond of engraving ornaments and of carving. Many of their eating utensils are made of silver. Taxes are paid in gold, silver, pearls and perfumes. They have books and depositories of archives, the writing being like that of the Hu.' Hu is the Chinese term for the people of central Asia, who use an Indian script.

The three embassies that went from Fu-nan to China between 285 and 287 were perhaps the result of the revival of maritime trade after 280, the year in which China was reunified under the Chin – an event which stimulated the demand for luxury goods at the Court.

When we reach the middle of the fourth century, the Chinese sources record that in 357 Fu-nan was ruled by an Indian whose name, or rather whose title of *Chandan*, seems to indicate that he was of Iranian origin – probably a Kushan.[5]

357 is the only date recorded during the reign of Chandan, and after that there is no further mention of Fu-nan until the end of the fourth or the beginning of the fifth century. This was a period marked by the revival of Indian influence throughout the whole of South East Asia. The Chinese historians refer to a second Kaundinya, who is said to have come from India via the Malay Peninsula and to have renewed Indian traditions in the country. His successors regularly maintained relations with China, and Jayavarman who died in 514 after reigning for over thirty years, was honoured by the Court of China by having the title of 'General of the Pacified South, King of Fu-nan' conferred upon him.

His reign marks a period when Fu-nan reached the height of its grandeur and apparently gave rise to a civilization of great brilliance. Fu-nan was then centred on the lower course and the delta of the Mekong. Its capital, Vyadhapura, the 'city of the hunter', was situated near the hill called Ba Phnom – a name which perhaps perpetuates to this day the ancient name of the country. The Chinese say that the capital lay at a distance of 120 miles from the sea. This is approximately the distance between Ba Phnom and the site of Oc Eo, which lies on the Gulf of Siam west of the delta, and which must have been, if not the main port of Fu-nan, at least a centre for foreign merchants. The remains of an ancient seaport have been found there, and excavations have disclosed the foundations of buildings, and many objects bearing witness to Fu-nan's contact with the west, such as Roman medals with the effigies of Antoninus Pius and Marcus Aurelius, a cabochon with a Sassanid effigy, rings with inscriptions in Indian script of the second to the fifth century, and intaglios engraved with motifs inspired by Hellenistic art.[6]

The Chinese sources provide some information about the civilization that flourished in Fu-nan at this time. They note that slavery was practised and raids carried out against neighbours to keep up the supply of slaves; that there was trade in gold, silver, and silk, and that gold rings and bracelets and silver vessels were made. They describe how the king lived in a multi-storeyed palace and the common people in dwellings built on piles and roofed with the leaves of 'a large bamboo growing by the seashore'. They mention boats eighty to ninety feet long and six or seven feet wide, the bows and stern of which were like the head and tail of a fish. They also say that the king rode about on an elephant, that the pastimes of the people were cock-fighting and pig-fighting, and that there was trial by ordeal: 'they throw gold rings or eggs into boiling water from which these objects have to be retrieved, or they make a chain red-hot which then has to be carried in the hands for a distance of seven paces; a guilty person's hands are completely scorched, while the innocent person remains uninjured; or else the accused is made to dive into water; an innocent person goes into the water but does not drown, while a guilty person drowns'. Another text adds the following details: 'They do not dig wells by their dwellings but share a pool, from which they draw water, between several tens of families. They have a custom of worshipping the deities of the sky. They make bronze images of these deities. Those with two faces have four arms, those with four faces have eight arms; each hand holds something, sometimes a child, sometimes a bird or a fourfooted animal, or else the sun or the moon. . . . When the king sits down, he squats on one side with the right knee raised and the left on the ground. A piece of cotton cloth is spread before him on which are placed gold vases and incense-burners. For mourning it is customary to shave the hair and beard. There are four ways of disposing of the dead: by throwing the corpse into the current of a river, by burning it to ashes, by burying it in a trench, and by exposing it to the birds.' To these items of information (many of which, such as houses on piles, trials by ordeal, the common pool (*trapeang*), and the custom of shaving the head and beard for mourning, still apply to the Cambodia of today) one might add that the rulers of Fu-nan must certainly have known advanced techniques of agricultural hydraulics. From the air it can be seen that the area that once formed the kingdom of Fu-nan is covered by a network of canals that link the ancient sites and date back to the time of that kingdom. Furthermore, a Sanskrit inscription of Funanese provenance found in the Plaine des Joncs in southern Viet-nam mentions a region 'reclaimed from the mud', which means that it was put under cultivation after drainage operations.[7]

There is evidence that all the various Indian cults existed in Fu-nan, either simultaneously or in succession. In the reign of Jayavarman, 'it was the custom to worship the god Maheshvara (Shiva), who ceaselessly descends upon Mount Mo-tan'. This apparently refers to the sacred mountain from which the country and its kings took their name. It was the place where heaven and earth were in communication – hence the Chinese expression about the god 'ceaselessly' descending. No doubt he materialized in the form of a linga, the phallic emblem of Shiva Girisha, Shiva 'residing upon the mountain', mentioned in the inscriptions. That the Vaishnavite cult existed is shown by the inscriptions of Prince Gunavarman (probably a son of Jayavarman) and of his mother. Lastly, Hinayana Buddhism, with its Sanskrit canon, is attested for the fifth and the sixth centuries in the inscriptions of Jayavarman and his successor Rudravarman.[8]

Of the architecture of Fu-nan, nothing seems to have survived except for a few foundations of buildings found at Oc Eo, and even these are difficult to interpret. But an interesting hypothesis[9] has been put forward which gives reason to suppose that certain buildings of the seventh century belonging to Khmer art of the pre-Angkor period, with roofs containing many minute storeys with decorated niches, reproduce the characteristic features of the architectural monuments of Fu-nan. As for its sculptural style, a number of statues found at Angkor Borei, the last capital of Fu-nan, may be regarded as belonging to it, particularly some representing Vishnu-Krishna, and perhaps also some of the Buddha in the Gupta style.[10]

Fu-nan dominated the Indochinese peninsula for five centuries, and its prestige lived on long after its fall. The pre-Angkor kings of Cambodia adopted its dynastic legends, and those who reigned at Angkor traced their ancestry to the supreme rulers of Vyadhapura.

We could wish for fuller documentation on the kingdom of Fu-nan, and it is to be hoped that excavation of the numerous supposedly Funanese sites that have been discovered in the Mekong delta will provide us with further information. Its culture seems to have been a result of the extension of the process of Brahmanization, which had been operating in India, to countries overseas. The absence of any texts in the vernacular dating from the Fu-nan period means that we are unfortunately left in ignorance as to what language was spoken by its people, and hence we do not know to what ethno-linguistic group they belonged. Nevertheless we can assume it to be highly probable that the Funanese belonged in the main to the Mon-Khmer group. The very name of the country given in the Chinese texts would seem to indicate this, if it does indeed represent the word *bnam*, 'mountain', which is typically Mon-Khmer. It has moreover been established[11] that the Khmer language spread along the routes that must have been followed by the conquerors of Fu-nan in the sixth century. As a result of this diffusion, various related dialects are dispersed around the periphery of present Cambodia. These dialects show great similarities, and also have features in common differentiating them from Khmer, which leads to the supposition that they are modern versions of the spoken language of the people of Fu-nan.

The people were described by the Chinese as being black-skinned and frizzy-haired – features which are common to most of the mountain tribes and even found in those Cambodians whose skin has not been lightened and whose hair has not been straightened by miscegenation with the Chinese. Their 'raised' dwellings (that is, dwellings built on piles) belong to the type widespread in South East Asia. Certain customs, such as the various kinds of trial by ordeal and cock-fighting and pig-fighting, are still practised by backward tribes of the eastern mountain chain. But it was from India that the cultured section of Funanese society acquired their religion, their burial customs, their art, their writing as found from the third century onwards, their knowledge of Sanskrit, and no doubt many features of their material culture, in particular their highly developed irrigation system. Fu-nan certainly played an important role in the spread of Indian cultural influence in Indochina.

Before narrating how in the sixth century Fu-nan lost its supremacy over southern Indochina to one of its dependencies, I must first describe how the kingdom of Champa on the east side of the peninsula, and the kingdoms of Dvaravati and Shrikshetra on the west, came into being.

2. THE SPREAD OF INDIAN INFLUENCE IN THE EAST OF THE PENINSULA: CHAMPA

The Chinese give A.D. 192 as the year when, in the region around the present city of Hué, a kingdom was founded to which they gave the name of Lin-i, and which later Sanskrit sources call Champa.[12] According to the Chinese sources, it was founded by a native – that is, a non-Chinese – official called Ch'iu-lien, which is the name also given to a band of 'barbarians' from the same region – the region being described as being 'beyond the frontiers of Jih-nan', which was the southernmost of the Chinese coastal commanderies – who in 137, before the kingdom was founded, made their first attempt at invasion. One is tempted to suppose that the founder of Lin-i was descended from these 'barbarians'.

Where had they come from? The commandery of Jih-nan lay along the east coast, and was bordered on the north by the Chinese commandery of Chiao-chih; so they could only have come from the south or – more probably – from the west, perhaps from the valley of the Mekong. As for their name, it is impossible to reconstruct it with any degree of accuracy from the Chinese characters which give the only written record of it, especially as the characters differ in the two versions of the name, although the pronunciation is the same for both.

There is no evidence of any Indian influence having reached Lin-i at the end of the second century. Indeed it is not until the fourth century that Sanskrit inscriptions, found it is true in a region farther south, provide direct evidence of the Indianization of Champa.

The descendants of Ch'iu-lien, profiting from the partition of China during the Three Kingdoms period, were able to expand northwards as far as the mountain spur of Hoanh-son, which forms a perfect natural frontier. In 220 and again in 230 an embassy was sent from Lin-i to the Chinese governor of Chiao-chih, Lü Tai by name; but this did not prevent the people of Lin-i from pillaging the towns of the north in 248. Their raids gained them the territory of Ch'iu-su, which coincides with the present region of Badon on the Song Gianh river, and this territory for some time formed a sort of march on the northern frontier of the country.[13] It was there, roughly in the area between Hoanh-son and the Col des Nuages, that the first struggles took place between peoples belonging to the zones of influence of the two great Asiatic civilizations, here represented by the Indianized Chams, who were endeavouring to expand northwards, and the sinicized Vietnamese, who were seeking for new territories in the south.

The first kings of Lin-i are only known by the names given them by the Chinese: Fan Hsiung (270), Fan I, Fan Wen (336–49), who went to China in 313 and 316 and learnt various techniques there, Fan Fo (377), Fan Hu-ta (380–413), and Ti Chen. Their devious dealings with the Chinese governors of Chiao-chih were motivated by their continual attempts to expand northwards, such for instance as the attacks against Jih-nan carried out by Fan Hu-ta in 399, 405, and 407, which were followed by an expedition which he launched against the territories to the north of Jih-nan in 413, from which he did not return.

In the second half of the fourth century a king appears bearing the Sanskrit name of Bhadravarman,[14] with whom are associated the earliest Sanskrit inscriptions found in the present provinces of Quang-nam and Phu-yen, to the south of the bay of Tourane (Danang). He it was who, in the My-son area, founded the first shrine for the worship of Shiva Bhadreshvara. The name of the god is linked with that of the founder of the cult. Later inscriptions tell us that the god Bhadreshvara was represented by a linga – the earliest royal linga on record in Indochina. Bhadravarman's capital must have been situated to the east of My-son, on the site of the present village of Tra-kieu, in the neighbourhood of which three rock inscriptions have been found with writing identical to that of the royal inscriptions. One[15] of them, which is the oldest extant text in the Cham language (and indeed in any Indonesian language) proves that during the fourth century the country to the south of the bay of Tourane (Danang) was inhabited by a people speaking Cham.

Attempts have been made to identify Bhadravarman either with the Fan Hu-ta or the Fan Fo mentioned in the Chinese sources, but it may well be that the kings of Lin-i recorded by the Chinese as reigning in the region of Hué belonged to a different dynasty from that of Bhadravarman and his successors (who also had Sanskrit names), who reigned in Quang-nam. It is only from the fifth century onwards that the names of the kings as given in the inscriptions can be identified with the transcriptions or translations of these names found in the Chinese sources.

The interest of the Sanskrit inscriptions of Bhadravarman lies in the evidence they provide of the introduction of Indian culture in the region of present Quang-nam, which, as the sites of Tra-kieu, My-son, and Dong-duong show, was to become the very heart of Champa, and which became known by the purely Indian name of Amaravati. These inscriptions are the earliest documents concerning the religion of the ancient Chams, and bear witness to the predominance of the cult of Shiva, in association with that of his wife Uma. A Chinese encyclopaedist gives additional information regarding the customs of Lin-i at that time.[16] He quotes sources which tell how 'the people build the walls of their houses with baked bricks covered with a layer of lime, and the houses are surmounted by a platform terrace known as *kan-lan* (in Cham, *kalan*)'. The people of Lin-i are described as having 'deep-set eyes, straight prominent noses, and black frizzy hair. The women wear their hair in a knot on top of the head. . . . Both men and women wear nothing but a length of *chi-pei* (cotton?) cloth wrapped round their bodies. They pierce their ears so that they can hang small rings in them. The upper classes wear leather shoes, while the common people go barefoot.' The headgear worn by the king is described as being 'a tall cap with flower embroidery in gold, decorated with a silk tassle. When he goes about he rides on an elephant.' With regard to marriage, the Chinese note that it is not forbidden for people with the same surname to marry each other. The arms carried by these 'cruel and warlike' people include bows and arrows, sabres, lances, and cross-bows made of bamboo. 'The musical instruments they use are very like those which we ourselves (i.e. the Chinese) have: the zither, the five-stringed fiddle, the flute, etc. They also use conches and drums as warning signals.' Lastly, here is what is said about burial customs, these being borrowed direct from India: 'the burial of a king takes place seven days after his death, great mandarins are buried three days after their decease, and ordinary people the day following it. Whatever the social status of the deceased may have been, the body is carefully shrouded, carried to the sea-shore or the banks of a river to the sound of drums and the accompaniment of dances, and then delivered to the flames on a pyre prepared by the mourners. The bones which survive the flames are enclosed in a gold vase and thrown into the sea when it is the body of a king that has been burned. The remains of a mandarin are enclosed in a silver vase and thrown into the waves at the mouth of a river. For the dead who have enjoyed no special distinction an earthenware vase is considered good enough and it is consigned to the waters of a river. The parents of the dead of both sexes follow the procession and cut their hair before leaving the riverbank, this being the only sign of a mourning period which is brief.'

The son of Fan Hu-ta (whatever the correct identification of the latter may be) abdicated in favour of a nephew and went to India; no doubt it is he to whom a seventh century inscription mentioning a king called Gangaraja, 'the king (who went) to the Ganges', refers. Little is known of events subsequent to this. After a period of internal struggles a new dynasty appeared in 420, whose kings are only mentioned in Chinese sources.

In 431, after a Cham fleet had pillaged the coasts of Chiao-chih, the Chinese laid siege to Ch'iu-su without success, and after a further series of Cham raids, the governor T'an Ho-chih carried out severe reprisals in 446 and took first Ch'iu-su and then the capital.

Possibly Fan Shen-ch'eng (*c.* 455-72) can be identified with King Devanika who will be mentioned in connection with Cambodia.[17] About 529 a king called Rudravarman appears, who was a descendant of Gangaraja. His reign was marked by unsuccessful raids carried out against the north in 543, and by several embassies to China (in 534, 568, and 572). His successors will be discussed in connection with Cambodia, with which Champa had close relations from their time onwards throughout the seventh century.

We are better informed about the linguistic affiliations of the early inhabitants of Champa, or at least of those inhabiting the region of present Quang-nam, than is the case with Fu-nan, owing to the rock inscriptions of the fourth century which I have already mentioned, the language of which is archaic Cham. Did these people belonging to the Indonesian linguistic group receive Indian cultural influence directly by way of the sea, or indirectly through the medium of neighbouring countries either to the west or to the south which had already been Indianized? The celebrated Buddha discovered at Dong-duong in Quang-nam[18] – a bronze statue in the Gupta style which is perhaps of Indian origin and probably dates from the fourth century – does not tell us much about where Indian influence came from. Nor does it necessarily indicate that there was an early period of Buddhism in Champa, which was a country chiefly characterized by its deep attachment to Hinduism, apart from the period of Buddhist expansion at the end of the ninth century. Statues are easily transported, and there is nothing to prove that this one was brought to Indochina immediately after it was cast.

Another question that is not easy to answer is whether, as has been supposed, the area on the east coast of the peninsula that became affected by Indian cultural influence had already been steeped in the Dongsonian culture of which remains have been found to the north of the natural frontier of Hoanh-son.

The important point is that although Indian cultural influence was brought by the Chams as far as that frontier, it never succeeded in crossing it. On the other hand, once the Chams – whose country, with its many internal geographical barriers, did not lend itself to the founding of a strong centralized State – had assimilated Indian culture, they were for centuries able to withstand the pressure of Sino-Vietnamese cultural influence. The history of Champa is so closely bound up with the expansion of Viet-nam towards the south, that for clarity's sake it has seemed better, in subsequent chapters, to treat the history of Champa after the seventh century along with that of Viet-nam. This does not in any way mean that the Indianized culture of the Chams had any influence whatsoever on the culture of the Vietnamese, who destroyed rather than assimilated the culture of the countries into which they expanded.

3. THE SPREAD OF INDIAN INFLUENCE IN THE CENTRE AND THE WEST OF THE PENINSULA: SHRIKSHETRA AND DVARAVATI[19]

Having seen how Chinese cultural influence was introduced into the north of Indochina by China's conquest of the delta, and how Indian cultural influence penetrated into the south and east of the peninsula with the founding of Fu-nan and Champa, let us now see what happened during the same period – that is, during the first centuries A.D. – in the west and in the centre, or, roughly speaking, the area covered by the valleys of the Irrawaddy and the lower Menam.

As regards the history of the valley of the Irrawaddy before the fourth century, external sources tell us practically nothing, and the indigenous sources of a much later date only give dynastic lists, the accuracy of which it is impossible to check. All that can be inferred from the few available documents is that a kingdom with Mon inhabitants in the low-lying lands of the delta existed contemporaneously with another kingdom, with Pyu inhabitants, on the middle Irrawaddy.

In the third century the Chinese entered into contact, via Yunnan, with a kingdom which they called P'iao, this being the Indianized kingdom of Pyu centred on the region surrounding the present town of Prome, where fragments of the Buddhist canon in Pali have been found. This is the kingdom to which the Chinese pilgrims of the seventh century gave the name of Shrikshetra, which was apparently derived from the ancient name of the Indian city of Puri in the Orissa. The Pyus (who called themselves the *Tirchul*) were perhaps the advance guard of the Burmese migration from the Tibetan borders. This migration had not yet reached the rice-growing plain of Kyaukse which later was to become the area where the kingdom of Burma arose and the centre from which it expanded. Seventh-century evidence shows that at that time the Pyus were still at Halin, farther to the north. The delta was occupied by the Mons, who were known as Talaing to the Burmese, from the Indian word Telingana (the name for Madras), and as Peguans to the Europeans, because the city of Pegu was their capital from the ninth century. Their main centre was Sudhammavati (present Thaton), where legend has it that Buddhaghosa, the famous fifth-century commentator on the Buddhist scriptures, was born and died. The western part of the peninsula which was later to form the territory of the Burmese State seems to have been the first of the overseas regions to benefit from Indian influence. This was because of its proximity to India, from which it is only separated by the Bay of Bengal, and with which it can communicate by a land route as well (although the use of this route in early times has been contested).[20] There is a Buddhist tradition according to which the emperor Ashoka, in the third century B.C., sent two monks to the country of Suvannabhumi, the Land of Gold, which is usually identified with the country of the Mons. But the first tangible evidence of Indian penetration into the Irrawaddy valley – namely, the fragments of the Buddhist canon found at Maungun, near the ancient site of Prome – dates from no earlier than the end of the fifth century.

Information about Indian penetration in the Menam valley is even more scanty and from a still later date. The existence of a kingdom situated between the Khmer kingdom and the Pyu kingdom of Shrikshetra is attested by the Chinese pilgrim Hsüan-tsang, who called it T'o-lo-po-ti. This name corresponds to Dvaravati,[21] a place-name which is given in Indian legend to the capital of the god Krishna in Gujerat.

Almost nothing is known about the origins and early history of this kingdom. Perhaps it was at one time one of the vassal kingdoms of Fu-nan. It seems reasonable to suppose that the Buddhist archaeological remains that are scattered over the lower valley of the Menam, from Lop Buri in the north to Rajapuri (*Rat Buri*) in the west and Prachin in the east, belong to it. Evidence that the people of Dvaravati were originally Mon-speaking is provided by the fragment of an inscription in Indian script found at the chief site at Nagarama Patha (*Nakhon Pathom*, or more usually, Phra Pathom), and by another text carved on a pillar at Lop Buri. Both texts are in archaic Mon, and the first dates perhaps from the sixth and the other perhaps from the seventh century.[22]

Curiously enough, Mon historical traditions locate the original centre of the Mon people at Sudhammavati (Thaton), at the mouth of the Sittang, where there are no archaeological remains of any importance, and say nothing about the Menam valley, where the Mons have virtually disappeared, but where there is a considerable number of remains, which, however, date from no earlier than the sixth or seventh century.

As regards architecture,[23] there is at Phra Pathom the lower part of a Buddhist temple which has a two-layered stepped base, upon each face of which seated Buddhas are placed in niches flanked by colonettes and pilasters. Other foundations, perhaps even older, have been found farther west at Phong Tuk on the river Kanburi, along with a bronze lamp in Hellenistic style and statuettes of the Buddha in post-Gupta style. In Phra Pathom were also found large stone wheels, often in association with statues of stags, recalling Mrigavana where the Buddha set the Wheel of the Law in motion. These wheels are probably contemporary with the Buddhist statues and bas-reliefs in the Gupta style found at Prachin in the east, Lop Buri in the centre, and Rajapuri and Jaiya (*Chaiya*) in the south of the territory belonging to the ancient kingdom of Dvaravati. These same sites have also produced statues of Vishnu wearing a cylindrical mitre, similar to those found in Cambodia dating roughly from the seventh and eighth centuries.

From what has been said it can be seen that during the first centuries A.D. the people who played the role of recipients and propagators of the main features of Indian culture in the west of the peninsula were the Mons. Many traces of Hinduism are found in Lower Burma, but in Mon country Theravada Buddhism was the main influence. Buddhism is not so bound up with the inner workings of Indian forms of social structure as Hinduism is, and with its claims to be a universal religion, it can reach deeper among the masses of the common people; so no doubt the upper classes in western Indochina were less moulded by it than were the upper classes of Fu-nan and Champa by Hinduism.

This prevalence of Buddhism in the west and of Hinduism in the east of the peninsula was a distinctive feature of Indochina from the first centuries of the Christian era, and one which was to have important consequences for later social developments.

PART THREE

---

*The Indochinese States from the
Sixth to the Thirteenth Century*

IN THE FOREGOING CHAPTERS I have attempted to show how both Chinese and Indian cultural influence was introduced into Indochina among ethnic groups whose origins and distribution in prehistoric times I have tried to trace. Under Chinese or Indian influence, several Indochinese societies situated in the plains and the deltas became organized States, and we must now follow the history of these States.

The first period to which we must give our attention is the period from the sixth century, when historical and archaeological documentation becomes fairly abundant, to the thirteenth century, when the upheavals in Asia brought about by the Mongols led to great changes in Indochina and to the birth of new States. During these centuries no new ethnic strain entered the peninsula from beyond its borders, except in the Irrawaddy valley, where the Burmese from the north took over from their advance guard, the Pyus, and founded the kingdom of Arimaddanapura (Pagan). The T'ais had not yet begun to infiltrate to any great extent, and were not found in large numbers anywhere except on the northern frontiers. The main changes that occurred during this period had nothing to do with any redistribution of ethnic groups, but were brought about by political events within the peninsula. Viet-nam liberated itself from Chinese domination and began to put pressure on its neighbours to the south, the Chams. Fu-nan disappeared, making way for the kingdom of Kambuja, which at first was confined to the basin of the Great Lake and the Mekong delta, but later expanded at the expense of the kingdom of Dvaravati to include the plateau of Korat and the lower and middle Menam valley. The area over which the Mons exercised political authority was thereafter restricted to the Burmese delta and the upper Menam valley.

Three great civilizations arose, each with its period of grandeur and expansion during which it exerted some influence on its neighbours. These were: the civilization of Viet-nam, which, once rid of Chinese domination, expanded into the delta of the Red River and enjoyed a brilliant period under the Ly dynasty (eleventh and twelfth centuries); the Khmer civilization, the successor to Fu-nan, with its capital at Yashodharapura (Angkor), which enjoyed great prestige in the centre of the peninsula from the ninth to the twelfth century; and the Burmese civilization, which, as the ruins of Arimaddana (Pagan) show, flourished from the eleventh to the thirteenth century.

Cham civilization, although its monuments are scattered over the coastal plains between Hoanh-son and the Mekong delta, suffered from the fact that the country occupied a narrow strip of territory cut up by natural barriers, which did not favour the founding of a centralized State; and this, together with its frequent struggles with Viet-nam, prevented it from exercising much influence on its neighbours (except for a brief period in the ninth century).

The sources available for the study of Indochinese history between the sixth and the thirteenth century are in the main epigraphic material and Chinese texts.

The epigraphic material consists for the most part of charters relating to the foundation of religious establishments. They have enabled us to draw up the chronological framework in which to place the names of kings and the principal events – especially those concerning religion – of their reigns. They have also enabled us to date with accuracy most of the monuments and other archaeological remains. But epigraphic studies are still far from having exhausted the primary documentation provided by inscriptions. Although the Sanskrit texts are somewhat limited in scope, being almost entirely confined to matters relating to the thoroughly Indianized Courts, the vernacular texts have much to teach us about the institutions, administrative and legal systems, economic structure, social organization, and material culture of the Khmers.

The documentation in Chinese, whether the sources are of Chinese or Vietnamese provenance, is a mine of information which is of great value because of the chronological accuracy of these sources, and because the information was acquired directly either from Chinese envoys, who had collected it during their missions to Indochina, or from Indochinese envoys to China.

But neither the inscriptions nor the Chinese texts (except those of Viet-nam) give a continuous account of historical events in Indochina, and it is the historian's task to reconstruct the sequence of events from source material which leaves many aspects in darkness and contains many gaps. The other available sources, such as accounts written by travellers or by Arab and Persian merchants, and legendary tales transmitted by oral tradition, are, except for a late and untrustworthy chronicle of the Burmese kingdom of Pagan, of a nature which only enables one to add a touch here and there to the picture built up from the inscriptions and the Chinese written documents – and also, of course, from the archaeological evidence, since often the remaining buildings are the only source of information about the past.

I

Viet-nam[1]

WE SAW EARLIER how Viet-nam, under Chinese domination, started quarreling with Lin-i or Champa shortly after this kingdom was founded in 192. Mention was made of the unsuccessful expeditions launched by the Cham king Fan Hu-ta against his northern neighbours at the end of the fourth and the beginning of the fifth century, and an account was given of how, in 431, after a Cham fleet had come to pillage their coasts, the Chinese laid siege to Ch'iu-su without success, and of how, in return, after further Cham incursions, the reprisals undertaken in 446 by the Chinese governor T'an Ho-chih (*Dan Hoa-chi*) resulted in the capture first of Ch'iu-su and then of the capital.

In the following century the Cham king, Rudravarman, who had founded a new dynasty in 529, attempted a raid against the north in 543, but was defeated by Pham Tu, a general of that same Ly Bon who, as we have seen, had just gained mastery over the delta area. The Chinese general, Liu Fang (*Luu Phuong*), regained this territory from Ly Phat-tu, and then in 605 conducted a campaign against Champa, where Shambhuvarman, the son and successor of Rudravarman, was reigning. The campaign was probably undertaken for the purpose of opening up the region for trade. Liu Fang took Ch'iu-su and then occupied the capital, which was then at Tra-kieu, removing from it some gold statues and a large number of writings. After his departure, Shambhuvarman took possession again. Shambhuvarman died in 629, after having reconstructed the great temple of Bhadravarman at My-son, which had been destroyed by fire in the previous reign, and

77

which was renamed Shambhubhadreshvara. He was succeeded by Kandarpadharma (630, 631), and then by his grandson, Prabhasadharma, who died in 645.

Owing to the powerful rule of the T'ang dynasty in China at that time, Viet-nam enjoyed a period of tranquillity during the eighth century. Its only troubles were a few brief internal revolts of minor importance, the most notable being the revolt of a certain Mai Thuc Loan, who in 722, aided by the Chams and the Khmers, succeeded in capturing the capital; and the revolt of Phung Hung (787–94), who in his lifetime only enjoyed the title of governor, but who was later venerated under the posthumous title of king.

Another type of occurrence during the eighth century consisted of incursions of Indonesians or Melanesians, which were perhaps connected with events that were taking place in the archipelago at that time. The Vietnamese Annals record that in 767, the delta area was invaded by bands from Java and the southern regions in general, upon whom the Chinese governor, Chang Po-i (*Truong Ba-nghi*), inflicted a defeat, driving them back to the sea. In 774, according to a Sanskrit inscription of Nha-trang, 'men born in other countries, men living on food more horrible than corpses, terrifying, thin, and entirely black, as fierce and as remorseless as death, who came in ships', burnt down the temple of Po Nagar near Nha-trang. They were routed and driven back to the sea by the king of Champa. In 787 armies that had come by ship from Java burnt down another temple.

Until the middle of the eighth century the heart of the Cham kingdom was first in the region of Hué, and then in the Quang-nam area, south of the bay of Tourane (Danang), where some of the most remarkable archaeological sites of Champa are found, the most outstanding being that of My-son, which was a kind of holy city. The little that remains there of the art of the eighth century (a pediment and a magnificent pedestal) shows features that still bear signs of fairly direct Gupta influence and great affinity with other types of Indian-style South East Asian art, particularly with Khmer art of the pre-Angkor period.

We know that in the middle of the eighth century the political centre of Champa was moved farther south to Panduranga (Phan-rang) and Kauthara (Nha-trang), and in 758 the Chinese use the name Huan-wang in place of Lin-i. This southern dynasty will be mentioned when Cambodia is discussed. Here it will suffice to say that in 803 King Harivarman I went to war against the Chinese provinces north of Hoanh-son, and had some success – a success which was, however, cancelled out by the failure of another expedition in 809. This is the dynasty to which may be attributed one of the most ancient forms of Cham architecture known to us – the towers of Hoa-lai, the oldest of which has a form of horseshoe niche on its superstructure which is almost identical with that known as *kudu* in the Dravidian art of the eighth century.

In 875 a dynasty appears with its capital at Indrapura in Quang-nam. The Chinese once more changed the name they gave to the country, this time to Chan-ch'eng, or the 'town of Chan', corresponding to the Sanskrit Champapura. The founder of the new dynasty, Indravarman II, was not related by blood to his predecessors. He was a Buddhist, and erected the great temple of Dong-duong, near the capital – the first evidence of the existence of Mahayana Buddhism in Champa. The style of architecture is far removed from its Indian origins, of which scarcely anything remains except the love of over-elaboration and the use of plant-motifs in ornamentation. Instead, it bears signs, especially in the facial expression of the statues and the representation of the human form in bas-relief, of indigenous influence such as only appeared much later in the art of neighbouring countries, when there was a kind of resurgence of native trends at the end of the Indian period. These sculptures and the exuberant and all-invading decoration of the buildings give an impression of barbarian vitality which cannot be accounted for by any known factors.

Meanwhile, towards the middle of the ninth century, the delta area found itself exposed to the attacks of Nan-chao, a kingdom which had come into being during the first half of the eighth century within an area extending over the west and north-west of Yunnan. The people of Nan-chao, whose aid had been sought by the mountain tribes of Viet-nam who had grievances against the Chinese governors to settle, came to attack Vietnamese strongholds in 858. Forced to retreat after their first attack, they returned in 862, when they succeeded in taking the capital, and thereafter proceeded to organize the country in their own way. The Chinese general Kao P'ien (*Cao Bien*) was put in command of reprisals, and he chased the invaders away in 866–67 and built the fortified town of Dai-la-thanh, to the north-west of present Hanoi.

The fall of the T'ang in 907, followed by the partition of China during the period of the Five Dynasties, marked the end of any effective control exercised by the empire over the provinces of the south. The Later Liang dynasty (907–23) recognized a native chief called Khuc Thua Du as governor of Viet-nam, and he was succeeded by his son, Khuc Hao. The latter sent his son, Khuc Thua My, who later succeeded him, to the Court of one of the rulers of the Southern Han dynasty. But the Southern Han emperor, hoping to reincorporate Viet-nam within his territory, sent an army which captured the new governor. In 923 a former general of Khuc Hao called Duong Dien Nghe organized a successful resistance against the Chinese, and he in his turn took the title of governor. In 937 he was killed by one of his officers who had given his allegiance to the Chinese, and who seized power on their behalf. But he in turn was killed by another officer, Ngo Quyen, who espoused the 'nationalist' cause, and who in 938 defeated the Chinese and got himself recognized as king the following year. He once more gave the country its former name of Nam Viet, and made the ancient city of Co-loa his capital. He reigned until 944.

His two sons had to wrest power from one of their uncles, and reigned jointly. They do not seem to have come into conflict with Champa, whose king, Indravarman III (*c.* 915–60), was busy fighting Cambodia, which had invaded the region of Nha-trang about 950. One of Ngo Quyen's two sons died in 954, and the other continued reigning alone. But as a result of the troubles following upon the death of Ngo Quyen, some feudal lords, known as *su-quan*, had reorganized the country on the old lines much to their own advantage, and each regarded himself as ruler of his own principality. This is what is known as the 'Twelve Su-quan' period, which lasted for a decade. On the death of Ngo Quyen's second son, killed in 965 during a campaign against the feudal lords, Dinh Bo Linh, the adoptive son and successor of one of the feudal lords, entered into the fight and reduced his rivals one by one.

While Viet-nam was rulerless during the Twelve Su-quan period, Champa remained more or less at peace. Does this account for the revival in its art? Cham art of the tenth century, of which the most perfect example in the architectural field is the great tower of My-son, is characterized by an abrupt change in style from the art of Dong-duong, as if in reaction against indigenous trends. Foreign influences, chiefly Khmer and Javanese, account for the innovations apparent in the new style. The sculpture, many examples of which are found at Tra-kieu, is supple and graceful, and its realism is in marked contrast to the fantastic style of the preceding period.

After Dinh Bo Linh had gained mastery over the country in 968 he had himself proclaimed emperor, taking the title of Dinh Tien-hoang. He set up his capital at his native town, Hoa-lu, where he had taken refuge during the troubles, and bestowed upon the country the name of Dai Co Viet. In 970 he sought recognition from the recently founded Sung dynasty in China, which had been in power since 960 and was to remain in power for three centuries. As the Sung emperor did not have the means at his disposal for reconquering the lost provinces, he was willing to accept the new ruler of the now independent Dai Co Viet as a vassal; the new ruler was in turn glad to accept a nominal vassalage from which he could derive a certain amount of prestige in the eyes of his subjects and neighbours. As regards internal affairs, the first Dinh emperor is remembered for having taken the first steps towards organizing the religious life of the country. He created an administrative hierarchy of priests, founded some monasteries, and built several temples.

The Vietnamese Annals describe the capital, Hoa-lu, as being of great magnificence, but a Chinese envoy who visited it in 990 does not seem to have been particularly impressed, and only mentions several thousand huts built of bamboo or straw which served as barracks. 'The palace,' he says, 'is quite small. The wooden towers raised for the defence of the city are as simple in construction as they are ugly in form.' None of the buildings to be seen today at the Hoa-lu site date back to the time when the capital was first founded.

In 972 a king of Champa appears whose name, as reconstructed from the Chinese characters, must have been Parameshvaravar-man. He was the first Cham king to come into conflict with Dai Co Viet since it had become independent. A member of the Ngo family who had fled to Champa requested his help in an attempt to regain the throne which his family had held from 939 to 965, the latter being the official date of Dinh Bo Linh's final victory. A sea-borne expedition organized by the Chams in 979 perished in a storm as it was approaching Hoa-lu.

On the death of Dinh Tien-hoang and of his eldest son, both of whom were assassinated in 979, a younger son succeeded. But the throne was almost immediately usurped by the minister Le Hoan, the leader of a powerful faction. In 980 he took the imperial title of Le Dai Hanh. He then fought against a Chinese army that had hoped to take advantage of the troubles following upon the death of Dinh Tien-hoang to bring the country under submission. The army was defeated in 881, near Lang-son. After his victory, the founder of the new dynasty, known as the Former Le dynasty, decided that it would be good policy to re-establish formal relations with China. He therefore dispatched an embassy, and returned the prisoners he had taken during the campaign.

In 980, the year of his accession, Le Dai Hanh also sent an embassy to Champa, which the Chams were imprudent enough to detain there. Le Dai Hanh immediately organized an expedition of reprisal, during which Parameshvaravarman lost his life, and in 982 his capital was destroyed. The new Cham king, Indravarman IV, had managed to escape in time from Indrapura, and had taken refuge in the south. Meanwhile a man of Dai Co Viet named Luu Ke Tong seized power in the north, and in 983 successfully resisted Le Dai Hanh's attempts to depose him. On the death of Indravarman IV he proclaimed himself king of Champa, and in 986 notified the Chinese Court of his accession.

In 988 the Chams united round a claimant of their own, whom they enthroned at Vijaya (in present Binh-dinh province), and when Luu Ke Tong died in the following year, the new king was crowned under the name of Harivarman II. No sooner had his reign begun than the northern part of his kingdom was again invaded by Dai Co Viet (990). There followed a short period of peace, during which, in 992, the Cham prisoners held by Dai Co Viet were set free; but soon fighting began again, this time because the Chams renewed their raids on the northern frontier in 995 and 997. Yang Po Ku Vijaya, who became king of Champa in 999, finally abandoned Indrapura, in Quang-nam, in the year 1000, and removed his capital to Vijaya, in Binh-dinh province. From then on Champa was ceaselessly subjected to ever increasing pressure from its neighbour to the north. Its political decline led to decadence in its art, betrayed by a heaviness and impoverishment of form. This change can be observed in the temple of Po Nagar at Nha-trang and in the oldest buildings of Binh-dinh.

Le Dai Hanh died in 1005, and two of his sons disputed the

succession. It was Le Long Dinh who came to the throne, but he died the following year, leaving only one son, who was still a child. The State dignitaries then raised one of themselves to the throne. This was Ly Cong Uan, who came from the province of Bac-ninh. He was proclaimed emperor at the beginning of 1010, and is known by his posthumous title, Ly Thai-to.

The new emperor, after having sought recognition from China, resided at Hoa-lu for two years, and then established his capital at the former capital of the Chinese governors, Dai-la-thanh, which he renamed Thang-long. The earthworks which were the ramparts of his new capital still stand to the west of the city of Hanoi, forming a vast quadrilateral by the side of the road to Son-tay. A number of objects have been discovered at this site, which were either turned up during the process of tilling the soil, or were found by means of clandestine diggings. They include terracotta tiles, fragments of cloth, pieces of the turned-up corners of ridge-tiles, and ceramics, many of which are celadon ware imported from China.

The reign of Ly Thai-to seems to have been a peaceful one. It was marked by new regulations concerning taxation and by the institution of rights of entry for imported goods. During his lifetime, Ly Thai-to appointed his eldest son, Phat Ma, as his heir apparent. In 1021 Phat Ma led a victorious expedition against Champa, where Parameshvaravarman II was reigning, and crossed its northern frontier. The Chams suffered a fresh defeat in 1026.

When Ly Thai-to died in 1029, trouble arose over the succession, and Phat Ma had to fight against his three brothers before he finally came to the throne. He reigned from 1028 to 1054, under the reign title of Ly Thai-tong. An important event in his reign was the promulgation, in 1042, of a new penal code, and history has recorded other measures, such as exemption from taxation after a war, the distribution of rice in times of famine, the creation of a relay postal system, the construction of numerous pagodas, and the quest for religious texts in China. After the Chams had pillaged the coasts of Dai Co Viet in 1042, Ly Thai-tong led a sea-borne expedition in 1044 which succeeded in routing the Chams and in which their king, Jaya Simhavarman II, lost his life. Ly Thai-tong pressed on as far as the capital, Vijaya, whence he brought back the royal harem, and 5,000 Cham prisoners who were settled in villages built by them in Dai Co Viet. The succeeding Cham king, Jaya Parameshvaravarman I (1044–60), seems to have reigned in the south, where he had to put down a revolt in Panduranga, and where he created some religious foundations, such as the one connected with the temple of Po Nagar. He remained on good terms with his neighbour.

The next emperor of Dai Co Viet was Ly Thanh-tong (1054–72), the eldest son of his predecessor. He changed the name of the country to Dai Viet. There are some interesting archaeological remains dating from his reign, in particular, parts of an ancient building at Phattich (in Bac-ninh province), dating from 1057. In 1068 he led a campaign against Champa, whose king, Rudravarman III, had attacked him. He won a complete victory. The capital, Vijaya, was set on fire, and the Cham king made a prisoner and taken to Dai Viet, regaining his liberty, however, in 1069 in exchange for the three provinces to the north of the Col des Nuages. Rudravarman III died in 1074, and was succeeded by Prince Thang, who took the reign title of Harivarman IV. At the very beginning of his reign he had to repel a new attack by Dai Viet, and gave only reluctant support to the campaign waged by his neighbour against the Chinese in 1076.

The eldest son of Ly Than-tong, who was only seven years old at the death of his father, at first reigned under the regency of his mother. Upon his accession he took the name of Ly Nhan-tong. His long reign, which lasted until 1128, was mainly occupied with wars against Champa and against China, in which General Ly Thuong Kiet made a name for himself. In China, by command of the powerful minister Wang An-shih, a large number of young men were recuited and trained with a view to waging war against Dai Viet. Ly Thuong Kiet forestalled the Chinese attack by going into action first and laying siege to Nan-ning (in Kwangsi), which was taken and sacked on 1 March 1076. A Chinese relief force then succeeded in taking several districts of the province of Cao-bang; but in 1078 a deal was made between China and Dai Viet exchanging these districts for Chinese prisoners. The fact that Dai Viet was now able to treat with China on a footing of equality shows the extent to which it was freed from Chinese domination.

Ly Nhan-tong next had to turn his attention to Champa, which had sent no tribute since 1091. Its king, Jaya Indravarman II, had begun reigning in 1080, but his reign had been interrupted from 1081 to 1086, when his uncle, Paramabodhisattva, had usurped the throne. When called to order, he again fulfilled his duty as a vassal from 1095 to 1102. But in 1103 he thought he might try to regain the three provinces that had been lost in 1069, and succeeded in doing so, but only held them for a few months. He reigned until 1113, continuing to build temples in the My-son area as his predecessors had done before him, and as his successors Harivarman V (1113–39) and Jaya Indravarman III (1139–45) were likewise to do.

Ly Nhan-tong, to whom the Long-doi-son pagoda, built in 1121, is attributed, was succeeded in 1127 by his nephew, Ly Than-tong, who reigned for eleven years. He had to repel a direct attack from Cambodia, where Suryavarman II was reigning. A Khmer army, 20,000 strong, threatened invasion in the year of Ly Than-tong's accession, but was repulsed by General Ly Cong Binh. Renewed attacks by Suryavarman II in 1132 were no more successful. Ly Than-tong died in 1138, leaving as successor his three-year-old eldest son.

The Cham king, Jaya Indravarman III, after supporting the Khmers in their expedition of 1131, entered into friendly relations again with Dai Viet. His own country suffered from a Khmer attack in 1145, in the course of which he disappeared, nothing being known as to what happened to him.

There is little to recount of the long reign of Ly Anh-tong, who ruled over Dai Viet from 1138 to 1175. He intervened in the internal struggles of the Cham kingdom by giving his support, between 1150 and 1160, to the faction led by a certain Vamsharaja, brother-in-law and rival of King Jaya Harivarman. The latter had emerged victorious from the attack of Suryavarman II in 1148, and in 1149 he had recaptured Vijaya, the capital where he had been crowned, from the Khmer prince, Harideva. His inscriptions celebrate his victory over Vamsharaja and his Dai Viet supporters. He brought the region of Quang-nam to submission in 1151, and that of Panduranga in 1160. He died in 1166–67. His son was supplanted by a certain Jaya Indravarman, who entered in 1170 into an agreement with the Dai Viet emperor, Ly Anh-tong, in order to be free to conduct operations against Cambodia; and in 1177 he went up river to Angkor, which was taken and sacked.

The twelfth century might be said to be the time when a new style of Cham art flourished, although in actual fact what is known as the Binh-dinh style lasted from the eleventh to the thirteenth century. When Vijaya was finally established as the capital in 1000, a number of buildings were erected in its vicinity, the oldest of which are Binh-lam and the Silver Towers. Many of the towers of Binh-dinh are built on heights. The details of the superstructure of the Hung-thanh tower, which is reminiscent of Angkor Vat, are due to Khmer influence which a concatenation of historical events had introduced into Champa, the two Khmer occupations – the first in the middle of the twelfth, and the second at the beginning of the thirteenth century – being the main causes. Khmer influence also accounts for the ground-plan of the Ivory Towers, which are built in a group of three along the same axis, and for the rounded silhouette of their superstructure, without projections or elaboration of the corners, and the style of their lintels, which are very similar to those of the Bayon at Angkor Thom. The three buildings that best represent the Binh-dinh style are Thu-thien, the Copper Tower, and the Golden Tower, which combine these features. A certain amount of foreign influence, both Khmer and Vietnamese, is discernible in the sculpture – especially that of Thap-mam – and the ornamentation, along with a resurgence of underlying indigenous trends showing that love of the fantastic which has already been remarked upon with reference to the Dong-duong style.

The sixth son of Ly Anh-tong succeeded him in 1176 at the age of three. He is known under the name of Ly Cao-tong. His reign, which more or less coincided with that of the Khmer king, Jayavarman VII, lasted until 1210, and marked the beginning of the decline of the dynasty.

His eldest son, Ly Hue-tong (1210–24), was the last of his line. In 1216 and 1218 there was again a threat of invasion from the Khmers, but they and the Chams, who were operating in concert with them, did not penetrate beyond the southern provinces of Dai Viet. In 1224 Ly Hue-tong, being ill and without a male heir, appointed as his successor his second daughter, Phat Kim, aged seven. He abdicated in her favour and became a monk. A court dignitary, Tran Thu Do, arranged a marriage between his eight-year-old nephew, Tran Canh, and the young princess, and at the end of December 1225 had the nephew proclaimed emperor under the name of Tran Thai-tong. The Ly dynasty had come to an end after reigning for 216 years.

It was the first of the great dynasties of Viet-nam. Its history is largely dominated by military events, since this was the period when the slow but large-scale expansion towards the south began which gradually displaced Champa. But the internal achievements of the dynasty were none the less important. They included a re-organization of the administrative system of the country, the establishment of a more rigid hierarchy of officials, the replanning of the armed forces, which henceforth were divided into a land arm and a sea arm, and the creation of social roles in the villages to form a basis for tax assessment and for recruitment to the army. The dynasty also initiated a programme of public works to protect the rice-fields against floods, an important feature of which was the building of the first embankment on the Red River. It was constructed in 1108, at the point where the capital was situated. The Ly encouraged Chinese studies, and the Van-mieu or 'temple of literature', consecrated to the cult of Confucius, was built at the capital in 1070. A national university was created in 1076, a year after the first literary examinations were held.

A large part of Vietnamese literature is in Chinese; but although this part of the literature, because of the language in which it is written, may legitimately be regarded as forming a chapter in the history of Chinese literature, it is nevertheless sufficiently Viet-namese in character as to form part of the national cultural heritage of Viet-nam. No work of literature from the brush of a Vietnamese survives from the period of Chinese rule prior to the rise of the first national dynasties; and from the Dinh, Former Le, and Ly dynasties, all that remains are some poems by Lac Thuan (end of the tenth century), Khuong Viet (same period), and Ly Thuong Kiet (last quarter of the eleventh century). Those competent to judge consider these works to be quite up to the best standards of Chinese literature.

There is a building in Vinh-yen province which dates from the end of the Ly dynasty: the multi-storied tower of Binh-son, ornamented with plaques and medallions of terracotta. It gives some idea of the style of architecture and the Chinese type of ornamentation that was in favour in northern Viet-nam.

2

Cambodia[1]

THE KINGDOM OF CAMBODIA, sometimes called the Khmer Empire, not only occupied the same territory as Fu-nan had occupied, but was to some extent its successor State.

On the death of the Funanese king, Jayavarman, in 514, his son Rudravarman, born of a concubine, got rid of the half-brother who was the legitimate claimant and seized the throne for himself. He reigned until 539 at least, this being the date of the last embassy he sent to China. He is the last known king of Fu-nan. In the second half of the sixth century the country was attacked from the north by a kingdom to which the Chinese gave the name of Chen-la. The city near the hill of Ba Phnom must have been abandoned and the capital of Fu-nan transferred to the site of present Angkor Borei, on the other side of the river. Possibly this site was chosen because of its proximity to the hill of Phnom Da. There were probably kings of Fu-nan residing there up until the time when all their territory had finally been absorbed by Chen-la, sometime during the seventh century. But 'kings of the mountain' continued to exist after that, possibly in one of their former dependencies in the Malay Peninsula, for after the last mission to China from Fu-nan in 588, two later missions are recorded, the first dating from the reign-period 618–26, and the second from the reign-period 627–49.

No explanation has yet been found for the name Chen-la, but the Chinese have always used it when referring to Cambodia, the country of the Khmers. According to Cambodian inscriptions of the tenth century, the kings of 'Kambuja' claimed to be descended from a mythical eponymous ancestor, the wise hermit Kambu, and the celestial nymph Mera, whose name may derive from the ethnic term 'Khmer'. The Kambujas seem to have been originally centred in the region bordering the north-east shore of the Great Lake. The first kings known to us are Shrutavarman and Shreshthavarman (fifth century?), who were probably vassals of Fu-nan. The similarity in the names would suggest that it was the latter who founded the city of Shreshthapura on the site of Bassac, or, more correctly, Champasak, in the middle Mekong valley. An inscription has been found there,[2] engraved by order of a king called Devanika, who seems to be identical with the Cham king whom the Chinese called Fan Shen-ch'eng (*c.* 455–72). Thus Shreshthapura may have been founded on territory recently conquered from the Chams. This would confirm an oral tradition still current among the Cambodians, according to which the Khmer kingdom came into being on territory taken from the Chams of Champasak. It would appear that when the city was founded a cult was inaugurated at the foot of the hill of Vat Phu. This hill dominates Champasak, and has on its summit a huge natural linga in the form of a monolith – hence the Sanskrit name for the hill: Linga parvata, 'the mountain of the linga'. Inscriptions show that the cult of this linga, which was called Bhadreshvara, continued through the centuries. A Chinese text of the sixth century records that 'near the capital [of Chen-la] there is a mountain called Ling-chia-po-p'o [Lingaparvata], on top of which there is a temple which is always guarded by a thousand soldiers. It is consecrated to a spirit named P'o-to-li [Bhadre(shvara)], to whom human sacrifice is made. Each year the king goes into this temple and himself offers a human sacrifice during the night.' The name Bhadreshvara, which, as we saw earlier, was the name of the royal linga founded during the fourth century in the main sanctuary of My-son by the Cham king Bhadravarman, may have been chosen by Shreshthavarman to mark his victory over the Chams of Champasak.

Be that as it may, it was a princess belonging to the maternal line of Shreshthavarman, to whom a late text gives the name of Kambujarajalakshmi, 'the fortune of the Kambuja kings', who transmitted the heritage of Shreshthavarman to her spouse Bhavavarman. The only date known during the reign of

Bhavavarman is 598. In the inscriptions of his brother Chitrasena, who succeeded him under the reign-title of Mahendravarman, he is described as being the grandson of the 'universal monarch', which must refer to the king of Fu-nan, the only monarch reigning in the peninsula at that time who could claim such a title.

In the second half of the sixth century, Bhavavarman, aided by his brother Chitrasena, extended his territory in the Mekong valley – possibly at the expense of Champa – as far as the mouth of the river Mun to the north, and southwards from the plateau of Korat, where inscriptions commemorating their conquests have survived. They subsequently, or simultaneously, turned against Fu-nan and pushed southwards along the Mekong as far as Kratie, and westwards beyond the Great Lake. The Chinese historians attribute this conquest to Chitrasena (Chih-to-ssu-na) alone, but he may only have been in command of the military operations. The reasons for the attack which Bhavavarman and his brother seem to have carried out against Fu-nan are obscure. On the supposition that the root cause lay in the fact that the accession of Rudravarman, the son of a concubine and the murderer of the legitimate heir to the throne, was irregular, two possibilities suggest themselves: either Bhavavarman was a member of the legitimate line and took advantage of the death of Rudravarman to lay claim to his rights to the throne of Fu-nan; or else, since Bhavavarman was the grandson of Rudravarman, he was defending the rights inherited from his grandfather against an attempted restoration of the legitimate line. Perhaps, in addition to the dynastic struggle, religious motives also entered into the matter, for the Chinese pilgrim I-ching, writing towards the end of the seventh century, declares that formerly in Fu-nan 'the law of the Buddha prospered and spread, but now a wicked king has destroyed it completely and there are no more bonzes'. As has been mentioned, Buddhism flourished in Fu-nan during the fifth and sixth centuries; but the inscriptions of the conquerors of Fu-nan and their successors are exclusively Shivaite. This tempts one to identify the 'wicked king' mentioned by I-ching with Bhavavarman (or his brother).[3]

I have given prominence to the events leading to the founding of Chen-la because it is of interest to try to find out what the influences were that moulded Khmer civilization. For this was the civilization that was to dominate the south and the centre of the peninsula for several centuries; and upon its decline, its main features were transmitted to the new States which arose after the fall of the Khmer Empire. The Kambujas inherited from Fu-nan a large part of their material culture, especially their techniques of agricultural hydraulics, as well as all that part of their spiritual culture lying in the realms of art, religion, and the concept of universal sovereignty; while from Champa they took certain features of their architectural style. Authentically Indian in type as their civilization was, they nevertheless retained the desire to keep the centre of their political power in the area where their State had arisen – that is, on the north shore of the Great Lake, the waters of which not only provided a plentiful irrigation supply, but were also well stocked with fish.

We have seen that Bhavavarman was reigning in 598. His brother Chitrasena succeeded at some date unknown, taking the reign title of Mahendravarman. He reigned until around 615, and pursued a policy of friendship towards Champa, sending an embassy there which must have been received by King Shambhuvarman, of whom mention was made in the foregoing chapter.

Mahendravarman was succeeded by his son Ishanavarman, who during his reign completed the conquest of Fu-nan, which has led some Chinese historians to suppose that he was entirely responsible for it. His sway gradually extended until it covered a territory more or less coextensive with that of present-day Cambodia, except perhaps for the north-western provinces. The remains of his capital, Ishanapura, occupy the site of Sambor Prei Kuk, to the north of Kompong Thom. He continued to pursue the policy of friendship towards Champa initiated by his father, and sealed the alliance by giving one of his daughters, the princess Sharvani, in marriage to a Cham prince called Jagaddharma, who was an emigré or an exile in Cambodia. The offspring of this marriage, the prince Prakashadharma, became king of Champa in 653, taking the name of Vikrantavarman. During his reign, which lasted for thirty years, many religious foundations – most of them Vaishnavite – were created at My-son and at Tra-kieu, and even in the Nha-trang area.

Ishanavarman was succeeded first by Bhavavarman II, who was reigning in 639 but of whom little is known, and then by Jayavarman I, who had a long and apparently peaceful reign (*c.* 657–81), and whose sway extended from the coast of the Gulf of Siam to the

Bassac region in the middle Mekong valley. During the period between the conquests of Bhavavarman I and the end of the reign of Jayavarman I, the power of the Khmer kings was gradually consolidated in the territories formerly occupied by Fu-nan.

Jayavarman I seems to have left no male heir to succeed him, and this is probably one of the reasons accounting for the partition of Cambodia,[4] which by the beginning of the eighth century had returned to the anarchic conditions that had existed prior to the foundation of Fu-nan. From an inscription of 713 it would appear that at that time the country, or at least the region where in the following century the capital where the Angkor ruins now stand was to be built, was ruled by a woman, Queen Jayadevi, who in this inscription laments the 'misfortunes of the times'. From 717 onwards until the end of the eighth century the Chinese speak of a 'Land Chen-la', situated in the middle Mekong valley to the north of the Dangrek mountain chain, and of a 'Water Chen-la', which more or less corresponded with present-day Cambodia together with the Mekong delta. 'Water Chen-la' was divided into several kingdoms and principalities, the most important of which was Shambhupura (Sambor on the Mekong), founded in 716 by Pushkaraksha, whose seizure of power perhaps marks the beginning of the partition of Cambodia.

A Chinese text referring to the reign of Ishanavarman[5] throws light on the material culture of the country during the seventh century. It records that the king resided in the city of I-sha-na [Ishana(pura)], 'which contains over 20,000 families. In the centre of the city there is a great hall where the king gives audience and holds his court. The kingdom contains thirty other cities, each with a population of several thousand families, and each administered by a governor; the titles of the State officials are the same as those of Lin-i.' The text goes on to describe the hall of audience and the throne, the costume of the king and of the high officials, and the protocol observed for audiences. 'Those who appear before the king touch the ground three times with their forehead at the foot of the steps to the throne. If the king calls them to him and commands them to mount the steps, they then kneel down with their arms crossed and their hands resting on their shoulders. Then they sit in a circle round the king and deliberate on the affairs of the kingdom. When the discussion is over, they kneel again, prostrate themselves once more, and withdraw.' The rule of succession is described with great succinctness. 'The sons of the queen who is the legitimate wife of the king are alone eligible as heirs to the throne.' The text adds that on the day when a new king is proclaimed, his brothers are mutilated; but this is the only mention of such a practice. Regarding the customs of the people, there are some details that still apply, thirteen centuries after they were recorded. 'They regard the right hand as pure and the left as impure. They make ablutions each morning, clean their teeth with small pieces of wood, and never forget to read or recite their prayers. They make ablutions again before each meal, use their wooden toothpicks after it, and again say a prayer. Funerals are conducted in the following manner: The offspring of the deceased go seven days without eating, shave the head as a sign of mourning, and make loud cries of lament. . . . The corpse is burnt on a pyre made up of all kinds of aromatic woods; the ashes are placed in a gold or silver urn which is thrown into deep water. The poor make do with an urn of terracotta painted in many colours. Some simply leave the corpse in the open to be devoured by wild beasts.' That these customs have an Indian origin goes without saying.

Many archaeological remains survive – buildings, sculpture, inscriptions – belonging to the period described by art historians as 'pre-Angkor'. The oldest would appear to date back to the end of the sixth century – that is, to the last years of the kingdom of Fu-nan. The art of the period lasting from then until the end of the eighth century constitutes a stylistic whole which is quite distinct from the art of the later 'Angkor' period dating from the beginning of the ninth century. Pre-Angkor art falls into three periods, each with its own style which has been named after the site where it is best represented. These are:

1. The style of Phnom Da (end of the sixth to the beginning of the seventh century), which perhaps represents the last period of the art of Fu-nan, since after Chen-la had conquered the northern part of their territory, the kings of Fu-nan may have continued to reign for a while at Angkor Borei in the vicinity of Phnom Da. The statues found at Angkor Borei include both Hindu images and those of the Buddha which have obvious affinities with Indian art, although there are certain features which already indicate the predominant trends of Khmer art of later periods.

2. The style of Sambor Prei Kuk (first-half of the seventh

century). This site contains a collection of buildings consisting of three groups of temples which formed the ecclesiastical quarter of Ishanapura, the first pre-Angkor capital of Cambodia. They are brick towers, square in form, standing either alone or in the form of a quincunx. The framework of the doors is in stone, and consists of two cylindrical colonettes supporting a lintel carved to represent an arch made of wood decorated with garlands and pendants. The superstructure consists of a number of superimposed storeys, similar to the first, but each smaller than the one below. The statues, few in number, are for the most part small female figures in graceful attitudes. The rare statues of male figures are mostly carved in a frontal position. The style of the decoration shows an Indian influence dating from the first half of the seventh century.

3. The style of Prei Kmeng and of Kompong Prah (second half of the seventh, and eighth century). The architecture differs little from that of the preceding period, but the decoration is more elaborate and characterized by a profusion of foliage. Among the statues, which are of mediocre quality, there is one *chef-d'œuvre*: the statue of Harihara (Vishnu and Shiva together forming one body), in which the modelling and anatomical detail are of exceptionally high quality.

Inscriptions carved on steles or on the jambs of doorways, either in Sanskrit or in archaic Khmer, are the main source of information about the history and institutions of the country, but what they chiefly throw light on is its religious life. The main Hindu sects, particularly the Shivaite sect of Pashupata[6] and the Vaishnavite sect of Pancharatra, coexisted as in India itself. Both epigraphic and iconographic material indicate how important the syncretic cult of Harihara was at this period. The worship of Shiva, particularly in the form of the linga, enjoyed royal favour. The only evidence of the existence of Buddhism, apart from a very few Buddhist images, is found in one inscription which mentions two monks (*bhikshu*), and it seems to have lost ground after the favour which, as we have seen, it enjoyed in Fu-nan in earlier centuries. The authors of the inscriptions in Sanskrit derived their literary culture from the great Indian epics, the Ramayana and the Mahabharata, and also from the Purana, which provided the official poets with a rich source of mythological material. As for the material culture, the economic conditions, and the social organization of pre-Angkor Cambodia, some knowledge of it will be gained – at least, one hopes so – from systematic exploration of the information contained in the Khmer inscriptions. But this is work that still remains to be done.

The history of Cambodia during the eighth and the beginning of the ninth century can only be understood if we know something about what had been happening in Indonesia since the end of the seventh century. An important centre of Indian cultural influence, specifically Buddhist in character, had arisen in the south-east of Sumatra. Owing to an increase in the number of ships plying between China and India, the region of Palembang had acquired a new importance. The coast here is half-way between the Sunda Straits and the Straits of Malacca, and was the usual landing point for ships sailing from China with the north-east monsoon. It thus occupied a favourable position for controlling the trade between the China Sea and the Indian Ocean, from which much profit could be derived. Doubtless this explains why the kingdom of Shrivijaya[7] – the (Shih-li) fo-shih of Chinese documents – prospered so rapidly. A desire to command the straits must have accounted for its expansion north-westwards to the Malay Peninsula and south-eastwards towards the western part of Java, which enabled it to maintain a commercial hegemony over Indonesia for several centuries.

The prosperity of the Sumatran kingdom was sooner or later bound to arouse the envy of the Javanese kings. The history of Java only begins to take shape around 732, this being the date of an inscription from the centre of the island which tells of a Shivaite king called Sanjaya, whom later tradition credits with having undertaken distant expeditions to Bali, Sumatra, Cambodia, and even China – by which must be meant Chiao-chih, then under Chinese rule. There seems to be some truth in this tradition, since, as was mentioned in the chapter on Viet-nam, there were Javanese raids on the east coast of Indochina between 767 and 787, and Java may well have acquired rights of suzerainty over Cambodia during the period of partition in the seventh century, for, as we shall see, the founder of the Angkor kingdom inaugurated his reign by performing a ceremony designed to free him from all dependence upon Java. Possibly an incident such as the one of which an obviously embroidered account is given by an early tenth-century Arab writer[8] lies at the origin of this dependence. According to the source mentioned, a Khmer king expressed the desire to have the head of the Maharaja king of Zabag (Javaka) brought before him on a dish. News of this reached the Maharaja who, under the pretext of making a pleasure voyage round the islands of his kingdom, armed his fleet and prepared an expedition against Cambodia. He sailed up the river to the capital, where he seized the king and had him beheaded. He then ordered one of the Khmer ministers to find a successor, and after returning to his own country, he had the decapitated head embalmed and placed in an urn which he sent to the king who was now reigning in place of the one who had been decapitated. With it he sent a letter pointing out the conclusions to be drawn. It would be absurd to take this story literally, but there is justification in supposing that it may have been inspired by some historical event. Java may indeed have taken advantage of Cambodia's being partitioned and launched an expedition against it. But it is not by any means certain that Sanjaya was the king most likely to have launched such an expedition, for about 775 there appeared in central Java the dynasty of the Shailendra or 'kings of the mountain', whose title recalls that of the rulers of Fu-nan. These Javanese Shailendra were Buddhist, just as the last kings of Fu-nan had been, and constructed large Buddhist buildings in the centre of the island. Thus they may have had better reasons than Sanjaya for intervening in Cambodia. They may have felt that they had some claim to the rights of its former masters, the Funanese 'kings of the mountain'.

Be that as it may, it was in order to liberate Cambodia from the suzerainty of Java that the founder of the Angkor kingdom, who had ties of ancestry with former dynasties, especially with that of Shambhupura, returned from Java at the beginning of the ninth century. He had been either in captivity or in voluntary exile there – the exact circumstances are not known. During the forty-eight years of his reign (802–50), Jayavarman II made every effort to reunify the country. After making Indrapura (to the east of present Kompong Cham?) his capital for a while, he next established himself at Hariharalaya (the site of Roluos), which was not far from Chen-la's centre of origin, and better situated than the former capital Ishanapura. Then, after founding Amarendrapura, the site of which has not yet been identified, he finally established himself on the Mahendraparvata (the hill of Phnom Kulen). There he sent for a Brahman named Hiranyadama for the performance of a ceremony designed to consecrate him as sole sovereign, liberated from all dependence upon Java. The ceremony consisted in founding a linga on the hill. This symbolized that the king's omnipotence was the equivalent of that of Mahendra the great Indra, the king of the gods. It would seem that in order to free himself from the overlordship of the Javanese Shailendra – the 'king of the mountain' whose title conferred on him the character of universal monarch – it was necessary that Jayavarman II should himself become a universal monarch by receiving from a Brahman, on the hill of the great Indra, the linga symbolizing his royal power. During the following centuries, the consecration of Jayavarman II on Mount Mahendra was regarded as marking the beginning of a new era. In inscriptions he is usually called by his posthumous name, Parameshvara, 'the supreme lord' – one of the epithets of the god Shiva; and he is often referred to as 'the king who established his residence on the Mahendra'. It is to his reign that many families trace back their early ancestry, and the ownership of land is dated from then in the charters of several religious foundations.

Jayavarman II then established a capital (Hariharalaya) near the site where Angkor was soon to arise, and after he had consolidated his power in the region surrounding the Great Lake, he returned to it and resided there until his death. The art produced during his reign is transitional in style between pre-Angkor art, to which it is closely related, and Angkor art, which derives some of its features from it. It is characterized, as the historical circumstances might lead us to expect, by the reappearance of certain features found in the Kulen style which clearly show Cham and Javanese influence, and also – though to a lesser degree – by features deriving from the early forms of pre-Angkor art.

Jayavarman II was succeeded by his son Jayavarman III (850–77), who was in turn succeeded by Indravarman I (877–89), a somewhat remote kinsman of the royal house. Both monarchs kept Hariharalaya as their capital. Indravarman extended his sway over a territory larger in area than present-day Cambodia, his suzerainty being acknowledged as far to the north-west as the plateau of Korat. His interest in irrigation projects evinced itself as soon as he came to the throne, for the construction of a huge reservoir to the north of the capital which he set in train was obviously no mere act of piety, but a practical measure for providing irrigation supplies during the dry season. In 879 he built the six brick towers of the temple of Prah Ko to contain the funerary statues of Jayavarman II and of his own ancestors. Finally in 881 he erected the first terraced pyramid in stone (Bakong) as a shrine to contain the royal linga under the vocable Indreshvara, formed from his own name. Indravarman's successors continued to attach prime importance to the irrigation works laid out to keep the land surrounding the capital under cultivation, and we shall see how the Khmer kings devoted careful attention to the development of a network of canals in the Angkor region, for which purpose they had large reservoirs constructed for storing water during the rainy season which could then be distributed to the rice-fields surrounding the capital in the dry season.

Indravarman's son, Yashovardhana, was connected through his mother with the ancient Funanese and pre-Angkor dynasties. He became king in 889, taking the title of Yashovarman. In order to house the statues of his parents, he built the temple of Loley, with its four brick towers rising from an island in the reservoir dug out in his father's reign. He then began building a new capital, which he named Yashodharapura – a vast rectangle, each side being about two and a half miles in length. In its centre rises the hill of Phnom Bakheng, on top of which he built the temple of the royal linga, Yashodhareshvara. In addition, being as anxious as his father had been to ensure regular irrigation supplies for the surrounding countryside, he had an enormous reservoir constructed, four miles long by over a mile wide, to the north-east of the city, which was fed by the waters of the river which comes down off the hill Phnom Kulen. It is known as the Yashodharatataka, 'the reservoir of Yashodhara'. On its southern shore he founded three monasteries, one for each of the three religious sects – Shivaite, Vaishnavite, and Buddhist. His religious eclecticism was already evident in the very year of his accession, when he had about a hundred monasteries for one or other of the sects built throughout the various provinces by the side of ancient shrines, each bearing the name of Yashodharashrama, and each containing a royal pavilion for the king to reside in when he travelled round the country.

After his reign came the reigns of his two sons, Harshavarman I (900–22) and Ishanavarman II (925). But in 921 one of their maternal uncles founded a new city, Chok Gargyar, the remains of which are the ruins of Koh Ker, fifty miles to the north-east of

Angkor. This uncle had himself crowned king there under the title of Jayavarman (IV). The buildings he erected in the new city were larger than any that had been built before, the most notable among them being the five-storied pyramid, 115 feet high, for housing the royal linga, to which Jayavarman IV attached a wider significance: instead of being a symbol of the personal power of the king, the royal linga now became the symbol of universal monarchy. Jayavarman IV also dug a reservoir to provide an irrigation system for the neighbourhood of his capital. He died in 941.

It is not known what happened to his son, Harshavarman II, but the end of his short reign in 944 brought another nephew of Yashovarman to the throne, who took the title of Rajendravarman. He applied himself to the task of returning to the traditions which had been interrupted by his uncle, Jayavarman IV, and transferred the capital back to Yashodharapura. He undertook the restoration of this capital, and in 952 built the first temple for the worship of the royal linga Rajendreshvara combined with the worship of the funerary statues of his parents. This was the Eastern Mebon temple, set in the centre of the reservoir dug by Yashovarman. Then in 961 he built a second pyramid temple, to the south of the reservoir, for the worship of the royal linga combined with the worship of the linga Bhadreshvara and of the images of various relatives as well as his own. This is the temple of Pre Rup. In 950 his armies conducted a campaign against Champa, as has already been mentioned in the chapter on Viet-nam.

When his son, Jayavarman V, came to power in 968, he was still very young, and remained under the guidance of his spiritual adviser, Yajnavaraha – the founder, that same year, of the small temple of Banteay Srei. During his reign a new capital was built, the centre of which is probably marked by the unfinished temple of Ta Kev, outside the north-east corner of Yashodharapura. He died in 1001 and was succeeded by his nephew, Udayadityavarman I, who only reigned for a few months. There then ensued a struggle for power, about which no details are known, between a certain Jayaviravarman who was reigning at the capital (1003–1006), and a prince who was a descendant of the maternal family of Indravarman I. After a war lasting nine years, the latter succeeded in establishing himself at Yashodharapura in 1010, and was crowned under the name of Suryavarman. His reign is important for two reasons. Firstly, because it marks the expansion of Khmer power and civilization in the Menam valley, particularly in the former Mon centre of Lvo (Lop Buri), where Khmer inscriptions dating from 1022–25 have been found; and secondly, because it marks the inhabitation and cultivation of territories to the west of the Great Lake which had hitherto either been waste land or only partly cultivated. The method followed for bringing the land under cultivation was to create religious foundations[9] and to grant concessions of land for the purpose of founding monasteries. To maintain these, the soil had to be tilled and villages built, with all that that implied in the way of irrigation works and local organization. Suryavarman died at the beginning of 1050. Because of his leanings towards Buddhism – although this did not exclude sympathies for other sects – he was given the posthumous title of Nirvanapada, 'the king who has gone to nirvana'.

His successor, Udayadityavarman II (1050–66), built a huge pyramid for the royal linga – the Baphuon. It was in the centre of the capital, which covered approximately the same area as present Angkor Thom. He also had a very large reservoir constructed to the west of the city. It is over a mile wide and five miles long, and is known as the Western Baray. Its construction is perhaps accounted for by the partial drying-up of the reservoir dug by Yashovarman to the east of the city as well as by an increased demand for irrigation supplies. During the sixteen years of his reign Udayadityavarman II had to put down a number of internal revolts which occurred in the south in 1051 and in the north-east and east in 1065.

His younger brother, Harshavarman III, who succeeded him in 1066, had to restore order after the havoc caused by the troubles of the preceding reign. He himself had to counter attacks made by the Chams in 1074 and 1080. The Cham king, Harivarman IV, is said to have won a victory over the Khmer armies and to have captured the prince who led them. Perhaps it was during the same campaign that a brother of the Cham king, the future king, Paramabhodisattva, took the city of Shambhupura (Sambor on the Mekong) and destroyed its shrines. In 1076 the Chinese inveigled Champa and Cambodia into taking part in their war against Dai Viet, but their defeat led to the withdrawal of their Khmer and Cham allies, who had invaded the region of present Nghe-an.

In 1080, Divakara, a Brahman who had been in the service of

Harshavarman III, brought a new dynasty to the throne which was unrelated to the previous one, and crowned the new king under the name of Jayavarman VI. This king seems to have resided, not at Yashodharapura, but somewhere farther north, which is probably where his family came from. Upon his death in 1107, his elder brother, Dharanindravarman, was crowned by the Brahman Divakara; but five years later his grandnephew, who was still quite young, seized power and was in turn consecrated as king by Divakara in 1113 under the name of Suryavarman II.

His reign, from almost every point of view, marks one of the high points of the civilization of Angkor. It was filled with a whole series of military operations against neighbouring countries. In 1128, 1138, and 1150, Dai Viet was attacked and invaded as far as the provinces to the south of the Red River delta. In 1145 Champa was conquered, and remained under the occupation of Khmer armies until 1149. To the north-west, Khmer forces seem to have got as far as the Mon kingdom of Haripunjaya (present Lamphun), but apparently did not occupy the territory for any length of time. Evidence of Cambodia's territorial expansion during the twelfth century is provided by Chinese sources, according to which the area covered extended from Champa to the frontiers of the Burmese kingdom of Pagan, and to the country of Grahi (on the Bay of Bandon on the east coast of the Malay Peninsula). Suryavarman II renewed relations with China in 1116, and in 1128 he obtained recognition from China as a great vassal of the empire. He built many temples, the most remarkable of which is Angkor Vat, which was apparently intended as a temple to the god-king, now no longer represented by a linga, but by an image of the god Vishnu. This temple became the mausoleum in which Suryavarman II was worshipped under the posthumous title of Parama-vishnu loka, 'the king who has gone to the supreme sojourn with Vishnu'.

On one of the bas-reliefs on historical subjects carved on the wall of the first-storey gallery of Angkor Vat there is a march-past of the armies accompanying the king, and at its head is a group of warriors wearing an entirely different costume from that of the Khmers. Two brief inscriptions describe them as Syam. This name, along with mention of Chinese, Vietnamese, Khmers, and Burmese, appears in eleventh-century Cham inscriptions referring to prisoners of war, and is the origin of the name Siam. It refers to

T'ais from the middle Menam who were at that time subjects of Cambodia. They brought a new ethnic strain into Indochina, which they entered by a slow process of infiltration dating from quite early times and resulting from the general population drift from north to south which had led to the peopling of the peninsula. Their social organization seems to have been similar to the feudal system of the people of northern Viet-nam briefly described in an earlier chapter, vestiges of which are still found in the Laotian principalities and in the Shan States of Burma. Throughout the whole of their history the T'ais have always had a remarkable capacity for assimilation, and wherever they have settled, they have always been able to acquire the cultural traits necessary for the process of raising themselves to the level of the most en-lightened section of the society of their adoption. This explains the wide cultural diversity found among T'ais settled in different parts of the peninsula. It is worth recalling here the much quoted passage by Louis Finot[10] concerning the southward movement of the T'ais, which has sometimes wrongly been described as an 'invasion'. 'It might be better to use the word "inundation" to describe the advance of this extraordinary race, for they are like water, which is fluid and yet can insinuate itself with force, which can take on the colour of any sky and the form of any channel while at the same time preserving, under different outward aspects, its essential characteristics, just as the T'ais preserved their own characteristics and their language. Now they are spread, like a vast sheet of water, all over South China, Tongking, Laos, Siam, and even as far as Burma and Assam.'

The view is gaining ground that this 'inundation' was less a matter of large-scale migration than of a gradual infiltration of immigrants who began by holding positions of command over communities of sedentary agriculturalists, and ended by gaining control over the native peoples among whom they had settled and whose culture they had assimilated.

The death of Suryavarman II, probably sometime after 1150, gave the signal for the outbreak of internal revolts which will be discussed later. His reign marks the end, not of the prosperity of Cambodia – for the end of the twelfth century and the beginning of the thirteenth saw another period of grandeur based on a new conception – but of what might be called traditional Angkor civilization, which played such an important role in the cultural development of central Indochina, and exercised a great deal of influence on that of the T'ais of the Mekong and the Menam.

The brilliance of this civilization and the magnificence of its works presuppose a large and prosperous population, whose prosperity was based on the intensive agriculture made possible by the well-planned irrigation system which had brought large areas of land under cultivation.[11] This achievement of the Khmer kings is less spectacular than their architectural works, but is indirectly responsible for them because of the increase in wealth and population which it brought about. The available sources give practically no information about the commercial activities of the country, but there is every reason to suppose that in this respect Angkor inherited the advantages of Fu-nan, whose favourable position on the ancient sea routes has already been noted. Mention in inscriptions of Chinese and Indian textiles and of other imported wares makes this quite clear.

Inscriptions are the only source of information about the period extending over the eleventh and twelfth centuries, and it is not until the end of the thirteenth century that we find a fairly full and extremely lively description of Cambodia on the eve of its decline, as given in the account of a Chinese envoy. The inscriptions are mainly concerned with Court circles and the world of the high officials and superior clergy, and at the present stage of research we only catch a glimpse of the civilization of Angkor through this distorting mirror. But it is to be hoped that if a methodical examination of the information contained in the inscriptions in Khmer is carried out and analysis in depth of archaeological finds is made, further information about its economic life and social organization will be revealed.

What we learn from the Sanskrit inscriptions is that the whole political organization of the country was centred on the king, who, in theory, was the source and the sum of all authority, the custodian of the established order, the final judge of disputes between his subjects, the defender of the faith and the protector of the religious foundations entrusted to his care. He had to defend the country against its enemies without, and ensure peace within by imposing on everyone the obligation to respect the social order, which consisted in the division of the entire population into various classes and corporations according to hereditary occupation. The fact that the kings of Angkor did not always live up to this ideal is another matter!

The king, following the Indian pattern of kingship, was a god on earth, the representative of Indra, king of the gods. Hence the capital of the kingdom where the king resided, with its ramparts and its moat, was a representation in miniature of the universe with its encircling mountain chain and ocean. Its centre was marked by a replica of Mount Meru, the cosmic mountain. This was a temple-mountain in the form of a terraced pyramid, with an idol symbolizing the king's power and the permanent principle of kingship placed on top, like Indra on top of Meru.[12] In theory, each king was supposed to build his own temple-mountain which would become his mausoleum when he died. He was then given his posthumous title – the name of his abode after death. The official cult of divine kingship was to some extent independent of the various Indian cults – Shivaism, Vaishnavism, and Buddhism – each of which displayed marked syncretic tendencies in their doctrines. In addition there is ample evidence to show that there was worship of images bearing the attributes of one or other of the great figures of the Brahman and Buddhist pantheons, but with names which combined the name of the god represented and the name of a deceased person, or even sometimes of a person still alive. It was to this personal cult that most of the great Khmer monuments were consecrated. They were royal, princely, or high official foundations which served to some extent as mausoleums in which the worship of parents and ancestors could be maintained.

Angkor art is divided into several periods, each with its own distinctive style. The Kulen style (first half of the ninth century) is, as we have seen, characterized by the revival of a style in which Cham and Javanese influences can be discerned, as well as by features recalling the earliest forms of pre-Angkor art; the statues, although entirely freed from Indian stylistic canons, retain the lateral movement of the hip. The Prah Ko style (last quarter of the ninth century) has the first pyramid with superimposed terraces of stone, erected at Bakong in 881, and instead of the isolated towers of pre-Angkor art, has towers grouped together on a common terrace. The Bakheng style (end of the ninth – beginning of the tenth century) is characterized by further advances in the use of stone for building, and by the first appearance, at Bakheng itself, of the architectural features which from then on characterized the temple-mountain: the terraced pyramid with five towers arranged in a quincunx on the top terrace. The Koh Ker style (second quarter of the tenth century) shows tendencies towards the grandiose or even the colossal in its architecture and also in its statuary, which gives an impression of vigour and power. The Banteay Srei style (second half of the tenth century) is transitional, and has links with the Bakheng style; it is marked by the first appearance of long halls, at the Eastern Mebon (952), which at Pre Rup (961) become segments of galleries. In the Khleang style (end of the tenth – beginning of the eleventh century), these unite and develop into the surrounding gallery, roofed at first with bricks (as at Ta Kev, end of the tenth – beginning of the eleventh century), and culminating in the surrounding gallery at Phimea-nakas (beginning of the eleventh century), which is the first gallery to have a vaulted sandstone roof. The Baphuon style is marked by a greatly extended use of concentric galleries, by the lithe, slim figures of its statues with their calm facial expression, and by development in the technique of bas-relief. Lastly, the Angkor Vat style (first half of the twelfth century) is remarkable for its architectural masterpieces, Angkor Vat and Beng Mealea, for the harmony of lay-out achieved, for the hieratic quality of its statuary, and for the many large-scale compositions in bas-relief which cover the inner walls of the pillared galleries whose outer side is left open. The buildings must have been constructed according to models, and must have taken less time to complete than has generally been supposed. The stone-masons did not begin work on the decorations until each storey of the building was completed, but they got to work as soon as each of the lower storeys was in position. In general, the style of decoration, having gradually departed more and more from the Indian models to which it had been so close in the seventh century, had reached the point where Indian influence is no longer discernible. Although the type of decoration remained the same as that borrowed from Indian art, vegetable, animal, and other motifs had been introduced and treated in an entirely original manner.

This particular aspect of the civilization of Angkor has been stressed because it is the one which is the best known and the most spectacular, and because it was more influential outside Cambodia than any other aspect. It represents Cambodia's outstanding contribution to man's cultural heritage. But epigraphy and archaeology disclose other aspects of this civilization – for example, they give some indications of the social organization of the country. The important offices were held by members of the royal family, while the posts of chaplain to the king, high-priest to the god-king, and tutor to the young princes were reserved for the members of several great priestly families and were inherited through the female line, usually by a sister's son or a younger brother. The Brahman families could intermarry with the royal family, and Brahmans and princes (*kshatriya*) formed a class apart, above the mass of the people, and were the educated sector of society by which Indian culture was perpetuated. The inscriptions produced by this aristocracy are the only surviving works of literature, and give some idea of the extent of their Sanskrit culture, which was from time to time enriched through the arrival of Brahmans from India.

We also learn from these inscriptions that there was a whole hierarchy of officials, indicative of a strongly centralized and fully staffed administrative system. They reveal little about the life of the common people – the peasants and the villagers – except that many of them were brought into service to look after the shrines and hermitages which were constantly being founded all over the country owing to the piety of the ruling classes. Nevertheless, a careful study of the inscriptions in the Khmer language and a critical examination of the information they provide about the administration of provinces and villages and about landownership disputes and the value of land at various periods would, as I have already indicated, no doubt enable us to add to the information already obtained from the inscriptions in Sanskrit, and would furnish us with a number of interesting details about the material culture and the social and economic organization of the people as a whole.

Now we must take up the account of events which followed upon the death of Suryavarman II. He was succeeded by his cousin Dharanindravarman II, who, either from personal inclination, or under the influence of his wife, the princess Chudamani, more or less openly favoured Mahayana Buddhism. The date of the death of Dharanindravarman II is uncertain. He was succeeded by a certain Yashovarman (II), whose origins are unknown; but around 1165 he lost his throne to a high official who proclaimed himself king under the name of Tribhuvanadityavarman. About the same time the throne of Champa also fell to a usurper named Jaya Indravarman IV, who seized the opportunity to attack Cambodia. When he failed to gain a victory on the field of battle, he mounted a maritime expedition which sailed up the river in 1177, took Yashodharapura, and brought about the death of the usurper Tribhuvanadhityavarman. It was also at this time that Cambodian suzerainty over the country of Lvo (Lop Buri) in the lower Menam valley was being contested. In 1115 Lvo, which the Chinese call Lo-hu, had already sent a mission of its own to China. This was only two years after the accession of Suryavarman II, and doubtless he had not yet had time to establish his authority over the outlying dependencies of his kingdom. A second embassy in 1155, perhaps immediately following upon the death of Suryavarman II, may represent a second attempt to break the ties of vassalage to Angkor.[13] An inscription found in Siam in the region of Nagara Svarga (*Nakhon Sawan*) mentions a king reigning in 1167 named Dharmashoka. He may well have been the ruler of an independent kingdom of Lvo.[14]

The crisis, affecting both external and internal affairs, might have sounded the death-knell of Angkor's civilization if the country had not been saved by a son of Dharanindravarman II, a fifty-year-old prince who, like his father, was a devotee of Mahayana Buddhism, and who channelled the civilization of Angkor into new directions, especially as far as art was concerned. In his youth he had lived in Champa, whence he returned, too late, to defend Yashovarman II against the usurper Tribhuvanadityavarman. He was recognized as rightful claimant to the throne when the latter quit the scene in the turmoil of 1177; but first he had to get rid of the Cham invaders, which took four years of fighting. In 1181 he was crowned under the name of Jayavarman (VII). A new attack mounted by the Cham king Jaya Indravarman IV in 1190 provided him with the opportunity for waging a war of revenge against Champa. Its forces were defeated, and its territories annexed and incorporated as part of Cambodia from 1203 until 1220. Jayavarman's sway extended northwards as far as present Vientiane in Laos, and westwards, was re-established over a large part of the Menam valley and over the north of the Malay Peninsula. When Cambodia reached the fullest extent of its territorial expansion, the former boundaries of Fu-nan were restored and even surpassed towards the north. Jayavarman VII died in *c.* 1218 and was given the posthumous title of Mahaparamasaugata, 'the great and supreme Buddhist'.

His achievements during the four decades of his reign were considerable. He built and maintained 102 hospitals scattered throughout the kingdom, set up 101 rest-houses for pilgrims placed at regular intervals along the roads, and constructed roads linking the capital with the main provincial centres, where the temples were furnished with images which were probably copies of the one which, as we shall see, was placed in the main temple at the capital. He left many large architectural monuments, of which the most imposing are Ta Prohm, a funerary-cult temple built in 1186 for the worship of his mother; Prah Khan, another funerary-cult temple, built in 1191 for the worship of his father; Neak Pean, built on an island in the reservoir dug to the east of Prah Khan; many other temples in the environs of the capital, such as Banteay Kdei, and in the provinces, such as Banteay Chhmar; and finally, in the centre of the capital, which had been restored and surrounded with thick stone walls and a moat measuring nearly two miles along each of its four sides and corresponding to the circumference of present Angkor Thom, the temple of Bayon for the god-king, who was now represented by an image of the Buddha seated on the naga.

The inscriptions inform us that Jayavarman VII acquired his faith from his father, Dharanindravarman II; but he was probably also influenced in this respect by the two princesses whom he successively married, who were both ardent Buddhists. Yet although Buddhism was unquestionably the religion of the king and his immediate entourage, we find that the Brahman *élite* continued to play its role at the Court. An inscription gives the name of a Brahman from Burma whom Jayavarman VII made his chaplain, and who continued in office under the two succeeding kings.

The style of art typical of the reign of Jayavarman VII has been named the Bayon style, after the most important of the buildings he constructed. What distinguishes it from earlier styles is that it is exclusively of Buddhist inspiration, and was more directly influenced by the personal predilections of the king. Around the year 1190, he adapted the cult of the god-king to the Buddhist faith which he professed, and he also associated the secular funerary cult with the worship of the bodhisattva Lokeshvara, which he particularly favoured, this being facilitated by the rites of apotheosis connected with the worship of the bodhisattva. As a result, the towers of the buildings took on an entirely new aspect: they were adorned on all four sides with huge smiling faces which, it is generally agreed, represent the face of the king in the role of bodhisattva. The addition of towers of this kind, with surrounding galleries forming cloisters, to already existing buildings (Banteay Kdei, Ta Prohm, Prah Khan) resulted in a complicated and overloaded architectural lay-out.

No new feature of any importance appears in the decoration of the buildings of this period, and the workmanship is usually careless and hasty. But the statues, of which there are many, are remarkable for their facial expression which, under the influence of Buddhism, is radically different from that of earlier styles. It is tempting to trace an influence deriving from the Buddhist statuary of Dvaravati in the half-closed eyes and the smiling lips, which seem to express an inner joy and a state of mystical meditation. Gradually, as the Bayon style developed, the eyelids become completely closed and the mouth still more smiling, and in some statues an impression is conveyed that the sculptor, for the first time in the history of Khmer art, has tried to produce a portrait of a real person.[15]

The bas-reliefs carved on the walls of Bayon and Banteay Chhmar, although much more interesting historically and iconographically than the mythological bas-reliefs of Angkor Vat, are much inferior to them in quality. On the other hand, the scenes carved on the Elephant Terrace display a certain realism, and the figures on the so-called Terrace of the Leper King, which are almost in high relief, are remarkably fine.

3

Burma[1]

IN THE PYU KINGDOM which, as may be gathered from the accounts of seventh-century Chinese pilgrims, bore the name of Shrikshetra (Burmese: *Thayekhettaya*), two Buddhist sects coexisted: the Theravada, whose language was Pali, and the Mulasarvastivada, whose language was Sanskrit. The names of the kings written on their funerary urns have been deciphered, and are found to be Indian in type: Suryavikrama, Harivikrama, Sihavikrama, Prabhuvarman, Jayachandravarman; and on the basis of the figures found along with the names, which have been interpreted as dates, these kings are thought to have reigned at the end of the seventh and the beginning of the eighth century.[2]

The first detailed information about Pyu civilization provided by Chinese sources comes from the accounts of two embassies sent from Nan-chao to China in 802 and 807.[3] The Pyus were then on the eve of their decline as a political power. The accounts tell us that the walls embracing the area of the capital were built of brick with a coping of green enamel, and that they were pierced by a dozen gates, fortified with towers at the corners, and surrounded by a moat lined with bricks. The population numbered several tens of thousands of families, and the houses were decorated with plaques of lead or of tin. There were over a hundred Buddhist monasteries where children of both sexes were given religious instruction until their twentieth year. The people were forbidden by the tenets of their Buddhist faith to wear silk, which can only be obtained at the cost of the lives of silkworms. No shackles, manacles, or instruments of torture were ever used, and accused persons were merely bound. Those found guilty received no greater punishment than some strokes of a bamboo on the back. Only homicide was punished with the death penalty. The Pyus traded with neighbouring countries, to whom they sold white cloth and earthenware jars. They had native forms of music and dance of which the Chinese sources give a detailed account.

The ruins of the ancient capital are at Hmawza, about six miles to the east of Prome.[4] Numerous fragments of the brick wall surrounding it remain, describing a rough circle with an average diameter of two and a half miles. Since we know that the decline of Shrikshetra began in the ninth century, it may be assumed that none of the buildings are of later date than this. The stupas have cylindrical drums with hemispherical or ogival domes – a form of architecture that seems to be characteristic of this period, appearing only sporadically later. It probably originated, not in Ceylon, but in north-east India and the Orissa coast. Another characteristic form of Pyu architecture found at Hmawza is the type of building with an inner chamber surmounted by a tapering superstructure known in India as a 'shikhara', which also has its origin in the architecture of Orissa, and which was considerably elaborated during the Pagan period. The continuation of Pyu architectural traditions in the Burmese capital is not surprising in view of the fact that Burmese territorial expansion towards the south was over territory formerly ruled over by the Pyus.

North-east Indian influence, which predominated in the Indianization of the western part of the Indochinese peninsula, particularly in the valley of the Irrawaddy, is also found in the delta among the Mons of Ramannadesa who were centred on the city of Sudhammavati (Thaton). The use of the name Ussa (Odra = Orissa), by which the city of Pegu was known, indicates, like the name Shrikshetra, that there was some kind of relationship between this whole region and Orissa. The ancient monuments of the Mon country have unfortunately either disappeared or been rebuilt or enlarged during the course of the centuries. The stupa of Zokthok, however, gives some idea of what some of the earlier Mon stupas must have been like. It is conical in form with an octagonal base, and has four stairways leading up to it.[5]

The west of the peninsula, doubtless because of its proximity to India and the ease of direct communication by land and sea, seems to have been more deeply affected by Indian influence than any other part of South East Asia, particularly as regards art. Buildings consisting of a mass of masonry supporting a heavy superstructure of the 'shikhara' type, of which there are prototypes at Prome, abound at Pagan, and give us a hint of what the architecture of north-east India – especially that of Orissa before its decline and disappearance – must have been like. In sculpture, too, the Buddhist and Hindu statues of Prome are very similar to examples of late Gupta style, and those at Pagan to examples of the later Pala-Sena style.

The decline of the Pyu kingdom of Shrikshetra during the ninth century is evidenced by the removal of a large number of its inhabitants to Nan-chao in 832. Nan-chao, after conquering the upper valley of the Irrawaddy between 757 and 763, had come under Chinese domination in 791. Meanwhile the Burmese of Arimaddana (Pagan) were rising to power, partly due to the favourable geographical position they occupied near the confluence of the Irrawaddy and the Chindwin in the vicinity of the rice-bearing plain of Kyaukse, and at the crossroads of routes leading to Assam, Yunnan, and the valley of the Sittang.[6] There they came into contact with the Mons, a large number of whom had settled in the region, and learnt from them how to write in a script of Indian origin, besides being introduced by them to Hinduism and Buddhism.

The native chronicles place the beginnings of Pagan in the second century. At first it was a group of nineteen villages, each with its 'Nat' or local god. When the villages were combined to form a single city, the king, with the consent of his subjects, inaugurated the cult of a Nat to be worshipped by all in common, whose status was above that of the local gods, in order to weld the various tribes into a national entity by means of the common cult.[7] Mount Poppa, an extinct volcano not far from the city, which was already regarded as sacred by the Burmese, was the site chosen for the worship of twin gods, Min Mahagiri, 'Lord of the Great Mountain', and his sister Taung-gyi Shin, a Burmese name with the same meaning. Legend has it that they were a brother and sister who had been unjustly put to death by a neighbouring king and who had turned into a tree. The tree had been cut down and had floated down the river as far as Pagan, where the images of the twin gods were carved from its trunk. The interesting thing

about this legend is that it points to another instance of the inauguration of a cult of a god worshipped on a mountain after
territorial and religious unification had led to the founding of a
new State. Mahayana Buddhism was introduced into Pagan during
the seventh century, and the Ari sect soon gave it a pronounced
Tantrist tendency.[8] The city walls are thought to have been constructed in 849.

At this time, the delta ports, where Arab and Persian merchants
traded, belonged to the Mon kingdom of Ramannadesa. Its capital,
Hamsavati (Pegu), is thought to have been founded in 825.
Numerous Hindu remains in Lower Burma show that Buddhism
was not the only religion practised there.[9] Possibly Buddhism
received added stimulus from emigrants from the kingdom of
Haripunjaya (Lamphun in the upper Menam valley)[10] who fled
from a cholera epidemic during the first half of the eleventh
century, and perhaps also from the Khmer armies of Suryavarman I.

It is not until the beginning of the eleventh century that the
kingdom of Pagan emerges from legendary times with the
appearance of Aniruddha (Burmese, *Anawrahta*). Tradition has it
that his father, a descendant of a former governor of the city,
dethroned a usurper in 964, who, however, forced him to retire
to a monastery in 986. Aniruddha, after eliminating his rivals,
became king in 1044, whereupon he proceeded to enlarge his
territory and provide for its prosperity by improving the irrigation
system in the plain of Kyaukse. He was persuaded by the exhorta-
tions of a Mon monk to embrace Theravada Buddhism. In 1057 a
campaign against Thaton brought him mastery over the delta,
thus giving him access to the sea, while at the same time enabling
him to spread the doctrine of the Theravada among his Burmese
subjects and deliver them from the spiritual stranglehold of the
Ari. Contact with the Mons who were brought back from Thaton
with their king, Makuta, had a civilizing influence on the Burmese,
and from it sprang their religion, their literature, and their art.

Legend attributes vast conquests to Aniruddha, but there is no
way of checking the facts of the matter. Towards the west, he is
supposed to have conquered a part of Arakan – a kingdom that
had acquired its civilization from north-east India. Towards the
east he is said to have conducted a campaign against Cambodia
(but there is no mention of it in the historical records of that

country), and towards the north to have got as far as Nan-chao. Information about his relations with the Sinhalese king, Vijaya-bahu I (1056–1101), is more reliable. He it was who sent the famous tooth relic that was enshrined at Pagan in the Shwezigon temple, begun about 1059. Two more of Pagan's oldest monu-ments, the Nan Paya and the Manuha, date from Aniruddha's reign. They were built around 1060 by the Mon king who had been brought back in captivity after the expedition of 1057.

Aniruddha died in 1077, leaving a kingdom which extended from Bhamo in the north to the Gulf of Martaban or perhaps even to Mergui in the south. Theravada Buddhism was now firmly established in Pagan, and Mon cultural influence continued to affect Aniruddha's immediate successors.

After the rather brief reign of his son Sawlu, as he is known in the Burmese chronicles, or Vajrabharana, as the inscriptions have it, who was put to death by a rebel governor of the city of Pegu, another of Aniruddha's sons, called Kyanzittha (a corruption of *Kalan cacsa*, 'soldier-official'), came to power in 1084. He first had to reconquer the provinces in the south, and was then crowned in 1086 under the name of Tribhuvanaditya Dharmaraja. This name formed part of the title of all his successors. He was an admirer of Mon civilization,[11] and an ardent Buddhist. During the last years of the century he built the great temple of Anantapanna ('infinite wisdom') at Pagan. This temple, commonly called *Ananda*, is the *chef-d'œuvre* of Burmese architecture.[12] He also had repairs carried out at the temple of Bodhgaya in India. In 1103 and 1016 he sent the first official embassies to China. He died in 1112 or shortly after.

He was succeeded by his grandson Jayasura I (*Cansu I*, or *Alaungsithu*), whose reign began with a campaign against Arakan (1118). The chronicles say that he travelled far and wide through-out his kingdom, and he may even have got as far as Nan-chao. He built the Shwegu temple (1131) and the Sabbannu temple (*Thatbyinnyu*, 'the omniscient', 1150) at Pagan, and died some time after 1167.

His successor Narasura (*Narathu*) was assassinated in 1165 by foreigners, probably Sinhalese, who had invaded Burma in the preceding year. Native chronicles credit him with a son Narasimha (*Naratheinhka*), who is said to have reigned three years and to have been assassinated by his younger brother in 1173. In fact, no king seems to have reigned at Pagan between 1165 and 1174, when, with the help of Sinhalese, the lineage of Aniruddha was restored in the person of Jayasura II (*Cansu II* or *Narapatisithu*).

During his reign, spiritual ties between Burma and Ceylon were strengthened. 1190 is the date marking the introduction into Burma of the Buddhism that resulted from the reforms brought in by the Sinhalese king, Parakramabahu I (1153–86). This reformed Buddhism was introduced by the Mon monk Chapata, who had been to Ceylon to be ordained anew according to the rites of the Mahavihara sect, regarded from that time on as the only valid ones. The Sinhalese doctrine at first led to a schism in Burmese Buddhism, but gradually it ousted all others. Its orthodoxy was not, however, finally established until the end of the fifteenth century.

The reign of Jayasura II, whose sway extended southwards as far as Mergui and eastwards as far as the T'ai principalities, was on the whole a peaceful one. Among the buildings he erected at Pagan, mention should be made of the Chudamani (*Sulamani*, 1183), and the Gawdawpallin (before 1230). It was during his reign that the continuous decline of Mon cultural influence began, due to its being replaced by Sinhalese influence which, after the return of Chapata in 1190, gave rise to a profusion of literary works in Pali, including grammatical treatises, works on monastic discipline, and legal compilations.[13] The most ancient of Burma's law codes dates from the reign of Jayasura II. Its author was a Mon called Dhammavilasa.

Before his death in 1210, Jayasura II had appointed his young son Jayasimha (*Zeyatheinhka*) – also known as Nandaungmya and as Htilominlo (= Tilokamangala?) – as his heir apparent, who, however, handed over the power to his brothers. His eldest son, Narasimha Uccana (*Uzana*), then came to the throne sometime before 1231, and next came his younger son, Kyoswa, who endeavoured to restore law and order and to improve the finances of the kingdom. Kyoswa died in 1250 and was succeeded by his son Uzana, who reigned for four years. On his death, his son Simhasura (*Thingathu*) was supplanted by Narasimhapati (*Narathihapate*), the son of a concubine, and the last king of the dynasty that ruled over Pagan.

The dynasty filled the capital and its surroundings with Buddhist monuments, the most noteworthy of which have been mentioned in the account of each successive reign.[14] The architecture of Pagan shows Burmese art at its best, and is to some extent heir to the traditions of Shrikshetra, from which it borrowed its two main types of building, the stupa, and the cubiform shrine crowned with a shikhara – both of them of north-east Indian origin. In addition to coming under this early Indian influence, Pagan architecture has a few later buildings modelled on Indian prototypes. The Mahabodhi temple, for instance, built by King Jayasimha (1210–31), was a copy of the Bodhgaya temple in India; and there is a tradition according to which King Kyanzittha built the Ananda temple in imitation of the cave-temple of Nandamula on Mount Gandamadana, which has been identified with the Udayagiri temple of Orissa, or possibly with the temple of Paharpur. Lastly, Sinhalese architecture certainly influenced stupas such as the Pebingyaung and more especially the Sapada, named after the Mon monk Chapata who introduced Sinhalese Buddhism in 1190.

Art historians distinguish two periods in the architecture of Pagan. The first (1044–1113) includes the reigns of Aniruddha and of his son Kyanzittha. Here Mon influence is predominant, and is shown in the dimly-lit corridors with cloister windows and the Mon inscriptions on the frescoes, both being features found in the Manuha and the Nan Paya, the temples said to have been built by the Mon king brought back as captive from Thaton along with a large number of craftsmen after Aniruddha's campaign in 1057. The second period lasted until the capture of Pagan by the Mongols in 1287. Here new features appear: better lighting of the galleries, complicated lay-out, and the placing of the shrine above ground level. There was a transitional period during the reign of Jayasura II, and in point of fact Mon influence is sometimes perceptible after it, while Burmese features begin to appear as early as the reigns of Aniruddha's immediate successors.

A rough indication of the main architectural styles in chronological order may be given as follows:

1. Before Aniruddha came to the throne in 1044, none of the buildings erected at Pagan were any different in type from those which we know already existed at Prome.

2. The bell-shaped stupa was in great favour during the reign of Aniruddha (1044–77), as instanced by the Shwezigon, the Myinkaba, the Lokananda (1059), and the Shwesandaw, and remained

a favourite type of building throughout the dynasty until the building of the Mangalachetiya (*Mingalazedi*) in 1274. The Burmese stupa differs from the Indian and Sinhalese versions in being without a harmika, and in having a larger terraced platform and a higher and more soaring terminal spire.

3. The sanctuary with a central mass of masonry supporting the weight of a shikhara and surrounded by a gallery, such as the cave-temple of Kyaukku Umin which may date from as early as the reign of Aniruddha, reappears in the middle of the thirteenth century with the building of the Thambula in 1256. This is the type of building from which the Ananda, the Shwegu (1131), and the Dhammaramshi (*Dhammayan*, 1167–70) temples were evolved.

4. The sanctuary with central cella surrounded by a gallery lit by claustral windows is characteristic of the reign of Kyanzittha (1084–1121), as instanced by the temples of Nagayon, Abhayaratana (*Abeyadana*), and Kubyaukgyi. Hardly any later examples are found.

5. The sanctuary placed upon a solid block of stone, the first example of which is the Sabbannu (*Thatbyinnyu*) of 1150, predominates for three-quarters of a century and is the most characteristic creation of Pagan's architecture. To this type belong the Chudamani (*Sulamani* 1183), the Gawdawpallin, and the Tilokamangala (*Htilominlo, c.* 1211).

6. Lastly there are one or two buildings, erected at different times during the Pagan period, which are inspired by the architectural style of buildings constructed of perishable materials. Examples of these are the Pitakattaik (1060), the Mimalaungkyaung (1174), and the Upali Thein of the second half of the thirteenth century.

The strong Indian influence seen in the sculpture of Prome continues to be evident in that of Pagan, but at this later date the models are provided by the Indian Pala-Sena school of Bengal. Some of the statues even give the impression of having been made by Indian artists. The frescoes on the internal walls of the sanctuaries of Pagan show great affinity with the early style of painting found in Bengal and Nepal.

PART FOUR

---

*The Crisis of the Thirteenth Century
and the
Decline of Indian Cultural Influence*

FOR THE INDOCHINESE PENINSULA, and indeed for the whole of South East Asia, the thirteenth century meant the end of a world—the world that had come into being at the beginning of the Christian era with the introduction of Indian cultural influence into the societies that were then in existence in Indochina. Before recounting the events and assessing their consequences, a survey must first be made of the ethnic, political, and cultural situation in Indochina on the eve of this time of crisis.[1]

On the east coast, the Indianized kingdom of Champa had for long been the target for attacks by its neighbour to the north, the sinicized Dai Viet. In the year 1000 it had finally had to abandon Indrapura, its capital city, and transfer the capital from the Quang-nam to the Binh-dinh area. Dai Viet, which had been liberated from Chinese domination for three-quarters of a century, increased its pressure when the Ly dynasty came to power in 1010. In the twelfth century, another enemy of the Chams, Cambodia, twice succeeded in occupying their territory, first from 1145 to 1149, and then from 1190 to 1220. But between these two periods of occupation the Chams had been able to take advantage of the internal troubles that had meanwhile afflicted Cambodia, and had taken up arms against it, advancing as far as Angkor and sacking the city in 1177, thus giving proof of their fighting spirit. On the cultural side, their civilization was still a lively one; Sanskrit culture continued to flourish, as is shown by the inscriptions, and the artistic tradition was still strong enough to produce beautiful monuments such as the towers of Binh-dinh.

In Burma, the twelfth century marks the apogee of the Pagan dynasty founded in 1044. It was a time of great literary activity in the form of a number of works in Pali, and even more, a time that saw a great flowering of art. In 1190 Burma received a new contribution from the world of Indian culture – Sinhalese Buddhism, which was introduced by a Mon monk. This new stimulus within a society already profoundly impregnated with Buddhism had the happiest results. The same cannot be said of Cambodia, where Buddhism had taken a very different form in a culture that was predominantly Hindu.

The firm foothold of Sanskrit culture in Cambodia is evidenced by the numerous inscriptions dating from the twelfth century and by what they convey of the linguistic, literary, and religious background of their authors; and the flourishing condition of Cambodian art at this period is sufficiently indicated by the many temples that were built then, including P'imai, Beng Mealea, Angkor Vat, Banteay Samre, and the first of the Bayon style buildings (the later ones, and the Bayon itself, date from the beginning of the following century). The Khmer Empire in fact reached two high-points during the twelfth century – the first under Suryavarman II, who led his armies as far as northern Viet-nam and the upper Menam valley; and the second, after a period of troubles and the invasion of the Chams in 1177, under the Buddhist king, Jayavarman VII, who enlarged Cambodian territory until it extended from Vieng-Chan in the north to the Malay Peninsula in the south, and from the east coast of Indochina to the frontiers of Burma, and included, be it noted, the territory of the Syam who were established in the region of Sukhodaya, where authentic Khmer remains still stand today. It is from this period of Khmer power that the principal monuments of Lop Buri date: Vat Mahadhatu, with towers which, despite several restorations, have not lost their resemblance to those of Angkor Vat; the crumbling pyramid of Vat Nak'on Kosa, which must once have marked the centre of the city; and the three Khmer towers of Prang Sam Yot.[2] The statues of the Buddha found in large numbers at Lop Buri belong to a provincial school of Khmer art which produced some remarkable works.[3] Although it is clear from the Khmer inscriptions of Lop Buri that, during the eleventh century at least, Hinduism was practised there as well as Buddhism, the predominance of Buddhist temples and statues both at Lop Buri and in other western provinces of ancient Cambodia shows that, even under Khmer rule, Buddhism retained the pre-eminence it had enjoyed in this region during the time of the kingdom of Dvaravati.

In short, it may be said that in the twelfth, and even at the beginning of the thirteenth century, the great Indianized States gave every appearance of still being firmly rooted in their traditional ways of life. Indian culture was still very much alive, finding expression both in Sanskrit and in Pali as well as through the medium of the vernacular enriched with a vocabulary borrowed from Indian tongues, and inspiring great works of art.

Nevertheless, signs of internal weakness can be discerned within the societies that had been civilized by Indian culture – warning signals of a decadence which simply became accentuated by the events of the thirteenth century.

Champa was like a body deprived of its essential organs after its capital and political centre had had to be moved from the holy city of My-son, where, ever since the fourth century, the god Bhadreshvara, protector of the kingdom, had sat enthroned in a temple that had several times been rebuilt; and it still had to face yet another conflict over its northern provinces with Dai Viet, where a new dynasty was reigning.

The founder of this dynasty, Tran Thu Do, began his career by removing the last ruler of the Ly dynasty, who retired to a monastery. Later, during the reign of his nephew, the young emperor, Tran Thai-tong, who as yet had no male heir, he attempted to ensure the line of succession by arranging a marriage for his nephew with the sister of the empress, who was pregnant. This resulted in a temporary estrangement between the emperor and his brother-in-law, but ended in the uncle being exiled. In 1240 Tran Thai-tong at last had a son, upon whom he immediately conferred the title of heir apparent, and to whom he ceded the throne in 1258, thus inaugurating a custom which became habitual with the rulers of this dynasty. Upon retirement, the former king maintained most of the control over the affairs of state, and the new king after he had been crowned did not have much more authority than when he had been heir apparent. Tran Thai-tong died in 1277.

The years when Tran Thai-tong was actually on the throne (1225–58) were made illustrious by a number of reforms concerning provincial administration, the official hierarchy, the payment of taxes, and public works for irrigation and water control. These reforms were a completion of the reforms initiated by the preceding dynasty. Abroad, Tran Thai-tong himself led an expedition against Champa in 1252. The Khmers had ended their occupation of Champa in 1220, and a new king, Jaya Parameshvaravarman II, had been enthroned. Towards the end of his reign he demanded the retrocession of the three northern provinces which were an eternal bone of contention between the two neighbouring countries. The demand provoked Tran Thai-tong into sending an expedition which brought back a large number of prisoners and perhaps was responsible for the death of the Cham king. Shortly after this Tran Thai-tong was subjected to the first of the Mongol invasions. It followed upon the taking of Yunnan in 1253 by Kublai, the future founder of the Yüan dynasty in China.

In the thirteenth century Cambodia was already beginning to show signs of strain due to its territorial expansion, and even more to the crushing burdens that had been imposed on its people during the twelfth century by two great warrior and builder kings. The Cham invasion of 1177 had shown how vulnerable the kingdom was during periods of internal troubles, and its possessions and dependencies were beginning to loosen their ties of vassalage, some even breaking free of them altogether. Chen-li-fu,[4] which probably lay at the north-west corner of the Gulf of Siam, and which in 1225 was described by Chao Ju-kua as being, according to earlier sources at his disposal, a dependency of Cambodia, demonstrated its independence by sending embassies to China from 1200 onwards. Lo-hu, or the country of Lvo, was later to follow its example, but not until 1289, although as early as the second half of the twelfth century it had, as we have seen, taken advantage of Cambodia's internal troubles and attempted to throw off the yoke. In Champa the Khmer armies, after withdrawing in 1220, advanced again for the last time during the years 1216–18, reaching as far as Nghe-an. Their subsequent withdrawal was probably on account of the death of Jayavarman VII, which coincided with a certain amount of movement on the part of the T'ai tribes in the north of the peninsula. Jayavarman VII was succeeded by his son (?) Indravarman II, concerning whom only one date is known – that of his death in 1243. His successor Jayavarman VIII was to have quite a long reign, during which a small Mongol force invaded Cambodia from Champa in 1283.

It was during the first half of the thirteenth century that Cambodia lost its hold over the T'ais of the Menam – the Syam who figure on the bas-reliefs of Angkor Vat – whose main centre was at Sukhodaya (*Sukhothai*) and Shri Sajjanalaya (present-day Sawankhalok). These twin cities were situated on the frontiers of three political and cultural zones of influence: that of the Khmers, that of the Mons of Haripunjaya, and that of the Burmese of Pagan. The river Me Yom afforded an easy line of communication with Lop Buri and the former Khmer provinces of the lower Menam, and westward communications, particularly those with Ceylon, were assured by the fact that the cities lay at the end of the route from Lower Burma.

The archaeological remains of Sukhodaya, the earliest of which, Vat P'ra P'ay Luang, is a group of three towers in the purest twelfth-century Khmer style, attest to the presence of the Khmers in this region at that time.[5] It was towards the middle of the thirteenth century that the Syam freed themselves under the following circumstances.[6] A certain Pha Muong, the son of a person of some importance who had perhaps been a Syam chief under Cambodian rule, had had conferred upon him by Angkor the title of Indrapatindraditya, and had married a Khmer princess. Following upon events of which little is known, and with the help of another T'ai chief called Bang Klang T'ao, he entered upon a struggle with the Khmer governor of Sukhodaya, and got the better of him. Pha Muong replaced him with his ally Bang Klang T'ao, whom he then proclaimed king, conferring upon him his own title of Indrapatindraditya, thereby giving the revolution a semblance of legitimacy, since he seemed to be acting in the name of the Khmer chancellery. In the event, however, there was a break in allegiance, and the first independent T'ai kingdom, called Hsien (= Syam) by the Chinese historians, was founded. The loss of the territory of Sukhodaya was not in itself a catastrophe for Cambodia, but it was not long before the newly-founded kingdom displayed an expansionist policy towards its former rulers which was to bear fruit at the end of the century, during the reign of the founder's son.

Farther north, in the upper Menam valley, the kingdom of Haripunjaya (present-day Lamphun) was still under the rule of a Mon dynasty at the beginning of the thirteenth century.[7] In Lamphun there are inscriptions, dating from 1215 to 1219, by Sabbadhisiddhi, one of the kings mentioned in the local chronicle. They are in the Mon language with intervening passages in Pali, and give an account of the founding of Buddhist temples, two of which date from the reign of Adityaraja, a contemporary of the Khmer king, Suryavarman II. The first of these is Vat Kukut, a square tower the storeys of which decrease in size and are decorated with rows of standing Buddhas in stucco; it was formerly the Mahabalachetiya, which was built to commemorate a victory over the Khmer armies. The other temple is Vat Mahadhatu, which has several times been altered and enlarged. In its present form it is an elegant bell-shaped stupa, very slim and slender, and capped with gilded bronze plaques. After the reign of King Sabbadhisiddhi, the chronicles give a list of kings of whom nothing is known except their names. Their neighbours on the north-east were the Lao princes of Ngon Yang (present Chiang Saen), the last of whom succeeded his father in 1261. The following year he moved his capital farther south and founded Chiang Rai, and then began extending his territory to the north-east and also to the south-west, in the direction of Haripunjaya, still ruled by the Mon dynasty.

One gets the impression that in the second half of the thirteenth century the kingdoms that had been Indianized since the first centuries of the Christian era no longer had the resilience to withstand a major shock, or even to survive a minor disturbance of the foundations upon which their civilization rested. The shock administered by the Mongols was their undoing.[8]

As soon as Kublai became Grand Khan in 1260, and even before he had completed the conquest of China, he sought to obtain the vassalage of those countries that had been neighbours of the former Sung empire. As far as Japan was concerned, the Mongols met with complete failure, and their attempt ended in disaster in 1281. In the following year, 1282, Indochina experienced the first big impact of Kublai's armies. But already in 1257 Uriyangadai (son of the famous Subötai who had led his army as far as Russia in 1222) had invaded northern Viet-nam from the Red River valley and sent ambassadors to Tran Thai-tong, who took them prisoner. The Mongols had then descended towards the south as far as the capital, Dai-la, which they attacked in December, thus taking their revenge for the affront given to their envoys. But the heir-apparent was able to come to the aid of his father, Tran Thai-tong, with reinforcements, and the invaders were forced to make a temporary withdrawal. It was after these events that Tran Thai-tong abdicated in favour of his son, who reigned from 1258 to 1278 under the name of Tran Thanh-tong.

The reign of the new emperor was not marked by any important event. He died in 1290. Twelve years before his death he had

Ploughing.

Planting out the rice-shoots.

I. WET RICE CULTIVATION.

II. MEGALITHIC MONUMENTS: The Plaine des Jarres at Tran-ninh (Laos).

III. PEOPLES OF NORTHERN INDOCHINA: Mountain-dwellers from
northern Viet-nam.

A Cambodian house near Battambang.

Men of the Stieng tribe in southern Viet-nam.

IV. PEOPLES OF SOUTHERN INDOCHINA.

A Dongson bronze drum (3rd century B.C.).

A Chinese tomb of the Han period at Bac-ninh (1st cent. A.D.).

V. THE BEGINNINGS OF VIETNAMESE CIVILIZATION.

VI. ARCHITECTURE OF CHAMPA: *Left:* The great tower of My-son (10th century). *Right:* The temple at Po Romé (17th century).

VII. SCULPTURE OF CHAMPA: *Left*: Statue of Shiva, Dong-düöng style (end of 11th century). *Right*: A dancer carved on a pedestal at Tra-Kiêu (10th century).

The temple of Banteay Srei (968).

The pyramid-temple of Ta Keo (end of 10th-beginning of 11th century).

VIII. KHMER ARCHITECTURE.

IX. KHMER SCULPTURE: *Left:* Statue of Vishnu, pre-Angkor style (6th century). *Right:* Statue of Vishnu, Angkor period (middle of 11th century).

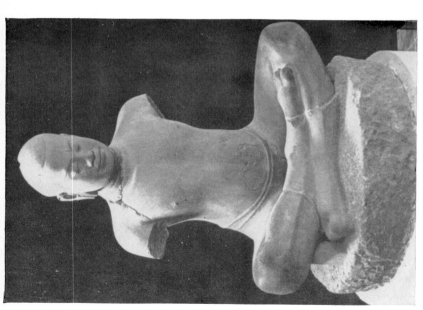

X. KHMER SCULPTURE: *Left:* Statue of Jayavarman VII (end of 12th century). *Right:* A statue which is thought to be of the first wife of Jayavarman VII.

XI. BURMESE ARCHITECTURE: Thatbinñyu or Temple of the Omniscient at Pagan (middle of the 11th century).

XII. SIAMESE ARCHITECTURE: Vat Mahadhatu at Sukhodaya (13th-14th century).

XIII. SIAMESE SCULPTURE: *Left*: Statue of the Buddha of the school of Sukhodaya (13th c.).
Right: Statue of the Buddha of the school of U Thong (13th c.).

Vat Mahadhatu at Svargaloka (end of 13th c.).

Stupa in the palace enclosure at Ayudhya (14th c.).

XIV. SIAMESE ARCHITECTURE.

Th'at Luang at Vientiane (1566).

Vat Ch'ieng T'ong at Luang Prabang (16th c.).

XV. LAOTIAN ARCHITECTURE.

XVI. LATER BURMESE ARCHITECTURE: Spire of a temple at Mandalay
(19th c.).

transmitted the power to his eldest son, who was crowned under the name of Tran Nhan-tong and reigned from 1279 to 1293. To him belongs the renown of having successfully resisted a powerful Mongol attack.

The aim of this attack, launched in 1282, was to bring Champa to submission. Champa had recovered its independence after the Khmer occupation of 1190 to 1220, and had been ruled since 1266 by Indravarman V, who, unlike other Cham kings, maintained good relations with Dai Viet, sending no less than four embassies there between 1266 and 1270. This policy bore fruit when it came to the fight against the Mongols. In 1278, and again in 1280, he was invited to present himself in person at the Court in Peking. He managed to avoid accepting this invitation by sending embassies and presents, but in 1281 the Mongol general Sögetu (Vietnamese, *Toa Do*), who was the conqueror of Kwangtung, and the Chinese Liu-shen were sent to Champa in order to 'maintain the peace' there, according to the expression used in the Mongol dynastic annals. The Cham people, incited by Prince Harijit, a son of the king, were little inclined to accept this form of protection, and the Grand Khan's commissioners had to return home. Kublai then organized a punitive expedition. Dai Viet, which, as mentioned above, happened to be on friendly terms with Champa, refused to allow the Mongol army to pass through its territory, so that Sögetu was obliged to take the sea route. In January 1283 he reached the Binh-dinh region, where the strongly fortified capital, Vijaya, was situated. King Indravarman had meanwhile had time to vacate it and take refuge with his troops in the mountains, whence for two years he conducted a gruelling guerrilla warfare against the Mongols. He sent embassy after embassy to the Mongol commander bearing the tribute of submission, but obstinately refused to come in person, giving age and ill-health as his excuse, although in fact he was busy all the time reorganizing his forces. These tactics finally exhausted the patience of Sögetu, and he returned to China in the spring of 1284. Another expeditionary force replaced his, but was no more successful. Kublai then decided to put an end to the matter and to send an expedition by the land route that Dai Viet had kept closed, whatever the cost might be. He sent a larger number of troops than before, under the command of one of his sons, Prince Toghan (*Thoat Hoan*). They went by Lang-son and attacked Dai Viet in

January 1285. Toghan won a battle near Bac-ninh, and advanced as far as Hanoi, but was then defeated in the delta area and forced to withdraw to China again. Meanwhile Sögetu planned to attack from the rear by advancing from the south. He disembarked in Champa and led his troops via Nghe-an and Than-hoa to meet Toghan, but they were ambushed and massacred.

This rid Champa of the Mongols. They had lost many officers and men there without having gained any appreciable advantage. But Indravarman V was anxious to prevent their return, and sent an ambassador to Kublai who presented himself at the Court on 6 October 1285.

An envoy from Cambodia was also present on that date, for Cambodia, as I have already mentioned, had also come under Mongol pressure, but had extricated itself at less cost. In 1282, Sögetu, at the beginning of his campaign against Champa, had sent a small troop of men commanded by two officers to attack the Khmer king. They probably followed the route from Quang-tri to Savannakhet. They were captured, but Jayavarman VIII thought it prudent not to exploit this success – hence his offering of tribute to Kublai in 1285. Kublai had been no more successful in persuading him to come in person to Peking than he had been in persuading the king of Champa. In 1295 Jayavarman VIII abdicated in favour of his son-in-law, Shrindravarman (1295–1327), during whose reign Cambodia received the visit of the Chinese envoy, Chou Ta-kuan, whose account, discussed later, is a source of primary importance concerning conditions in Cambodia in the thirteenth century.

The capital of Dai Viet was once again occupied by the Mongols in 1287, but they were unable to maintain their hold and had to withdraw from the country. The emperor, Tran Nhan-tong (1279–93), after having successfully withstood all attacks, returned in triumph to his capital. But in 1288 he, too, thought it prudent to enter into ties of vassalage with Kublai. The success of Dai Viet resistance was largely due to the valour of the general in command, a cousin of the emperor called Prince Tran Quoc Toan, nowadays worshipped as a god under the name of Tran Hung-dao. In accordance with the custom of the dynasty, Tran Nhan-tong abdicated in 1293 in favour of his eldest son, who took the name of Tran Anh-tong and reigned until 1314. The new emperor concluded a matrimonial alliance with Champa in 1306, giving the hand of his sister, the Princess Huyen Tran, to the Cham king, Che Man, in exchange for a final renunciation of rights over the provinces to the north of the Col des Nuages. This Cham king, who in the inscriptions is called Jaya Simhavarman (III), died in 1307. He it was who built the Po Klaung Garai temple at Phan-rang, which exhibits, along with features of earlier styles, some of the peculiarities of the late style, particularly the rounding-off of exterior angles, giving a flowing, curved effect to the lines of the building. Che Chi (Jaya Simhavarman IV), the succeeding Cham king, came to power in 1308. He did not respect the treaty concluded between his father and Tran Anh-tong, and the latter had to lead an expedition to reclaim the contested provinces, which resulted in the capture of the Cham king. The king died in Dai Viet in 1313, and one of his brothers, Che Nang, was appointed to administer Champa in the name of the Tran.

The Mongols, to make up for their defeat by Dai Viet in 1287, took their revenge on Burma during the same year. After they had annexed Yunnan in 1253 they had demanded that tribute should be sent to Peking by the Burmese king, Narasimhapati. Their mission was not received, and when another was sent to renew the demand in 1273, the ambassadors were put to death. In 1277 Kublai seized the opportunity afforded by a campaign conducted by the Burmese army in Mongol-controlled territory up-stream from Bhamo to avenge this outrage.[9] In the spring of 1277 the first phase of the operations was crowned with success, and during the following winter the Mongols occupied the fortress defending Bhamo. In 1283 their troops descended the valley of the Irrawaddy, without however reaching Pagan. King Narasim-hapati fled towards the delta, but in 1286 he was poisoned by his son Sihasura (Burmese, *Thihathu*) at Prome. The latter tried to take Pegu and died in the attempt. In 1287, after three unsuccessful campaigns, an expedition commanded by Prince Yesin Timur at last reached Pagan after suffering considerable losses. It is not known whether the capital suffered much damage from its occupation by the Sino-Mongol troops. The episode was of no permanent political significance for the Mongol Empire, but it had immense consequences for Burma and the Menam valley because it led to the T'ais gaining their independence.

Since the first half of the thirteenth century the southern borders of Yunnan had tended to be in a state of ferment. It was during this period that several T'ai principalities were founded which later became the Shan States of Burma; and, as we have seen, the Siamese kingdom of Sukhodaya was also founded at that time. During the same period the T'ais of Luang Prabang advanced down the Nam Hou valley. For the most part, what was happening was not so much a heavy influx of tribal peoples, but rather the taking over of power by people of T'ai origin who had already been members of the ruling class in the various countries for a shorter or a longer period.

The capture of Pagan by the Mongols in 1287 resulted in the temporary disappearance of Burmese kingship and the partition of the territory. Kublai seems to have followed the policy of divide and rule, and consequently to have made a habit of setting up the largest possible number of petty local chieftains as kings so that the territory could more easily be held in subjection. The T'ais were able to take advantage of this,[10] and it was they who got into positions of power – some in the south (in particular at Martaban), and others in the group of small fiefs in the rice-growing plain that lies in the bend of the river to the east of Pagan.

In the upper Menam valley – so an ancient text[11] informs us – Mangrai, ruler of Chiang Rai (who, as we have seen, was in process of extending his territory towards the south-west), Ngam Muong, ruler of Phayao, and Rama Khamheng, son and successor of the founder of the kingdom of Sukhodaya, 'met together at a propitious spot, concluded a solemn pact of friendship, and then returned each to his own country'. It was certainly no mere coincidence that 1287 was the year in which these three rulers concluded their alliance, for this was the year in which Pagan was taken. In the following year Mangrai sent an envoy to Lamphun, the capital of the Mon kingdom of Haripunjaya. The envoy succeeded in winning the confidence of King Yiba, and got himself appointed as tax-collector. When he had sufficiently exasperated the inhabitants of Lamphun with his demands and exactions, this agent provocateur sent a secret message to his master, Mangrai, who thereupon marched upon the city and took it – a fruit ripe for the plucking. In 1296 Mangrai founded the city of Chiang Mai, 'the new city', about twelve miles to the north of Lamphun. This city was to have a glorious future as the capital of the kingdom of Lan Na, 'the country of a million rice-fields'. It is today the second city of Thailand.[12]

During the same period Rama Khamheng, another signatory of the pact of 1287, achieved a kind of hegemony over several T'ai tribes and considerably enlarged the territory of Sukhodaya at the expense of Cambodia. By the end of the thirteenth century the States he ruled over extended northwards as far as the site of Luang Prabang, eastwards as far as Vieng Chan, southwards as far as Ligor, and westwards as far as Pegu. The conquest of the Khmer provinces in the Mekong and Menam valleys was apparently achieved during the course of the merciless war described, in 1296, by the Mongol envoy to Cambodia as follows: 'In the recent war against the Siamese, the entire Khmer people were obliged to take up arms and the country was completely devastated.' Rama Khamheng's conquest of the Malay Peninsula, where T'ai infiltration had already begun in the middle of the thirteenth century, must have occurred sometime around 1294, for a Chinese text of 1295 refers to it.[13]

If we now cast a backward glance over the events of the thirteenth century and attempt to assess their consequences for the Indochinese peninsula, we see that they brought about a decline of the Indianized kingdoms and at the same time the growth, at their expense, of a number of petty principalities and of one or two kingdoms all ruled over by the T'ais. But this political conjuncture seems to have been due rather to a change in the membership of the ruling classes than to a sudden disruption of the pattern of settlement in the peninsula.

In the Irrawaddy valley several T'ai chiefs succeeded to the heritage of the Burmese kings after the fall of Pagan in 1287; and in the valley of the Menam the position of the T'ais of Sukhodaya, who had won their independence in the first half of the thirteenth century after the death of the Khmer king, Jayavarman VII, strengthened rapidly during the second half of the century, and led to the decline of the Khmer Empire. In the following century the northern provinces of the Khmer Empire came under the rule of yet another T'ai chief to form the Laotian kingdom of Lan Ch'ang, 'the kingdom of a million elephants'.

This political upheaval, which weakened the States where Indian culture flourished, was accompanied by cultural changes that were to have far-reaching effects over several centuries.

By the fourteenth century, Sanskrit was more and more falling out of use. In Champa the last Sanskrit inscriptions date from 1253, and in Cambodia from 1330. In the Mekong and Menam valleys what remained of Hinduism and Mahayana Buddhism gave place, during the twelfth to the fourteenth centuries, to the reformed type of Buddhism from Ceylon that had been introduced at the end of the twelfth century by the Mons of Burma and was subsequently taken over by the T'ais.

In art, where direct observation makes it easier to draw conclusions, two trends can be discerned. The first consists of a return to an indigenous style of architecture in which the general lines of buildings are different from what they had been before, while sculpture begins to exhibit contorted forms, exuberant ornamentation, and an iconography that becomes further and further removed from that of the original Indian models. This is displayed in the fourteenth-century buildings and statues of Champa, and even more in those of the island of Java. The other trend is one of growing sterility in art, largely due to the influence of Sinhalese Buddhism, which was in principle hostile to the worship of individual persons, and which created an atmosphere that was not conducive to the flourishing of the plastic arts. In Cambodia, apart from a few small buildings at Angkor Thom that are still in the Angkor tradition, almost the only constructions undertaken were Buddhist terraces which are mere esplanades upon which buildings similar to modern pagodas, constructed of flimsy materials, could be erected. In Burma the art of Pagan ceased to flourish after the fall of the capital, and what took its place consisted mostly of large stupas similar in type to the Shwe Dagon in Rangoon. But from the ruins of the Khmer and Burmese art of the twelfth and thirteenth centuries a new art arose – the Siamese style of Sukhodaya.

Did the generations who lived through these critical times and the generations that followed realize that great changes were taking place before their very eyes? One is tempted to believe that they did when one reads what King Lu T'ai, the last sovereign of the kingdom of Sukhodaya, wrote in the fourteenth century. In one of his inscriptions, written in 1357,[14] he declares that one hundred and thirty-nine years before this date (that is to say, in 1218), 'the age of men, which used to reach to a hundred years, fell below this figure. From that year, the nobles and the high dignitaries, the Brahmans and the wealthy merchants gradually ceased to occupy the first place in society; also from that time, astrologers and physicians lost their prestige; from that time on they were no longer respected.' The year 1218 is roughly the closing date of the reign of Jayavarman VII,[15] the last Cambodian king to hold sway over the Syam of the middle Menam. It marks the beginning of the ferment in the T'ai principalities on the Yunnan border, and perhaps also the introduction of Sinhalese Buddhism among the T'ais.

It is difficult to say whether King Lu T'ai refers to any specific event, and if so, what this event might be. The death of the Khmer ruler? The declaration of Sukhodaya's independence by Lu T'ai's ancestor? The decline of Hinduism and Mahayana Buddhism due to the introduction of Sinhalese Buddhism? One thing only is certain: in Lu T'ai's opinion, the year 1218 marked the beginning of the decline in the influence of the aristocracy based on Indian cultural traditions, made up as it was of the various elements mentioned: nobles, Brahmans, merchants, astrologers, and physicians. I feel inclined to interpret this passage as an expression of satisfaction on the part of the king in being able to chronicle this 'transvaluation of all values' brought about by the break-up of the Indo-Khmer aristocratic society that was so alien to his own Buddhistic ideals.[16]

Although the decline of Indian culture which took place throughout South East Asia during the thirteenth century was accelerated by the commotions caused by the Mongols, it was by no means directly due to them, for premonitory symptoms can be discerned during the previous century. The underlying causes of the decline of Indian culture lay in the ever-increasing number of indigenous peoples who adopted it and in doing so adapted it to their own cultural traditions, and also in the gradual disappearance of a cultured aristocratic class, the members of which had been the guardians of the Sanskrit cultural tradition. Hinduism and Mahayana Buddhism, as practised in the form of the worship of kings and of other individual persons, were religions with little appeal for the masses; and this explains why the masses so quickly and so readily adopted Sinhalese Buddhism.

The net result of the commotions caused by the Mongol conquests was the falling apart of old political entities and old cultural complexes: the Khmer Empire, the Cham kingdom, and the Burmese kingdom. Their dismembered elements were later regrouped to form the new combinations which we shall see taking over from them. These were the Burmese kingdom of Ava followed by that of Pegu, and the T'ai kingdoms of Ayudhya, Lan Na, and Lan Ch'ang.

Although from this time onwards India – in contradistinction to China – ceased to be a source of inspiration and renewal for the Indochinese civilizations which were an extension of its own, it had already exercized so profound an influence that, as I shall argue in my conclusion, the effects are still felt today.

PART FIVE

The Indochinese States after the Thirteenth Century

AFTER THE CRISIS of the thirteenth century the history of Indo-china seems to take on an altogether new aspect, but the explanation for this lies perhaps in the different nature of the source material. In the countries where Indian culture had flourished, epigraphy supplies the main documentation for the preceding centuries, whereas there are almost no inscriptions referring to later times (except in the T'ai countries); and Chinese historical works, which, although a main source elsewhere, provide a subsidiary source of information for the Indianized countries, have not been explored so thoroughly for the period since the thirteenth century as they have for the earlier period, especially as regards Champa and Cambodia. Hence the main available sources are local annals and chronicles compiled at a somewhat later date than the events recorded. They have the advantage of giving a continuous narration of events, but too often they include legendary material or information that cannot be checked. After the sixteenth century sources include reports and correspondence of European merchants and missionaries, the advantage of which is that they supply precise and accurate dates; but they often relate events and pass judgements from a biased point of view, and thus lack objectivity. In the case of Viet-nam, the difference between its ancient and its modern history is less noticeable; there the sources, both national and Chinese, are the same after the thirteenth century as before.

There is, however, not only an apparent but also a real difference between the history of Indochina before the thirteenth century and its history since then – or rather, its history since the founding of the Siamese kingdom of Ayudhya and the Laotian kingdom of Lan Ch'ang in the middle of the fourteenth century. The difference is this: in the later period no major upheavals from either external or internal causes occurred, so that the patterns of settlement remained unaltered and there were no drastic changes in the political map of the peninsula such as the substitution of Chen-la for Fu-nan at the turn of the sixth to the seventh century, the disappearance of the Pyu kingdom of Shrikshetra and of the Mon kingdom of Dvaravati due to the rise of the Burmese at the turn of the tenth to the eleventh, or the establishment of Khmer power in the central and southern Menam valley at the expense of the Mons of Dvaravati in the tenth century and the rise of T'ai power in the north at the expense of the Mons of Haripunjaya in the thirteenth. At the beginning of the later period the States of Burma, Siam, Cambodia, Laos, and Viet-nam were already on the map, and stayed there, preserving their political and cultural entity despite being frequently torn by internal strife or involved in wars with each other that were often bloody, and despite fluctuations in their frontiers from time to time. Champa alone failed to survive, falling prey to the slow but continuous advance of Viet-nam towards the south. The external influences that now played the greatest part were those stemming from China, from Islam – by which only southern Indochina was affected, and then only slightly – and from Europe. Prior to nineteenth-century colonization, the European contribution consisted chiefly in the introduction of fire-arms, various commercial products, and Christianity.

As I explained in the Introduction, I shall treat the history of the post-thirteenth-century Indochinese States in much more summary fashion than I treated that of the States of the earlier period. I shall give only the general outline and mention only the outstanding events of each nation's history. At the end of each of the following chapters, which deal successively with Siam, Laos, Burma, Cambodia, and Viet-nam, there will be a few brief remarks about the cultural aspects of each State and about the various indigenous and foreign elements that contributed towards its culture as a whole. In most cases it will be mainly art and literature that come under discussion, since these are the aspects about which most is known, and often the only ones to which any serious study has been devoted.

I

Siam or Thailand[1]

WE HAVE SEEN ABOVE how the T'ais of the upper Menam shook off the yoke of Khmer domination and founded at Sukhodaya the first independent T'ai kingdom. The new State reached the apogee of its power under Rama Khamheng, third son of Indraditya and second king in succession to him. The stele erected by Rama Khamheng in 1292, bearing the oldest written text in the T'ai language,[2] records successively the invention in 1283 of the script used in the inscription, the construction in 1285 of a large stupa in the centre of the city of Shri Sajjanalaya, and the erection in 1292 of a stone throne for the king to sit on in order to show himself to his subjects and hold audience. It also mentions the king's conquests in all four directions: eastwards as far as Vieng Chan, southwards as far as Nagara Shri Dharmaraja (Ligor), westwards as far as Hamsavati (Pegu), and northwards as far as Java (site of the future Luang Prabang). All these conquests were achieved roughly between 1280 and 1295.

It was also during this period – in 1282 to be exact – that Sukhodaya first entered into relations with China. It is not known whether the imperial command of 1294,[3] enjoining the King of Hsien (= Syam) 'to come to the Court or, if he had reason to excuse himself, to send his son, his brother, and some envoys as hostages' was in fact carried out. According to Siamese tradition, P'ra Ruang – a name by which the first kings of Sukhodaya are jointly referred to, but here having special reference to Rama Khamheng – himself went to China, and brought back with him the secrets of Chinese ceramic technology. Certainly the first pottery kilns at Sukhodaya and at Shri Sajjanalaya were installed by Chinese.[4]

No exact date can be given for the end of Rama Khamheng's reign, but it cannot have been later than 1318. He was succeeded by his son Lo T'ai, whose fervent Buddhism earned him the title of Dharmaraja (I), the 'king of the Law'. During his reign closer relations between Sukhodaya and Ceylon, now become the religious metropolis, were entered into, largely because of a voyage undertaken by a member of the royal house who had been ordained according to the new orthodox rites.[5]

About 1340 Lo T'ai appointed his son Lu T'ai to be viceroy at Shri Sajjanalaya. The probable date of his death was 1347. Lu T'ai was a scholar 'learned in the whole of the Holy Scriptures, and in the methods of the traditional masters of the Vinaya and the Abhidharma; conversant with the Veda, the treatises and the traditions, the law and the maxims, beginning with the astronomical treatises . . .; conversant with the short years and the years with intercalary months, the days, the lunar mansions, and using his authority to reform the calendar'.[6] He wrote a Buddhist cosmological treatise, the *Traibhumikatha* ('The History of the Three Worlds'), in 1345, during his years as viceroy. The treatise has come down to us in its original Siamese version, almost intact.[7]

In 1347 Lu T'ai went to Sukhodaya, where trouble seems to have broken out on the death of his father. He took the city and had himself consecrated as king under the title of Shri Suryavamsa Rama Mahadharmarajadhiraja (Dharmaraja II). But two years later he had to acknowledge the suzerainty of a new State that had just been established in the southern part of the Menam valley.

According to the traditional account of the founding of this kingdom, a T'ai chief belonging to the family of the rulers of Chiang Saen (to which Mangrai, the founder of Chiang Mai, also belonged) set himself up in the south as ruler over territory formerly occupied by the Mon kingdom of Dvaravati, and married one of the daughters of the ruler of the city of U Thong in the region of Subarnapuri (*Suphan*). He succeeded his father-in-law as ruler of U Thong, but about 1347 he abandoned his capital following upon a cholera epidemic, and founded a new city on an island of the Menam situated at the confluence of several tributaries. He named the city Dvaravati Shri Ayudhya. In 1350 he was crowned at Ayudhya under the name of Ramadhipati, having during the previous year obtained the submission of King Lu T'ai, who now devoted himself entirely to religious activities and finally became a monk in 1361. Thus ended the first period of Siam's history – that of the kingdom of Sukhodaya, which lasted roughly from 1220 to 1350, and which saw the rise of an art style of which some interesting specimens have survived.

The T'ai monuments of Sukhodaya do not date back any earlier than the reign of Rama Khamheng. They assume a variety of forms due to the many different stylistic influences (Khmer, Mon, and Burmese) from neighbouring countries, not to mention the influence of Ceylon. Thus a stupa supported by caryatid elephants, in a style borrowed from Ceylon, may be found next to a conical tower in the Khmer manner (modelled on the towers of Vat P'ra P'ay Luang built at Sukhodaya during the period of Khmer rule), or to a bell-shaped stupa, or to a temple in the massive style, with interior cella, of Burmese inspiration. But although it is true that the T'ais were strongly influenced by the architecture of neighbouring countries, they must be given the credit for having invented a type of building of their own. Only four or five specimens survive, all placed in a central position, which shows that they were regarded as important buildings. They consist of a tower containing the shrine, which soars up from a foundation that is reminiscent of the massive type of temple in the Burmese style. This results in a curious composite structure, the main body of which is like a truncated Khmer tower topped by a tiny stupa. Its originality lies in the combination of the three main types of building in use at the time. The general effect is that of a reliquary urn. These temples usually bore the name of Vat Mahadhatu, 'temple of the great relic', and they were erected, like the one at Sukhodaya, in the centre of the city, in the same way as the temple-mountain of the royal linga stood at the centre of the Khmer capital.

Shri Sajjanalaya (present Svargaloka = Sawankhalok), twin city to Sukhodaya, now consists of two groups of ruins, the most ancient of which centres round the great tower of the Vat Mahadhatu, which is well preserved owing to its having been several times restored. The tower is in the late Khmer style, and is placed upon a foundation of considerable height and of harmonious proportions, surrounded by a rampart of huge monoliths. It dates from the reign of King Rama Khamheng, whose stele records that it was built between 1285 and 1288. The second group of ruins, corresponding to the actual city of Shri Sajjanalaya, consists of a large number of buildings as diverse in type as those of Sukhodaya, surrounded by an imposing rampart about two and a half miles in length.

All these buildings are Buddhist. Does this mean that already at this time Sinhalese Buddhism had completely supplanted the Hindu cults introduced by the Khmers and the traditional animism of the T'ais? This would be a mistaken assumption. Rama Khamheng's inscription, deeply imbued with Buddhism as it is, nevertheless contains a passage that throws a revealing light upon this question. '[To the south of Sukhodaya] a spring gushes forth from the hillside. Brana Khabung is the spirit (*p'i*) and god (*devata*) of this hill, and he is above all the other spirits of the land. If whatever prince who happens to be ruling over the country of Sukhodaya faithfully continues to worship him and to present him with the ritual offerings, then the country will remain stable and prosperous, but if he does not carry out the prescribed worship, and does not present him with the ritual offerings, then the spirit of this hill will no longer protect nor respect this country, which will then decline.' The hill in question must be the one that rises at a distance of several miles to the south-west of the city and bears the name of Khao Luang, 'the great hill'. Some people say that on top of this hill was a pedestal bearing a statue which has since disappeared. This may be a mere supposition; but the name of the spirit contains a Khmer word meaning 'high' or 'raised'. Brana Khabung means the Lord of the Height, or the Lord of the Mountain-top, a name which immediately recalls the Burmese spirit or Nat, Mahagiri, who, as has already been mentioned, resided on Mount Poppa, the sacred mountain situated to the south-east of Pagan, whose cult was inaugurated when several territorial units, each with its own spirit, were united under the rule of one man – the ruler of Pagan. We have also seen that in Fu-nan the mountain from which the country took its name, upon which a powerful god was thought to dwell, also symbolized the unification of various tribes under the rule of one monarch, the 'king of the mountain'; and the inauguration of the cult of the royal linga on the hill of Kulen by the Khmer king Jayavarman II, in 802 coincided with the re-unification of the country, which had been partitioned during the preceding century. One is therefore led to suppose that Brana Khabung of Sukhodaya – the Lord of the Mountain-top who was 'above all the other spirits of the land' – fulfilled the same protective and unifying role as the Burmese Mahagiri on Mount Poppa and the royal linga of the Khmers on top of the Kulen hill, and that he symbolized, in magico-religious terms, the unification of territories conquered and brought together by Rama Khamheng; that he was, in fact, a kind of national deity, dominating, from his height near the royal city, all the other local gods. During the reign of Rama Khamheng the cult was a purely animistic one, but in the course of time the worship of this national deity was incorporated within Buddhism, and the powerful spirit who was 'above all the other spirits of the land' came to be represented by, and was finally identified with, an image of the Buddha.[8]

In sculpture, the art of Sukhodaya is characterized by bronze images of the Buddha which are as different from the Khmer, Mon, and Burmese Buddhas as they could possibly be.[9] The Buddhas of Sukhodaya are often represented in the walking position – one of the four traditional positions of the Buddha (seated, standing, walking, and recumbent), but one which is never found in Cambodia, the Mon countries, or in Burma. They offer a striking contrast to the Khmer images of the school of Lop Buri, the treatment of the hair and of the facial features being entirely different. One gets the impression that the T'ai sculptors purposely sought to create a type as far removed as possible from the Khmer type, and their long-faced Buddhas with arched eyebrows, prominent noses, and the slightly effeminate flowing lines of the body, are the very opposite of the hieratic Khmer images. We know very little about the political and social aspects of Sukhodaya, but indications such as these seem to point to there having been some sort of democratic reaction on the part of the T'ais against the Khmer oligarchical pattern.

There are indications of Mongol influence in the forms of social organization. Just as the Mongol social pyramid had at its summit the 'golden family' with the Grand Khan at its head and the sons of the Grand Khan as its princes, so Rama Khamheng refers to himself in his inscription as *p'o khun*, 'khun father', and to the princes and high dignitaries as *luk khun*, 'khun sons'. And just as in Mongol society the aristocracy, the warriors (who were the free men *par excellence*), and the commoners were distinguished from the serfs, who were usually non-Mongolian, so a distinction was made between the T'ai warrior aristocracy and the conquered peoples – and so sharp a distinction, that the ethnic term 'T'ai' acquired the meaning of 'free man' (as opposed to serf) in Siamese, the role of serf in T'ai society being occupied by the indigenous peoples.

With regard to the Khmers, however, the Siamese of Sukhodaya, once they had gained their independence, seem to have made an express effort to go against everything that had been done by their former masters. No doubt they found Khmer rule irksome, since they belonged to an entirely different ethno-linguistic group with a political and social organization and a religion that were in complete contrast to those of Cambodia.

Some idea of the political ideals of the kings of Sukhodaya can be gained from Rama Khamheng's inscription of 1292, from various passages of the *Traibhumikatha* of King Lu T'ai, and from an inscription by the latter dating from 1361. Here is what Rama Khamheng has to say about his own government: 'During the lifetime of King Rama Khamheng the city of Sukhodaya has prospered. There are fish in its waters and rice in its rice-fields. The Lord of the country does not tax his subjects, who throng the roads leading cattle to market and ride horses on their way to sell them. Whosoever wishes to trade in elephants or horses does so; whosoever wishes to trade in gold and silver does so. When a commoner, a noble, or a chief falls ill and dies, or disappears, his ancestral home, his clothes, his elephants, his family, his rice granaries, his slaves, the plantations of areca and betel inherited from his ancestors, all are transmitted to his children. If commoners, nobles, or chiefs have a dispute, the king makes a proper inquiry and decides the matter with complete impartiality. He does not enter into agreements with thieves and receivers. If he sees rice belonging to others, he does not covet it, and if he sees the riches of others he is not envious. To whomsoever comes on elephant-back to seek him and put his own country under his protection, he will extend his support and assistance. If the stranger has neither elephants nor horses nor servants nor wives nor silver nor gold, he will give them to him and invite him to regard himself as being in his own country. If the king captures warriors or enemy soldiers, he neither kills them nor beats them.

In the gateway of the palace a bell is hung; if anyone in the kingdom has some grievance or some matter that is ulcerating his
entrails and troubling his mind, and wishes to lay it before the
king, the way is easy: he has only to strike the bell hung there.
Every time King Rama Khamheng hears this appeal, he interro-
gates the plaintiff about the matter and gives an entirely impartial
decision.' And here is how the pious king, Lu T'ai, boasts of the
way he governs his country: 'This king rules by observing the ten
kingly precepts. He has pity on all his subjects. If he sees rice
belonging to others, he does not covet it, and if he sees the wealth
of others, he does not become indignant. . . . When a father dies,
he lets the children have his possessions; when an elder brother
dies, he lets the younger brother have them. He has never once
beaten to death someone who has done wrong, whatever the
crime may have been. Whenever he has captured warriors or
enemy combatants, he has neither killed them nor had them
beaten, but has kept them and fed them so as to preserve them from
ruin and destruction. If he catches people who are guilty of
deceit and insolence – people who put poison in his rice so as to
make him fall sick and die – he never kills them nor beats them,
but is merciful to all those who display evil intentions towards
him. The reason why he represses his feelings and curbs his
thoughts, and refrains from anger when anger is called for, is that
he desires to become a Buddha and to lead all creatures beyond the
sea of suffering of transmigration.'

If the various features of this programme are compared with
what Cambodian epigraphy tells us about Khmer methods of
government, it will be seen that they differ on almost every point.
The Khmer king was regarded as being on such a superior plane
to that of ordinary men that he was designated by the epithet 'the
dust of his sacred feet'. He gave audience within his palace and
showed himself at a window framed in gold; and when he went
out, all who happened to be on the route had to prostrate themselves with their foreheads touching the ground; if they failed to
do so, 'they were seized by the master of ceremonies, who would
not on any account release them'.[10] A marked contrast to this
picture is presented by Sukhodaya, where King Rama Khamheng
had a stone daïs installed in his garden 'so that all could see the
king receiving homage from tributary peoples'. Everything
points to the existence in Cambodia of a system of extremely

heavy imposts and prestations, and of corvées which can have done little to conserve the energies of the people forced to carry them out. One has only to think of the amount of effort the Khmer people must have put into constructing the vast number of buildings erected during the twelfth century under Suryavarman II and Jayavarman VII! But the kings of Sukhodaya declare that there commerce was free and exempt from taxation, that imposts were moderate, that corvées must be proportionate to the capabilities of the forced labour employed and that the old must be spared, and that all property was transmitted to the natural heirs without any levy on behalf of the crown. Khmer justice does not seem to have been carried out very expeditiously, and the only means of recourse to the king was through the official hierarchy, which was a complicated procedure; sentences included, apart from the death sentence, appalling corporal punishments. In Sukhodaya, however, the plaintiff who wished to appeal to the king had only to ring at the gate of the palace, and neither the death sentence nor corporal punishment existed. The contrast is so striking that one is inevitably led to suppose that the kings of Sukhodaya were anxious to do away with a hateful past and to inaugurate a new régime.

With the foundation of the new Siamese kingdom of Ayudhya a complete reversal of this trend becomes evident. The new Siamese monarchy seems to have made every effort to continue the traditions of the rulers of Angkor instead of flouting them. Perhaps this was because the new kingdom arose in an area that had been impregnated for the past three centuries by Khmer civilization, and where the T'ai element was only an aristocratic minority. While it may be true that the ruler of U Thong had married into the T'ai family of Chiang Saen, he himself may well have belonged to a family of Mon or Khmer origins. However that may be, what now took place in the southern part of the Menam valley was the very opposite of what had happened in the north.

In Ayudhya, the king was not at all a fatherly figure. He may not have been a god on earth like the Cambodian king, but he was at least a sort of Living Buddha, to be addressed as 'Our master the Holy Buddha', while the Crown Prince was known as Buddhankura, 'Descendant of the Buddha.' Like the King of Angkor, the King of Ayudhya was referred to by the epithet 'dust on the holy feet', and the whole Khmer vocabulary reserved for the person and actions of the king was taken over *en bloc* for the protocol of the Court of Ayudhya. The Siamese king no longer made public appearances seated on a stone dais in his garden as had been the custom of Sukhodaya, but could only be seen in his palace, at a window inserted in the inner wall of the hall of audience; and when he went out, any subject who committed the sacrilege of raising his head to look upon the royal countenance was liable to receive an earthenware pellet in his eye, shot from the bow of one of the guards at the head of the royal procession. The laws that have been ascribed, whether rightly or wrongly, to the founder of Ayudhya seem for the most part, so far as one can judge, to revive the clauses of the old Khmer code. The regulations for the palace guards (*mandirapala*), which is a text so difficult to interpret that it has so far defeated the exegetists, would not be understandable at all without a thorough knowledge of the customs at the Court of Angkor. The type of Siamese prang found at Ayudhya is a slimmer version of the Khmer tower, while in sculpture what is known as the U Thong school, which it would be better to call the first school of Ayudhya, is characterized by a return to the Khmer tradition of Lop Buri, or is, rather, a continuation of that tradition with some new features, such as the flame on top of the head (of Sinhalese origin), and the tight curls of the hair. Apart from details such as these, all the features of the Khmer statuary of Lop Buri are found again here. The same thing happens in literature. The first poetic texts of Ayudhya, such as the curse upon the flood waters, the prayers addressed to the gods and the spirits by the clerk of the court before a trial by ordeal, and the oldest passages of the laws for the palace guards – all of them non-Buddhist texts, composed or inspired by Brahmans who inherited the traditions of Angkor – were probably very much influenced by Khmer models.

Ramadhipati (*Ramth'ibodi I*), the founder of Ayudhya, held effective sway over a territory covering the lower Menam valley and the major part of the Malay Peninsula, the principal towns being Lop Buri, Subarnapuri (*Suphan*), Rajapuri (*Rat Buri*), Bejrapuri (*Phet Buri*), Tenasserim, Tavoy, Ligor, Signora, and Chandapuri (*Chanthaburi*). His suzerainty extended northwards as far as Sukhodaya and southwards as far as Malacca. His reign was marked by an expedition at the beginning of it against Cambodia, and by an expedition in 1354 against Sukhodaya, which ended with the taking of the city of Jayanada (*Chainat*), which was later returned to King Lu T'ai in exchange for some concessions. Tradition attributes to Ramadhipati I the construction of the temple of Vat Buddhaishvarya (*P'utth'aisavan*) in 1353, and a juridical work of some importance, which consists of eight texts with preambles bearing dates that fall within the period of his reign. The eight texts are on laws concerning witnesses (1350), crimes against the government (1351), acceptance of pleas (1355), abduction (1356), crimes against the people (1357), theft (1350, 1366), marriage (1359), and miscellaneous matters (1359). But many of these laws are clearly of later date, and merely preserve preambles belonging to more ancient texts.

The history of the kingdom of Ayudhya can be divided into four periods. The first is from the middle of the fourteenth century to the middle of the sixteenth, when Siam expanded towards the east and the north; the second covers the second half of the sixteenth century, when there was a long war against Burma; the third covers the seventeenth century, when relations were opened up with foreign countries, especially with Europe; and the fourth lasted for most of the eighteenth century, beginning with a brilliant period during the second quarter of the century, followed by the decline of the kingdom and finally the fall of the capital to the Burmese in 1767.

Ramadhipati I appointed his brother-in-law P'o Ngua as governor of Subarnapuri, and his son Rameshvara (*Ramesuen*) as governor of Lop Buri. The latter succeeded his father in 1369, but had to abdicate a year later in favour of his uncle P'o Ngua, who had a large popular following, and who was crowned in 1370 under the name of Paramaraja (*Boromorach'a*). His reign lasted for eighteen years and was occupied with a series of campaigns against the kingdom of Sukhodaya (1371–73, 1375, 1376), which ended in that country's being brought under more direct subjection, the king being degraded to the rank of a mere provincial governor. In 1374 Paramaraja began the building of the Vat Mahadhatu at Ayudhya. In 1387 he intervened without much success in the troubles that arose in Chiang Mai over the succession to King Ku Na, the ninth successor of Mangrai.

The death of the founder of Chiang Mai in 1311 had given rise to a bitter struggle for the succession which resulted in the kingdom of Lan Na being divided into two, with the upper part centred on the city of Chiang Rai, and the part lying in the plain on Chiang Mai and Lamphun. The country had then been re-unified in 1325 by King Sen Phu, founder in 1327 of the city of Chiang Saen, who died in 1334. He was succeeded by his son K'am Fu, who died in 1336, and then by his grandson Pha Yu, who died in 1355, having enlarged Chiang Mai and surrounded it with a wall and a moat. The reign of his son, Ku Na, was marked by an event of great importance for the spread of Sinhalese Buddhism in Lan Na. This form of Buddhism was introduced by a monk named Sumana who had been ordained in Ceylon according to the rites there considered as orthodox. It was he who in 1369 founded Vat P'ra Yün, near Lamphun. In this temple were placed four standing Buddhas. These statues, or those of other founda-tions of Sumana, set an example for a new school of Buddhist art inspired by that of Sukhodaya, which flourished for about a century.

On the death of Paramaraja I during the course of an unsuccess-ful campaign against Lan Na, his son T'ong Chan (or T'ong Lan), aged fifteen, was prevented from coming to the throne by Rameshvara, who gave up his governorship of Lop Buri and returned to power, reigning from 1388 to 1395. Shortly after 1390 Cambodia invaded the piovinces of Jalapuri (*Chon Buri*) and Chandapuri, but its armies were repulsed and Siamese garrisons installed in both these provincial cities. Rameshvara was succeeded on his death by his son, Rama Rajadhiraja (*Ram Rach'ath'irat*), whose reign was more or less uneventful. He was dethroned by Indaraja (*Int'arach'a*), the younger brother of Paramaraja I.

Like his brother, Indaraja (1408–24) intervened in the internal affairs of Lan Na, particularly in 1411, but Chiang Mai put up a successful resistance against the Siamese army, which was under the command of the governor of Sukhodaya. When the latter died in 1419, the resulting unrest forced Indaraja to advance towards the north as far as Nagara Svarga (*Nakhon Sawan*). When Indaraja died, there was a struggle for the succession between his two elder sons, both of whom died on elephant-back during the fighting. This resulted in the third son coming to power. He was crowned in 1424 under the name of Paramaraja II.

The new king had the Vat Rajapurana built in which to inter the remains of his two brothers. The storehouse of this temple has recently been unearthed intact,[11] and in it were found weapons, princely ornaments, and a large number of Buddhist images of various styles and periods. The chief event of his reign was the siege and capture of Angkor in 1431, which finally put an end to the Angkor period of Cambodia's history. In 1438, Paramaraja II appointed his son Rameshvara as governor of Bishnuloka (*Phitsanulok*). This put an end to the dynasty of hereditary governors descended from the former kings of Sukhodaya. Next, Paramaraja II followed his predecessors in taking a hand in the internal affairs of Chiang Mai, where dynastic disputes had broken out in 1441–42 at the end of the reign of the renegade king, Sam Fang Ken, grandson of Ku Na, who had repudiated Buddhism and given himself up to an animistic cult. But the intervention of Paramaraja II was no more successful than that of his predecessors, and he died during the fighting in 1448.

His son Rameshvara succeeded him under the name of Paramatrailokanatha (*Boromotrailokanat*). His long reign, lasting for forty years, is one of the most important reigns of the first period in the history of Ayudhya. It marks the beginning of the consolidation and the centralization of the power of the king, to the detriment of that of the great vassals who shared between them the administration of the provinces, and whose titles and appanages came under the control of the king. This is the reign to which can be dated the final form of the laws concerning the functions of the palace guards, which, as has been mentioned above, give a valuable insight into the ways and traditions of the Court, largely modelled on those of Angkor. Paramatrailokanatha was greatly given to works of piety, and built a number of temples, the most important of which were the Vat Chulamani (*Chulamani*) at Bishnuloka, in which the design and the ornamentation in stucco are of Khmer inspiration, where he went into retirement for several months during the year 1465; and the Vat Mahadhatu (1482), in which was placed the fine bronze statue of Buddha Jinaraja (*P'ra Ch'inarat*) – a splendid specimen of the art of Sukhodaya, which may well date from the reign of King Lu T'ai.

Most of the reign of Paramatrailokanatha was taken up with hostilities with the King of Chiang Mai, whose name, Tilokaraja (*Dilokarat*), is synonymous with that of the Siamese king, and whose reign (1442–87) more or less coincided with his. Tilokaraja, in contrast to his father, the renegade king Sam Fang Ken, was a fervent Buddhist, whose reign was marked by the construction of many great monuments at Chiang Mai, and by the flowering of a remarkable school of bronze statuary. The most interesting of the buildings is the Mahabodharama (usually called the Vat Chet Yot, 'the temple with the seven spires'),[12] built in 1455 a mile beyond the north-west corner of the city. It reproduces on a smaller scale the ground-plan and general lay-out of the Mahabodhi at Pagan, which itself is modelled on the Bodhgaya Temple in India. In 1472 he built the Mahachetiya (popularly known as the Chedi Luang, the 'great chetiya') on a site in the centre of Chiang Mai where a building dating from half a century earlier had stood. The huge bronze seated Buddhas that were cast in large numbers during the reign of Tilokaraja[13] were inspired, it seems, by the Buddha Shakyasimha enthroned in the shrine of the Bodhgaya Temple. It was also probably during the reign of Tilokaraja that literature began to be written in Pali,[14] although the main works date from the reign of his successor, P'ra Muong Keo (1495–1525).

In order to be nearer the field of operations against Lan Na, Paramatrailokanatha resided for twenty-five years at Bishnuloka, leaving his eldest son to look after the capital, while taking his second son with him. He died in 1488 after occupying the port of Tavoy, which thereafter became a permanent bone of contention between Siam and Burma. It was during his reign that the poem *Lilit Yuen P'ay* was composed, which recounts in varied metres (*lilit*) the victorious campaign against Chiang Mai, and which is full of Sanskrit words. Also attributed to his reign is a poetic version of the Mahajati – that is, of the Vessantarajataka – which was the work of a group of scholars belonging to the royal house (1482).

The eldest son of Paramatrailokanatha, who had remained at Ayudhya as viceroy, succeeded his father and brought the Court back from Bishnuloka, where he installed his young brother, Jettharaja (*Ch'ettharat*), as viceroy. He reigned from 1488 to 1491 under the name of Paramaraja (*Boromorach'a III*). On his death, Jettharaja, who was descended through his mother from the former royal family of Sukhodaya, became king under the name of Ramadhipati (*Ramath'ibodi II*). During his reign the eastern and the central stupa of the temple of Shri Sarvajna (*Si Sanp'et*) which stands to the south of the royal palace, were built – the first for enshrining the ashes of King Paramatrailokanatha, and the second for those of Paramaraja III. Ramadhipati II was the first King of Ayudhya to come into contact with Europeans. As early as 1509, before the taking of Malacca in 1511, Albuquerque had sent an embassy to Siam. A second one arrived in 1512, and a third, in 1516, concluded a treaty by which the Portuguese were authorized to reside at Ayudhya, Tenasserim, Mergui, Patani, and Ligor.

The chronic state of hostilities between Siam and Lan Na continued, and in 1515 the Siamese armies reached Lampang, which was sacked. Ramadhipati died in 1529. His son Buddhankura (*No P'utth'angkun*), whom he had earlier made viceroy of Bishnuloka, succeeded him, taking the name of Paramaraja (*Boromorach'a IV*). The new king sent ambassadors to Chiang Mai for the purpose of negotiating a treaty to put an end to hostilities. He built the western stupa of the royal temple of Shri Sarvajna for the ashes of Ramadhipati II. He died an early death in 1534, and his half-brother, Jayaraja (*Ch'airach'a*), came to the throne in place of his son, who was a child of five.

The name of Jayaraja is associated with certain changes made in the course of the river, with the promulgation of a law concerning trial by ordeal, and with the engagement of Portuguese as guards and instructors. The first conflict with Burma, which, as we shall see, had just become unified,[15] dates from his reign. Tabinshweti, the new Burmese king, when conducting a campaign against Pegu in 1540, had occupied a locality in the province of Moulmein to which Siam laid claim. Jayaraja, with the aid of his Portuguese guards, succeeded in recapturing it, and this was what began the Burmese wars that occupied the second period in the history of Ayudhya.

Jayaraja's reign ended with a disastrous campaign against Chiang Mai in 1545–46. On his return from it, the king was poisoned by Queen Si Sudachan, a crime which was the first act in a drama of intrigue, the echoes of which were noted by Mendez Pinto during his sojourn in Siam. After the queen had become regent, she brought her lover, Khun Varavamsha (*Voravong*), to the throne. He was crowned in 1548. But before long the couple fell victims to a plot hatched by Khun Birendra (*P'iren*), who was descended through his father from the former royal family of Sukhodaya, and related through his mother to the late king, Jayaraja. The crown was then offered to a brother of the latter, who had prudently retired to a monastery. He became king in 1549 under the name of Mahachakrabarti (*Mahachakrap'at*).

The second half of the sixteenth century was a time of both internal and external troubles. In Siam the main protagonists were King Mahachakrabarti, his nephew – a son of King Jayaraja – Shri Shilpa (*Si Sin*), his sons Rameshvara (*Ramesuen*) and Mahindra (*Mahin*), his son-in-law Khun Birendra (*P'iren*) who had been given the title of Mahadhammaraja (*Mahath'ammarach'a*) in memory of his ancestors of Sukhodaya, and his grandsons Nareshvara (*Naresuen*) and Ekadasharatha (*Ekat'otsarot*); and in Burma, King Tabinshweti, his brother-in-law Bayinnaung, and the latter's son, Nandabayin.

Soon after his accession in 1549, Mahachakrabarti had to defend his capital against a Burmese attack from the direction of Martaban, Kanchanaburi, and Suphan. The city of Ayudhya withstood a siege of four months, during which Queen Suriyodaya (*Suriyot'ai*) and her daughter met a heroic death fighting in male attire. Mahadhammaraja, who had come down from his viceroyalty at Bishnuloka, was made a prisoner along with Rameshvara, but the two princes were released on condition that the Burmese troops, who lacked equipment to carry on the fighting, were allowed to withdraw without being harried. The king took advantage of this respite to strengthen the defences of the city and suppress slight signs of hostility on the part of Cambodia (1551, 1556).

In 1561, Prince Shri Shilpa, who had been adopted by his uncle, the king, escaped from the monastery where he had been ordained as a novice in 1555 and succeeded in entering the royal palace at night with a group of followers. The king had to make his escape; but the attempted *coup* failed, and its instigator was put to death by his cousins Rameshvara and Mahindra.

Burma had become partitioned after the death of Tabinshweti in 1550. His brother-in-law Bayinnaung had made himself king over Toungoo, Prome, Pegu, and Ava, and in 1556 had succeeded in taking Chiang Mai, thus providing himself with an excellent base for operations against Ayudhya. In 1563 he advanced towards the south, taking possession of the territory of the former kingdom of Sukhodaya, and arriving in front of Ayudhya in 1564. Under pressure of anti-war opinion, Mahachakrabarti treated with the enemy and delivered up the leaders of the party of resistance. Among them was his son, Rameshvara, who died shortly after while taking part in a Burmese campaign against a rebellion in Chiang Mai and against Vieng Chan.

In 1565 Mahachakrabarti abdicated in favour of his son,

Mahindra. But Mahindra proved useless as a ruler, and was unable to overcome the opposition of his brother-in-law, Mahadhammaraja, who was in favour of coming to terms with the Burmese. An attempt to reconquer the northern provinces with the help of Vieng Chan ended in failure, and in 1568 Mahachakrabarti, who had entered a monastery the previous year, once more had to take over the direction of affairs. By this time Mahadhammaraja had gone over to the Burmese side, and his wife, who was the king's daughter, was retained as hostage by her father. As a reprisal for the affront thus offered to one of his followers, Bayinnaung then launched another expedition against Ayudhya and set siege to the city. Mahachakrabarti died in January 1569, and Ayudhya was taken on the thirtieth of August the same year. Mahindra was led into captivity and died *en route*, and Mahadhammaraja was enthroned in his stead by the Burmese, who evacuated the city of all its inhabitants. In commemoration of his victory, Bayinnaung had a stupa built on the banks of a branch of the river, about a mile north-west of the island of Ayudhya. This was the Ph'u Khao T'ong, in the Mon style, which was restored and enlarged in the eighteenth century.

The liberation of Siam was the work of Nareshvara (*Naresuen* or *Naret*), the eldest son of Mahadhammaraja. He had been led into captivity in Burma during the invasion of 1564, and returned thence in 1571 to attend the coronation of his father and to take up the appointment of viceroy of Bishnuloka. He first made his name by crushing the attempts of Cambodia to take advantage of the difficulties Siam was undergoing because of Burma (1575–82). In 1581 Nareshvara went to Burma to represent his father at a meeting of vassals convocated by the new king, Nandabayin, who had recently succeeded his father, Bayinnaung. He returned to Ayudhya in 1582 convinced that the Burmese State was in a weak condition. So in 1584, after escaping an assassination attempt instigated by Nandabayin, he did not hesitate to repudiate all ties of vassalage to Burma, and set siege to Pegu, which Nandabayin had left in charge of the Crown Prince so that he himself could conduct a campaign in the north. Nareshvara had to raise the siege on receiving news that the king was returning, but he was fighting quite a successful rearguard action against the pursuing forces of the Crown Prince when two Burmese armies invaded Siam, one from the west through the Three Pagodas pass, and the other, under the command of the ruler of Chiang Mai, from the north. The delayed arrival of the latter army resulted in the defeat of the other at Subarnapuri, and the Burmese had to withdraw at the beginning of 1586. In November of the same year three Burmese armies renewed the attack and converged upon Ayudhya from the north, the west, and the east. The siege of the capital lasted from January to May 1587, but the Burmese were unable to overcome the resistance offered them by Nareshvara. Hardly had he got rid of the Burmese than he had to turn his forces against the Cambodians, who, in spite of a reconciliation sealed by treaty in 1584, had occupied Prachin. He dislodged them from there and pursued them right to the walls of Lovek, their capital.

When Mahadhammaraja died in 1590 Nareshvara became king and appointed his brother Ekadasharatha viceroy, not of Bishnuloka, but of Ayudhya. In 1592, when he was preparing to attack Cambodia, he himself was attacked by the Burmese, who were determined to put an end to the fighting once and for all. He thereupon decided to throw the forces he had in preparation into an offensive against the Burmese, who were gathering their forces to the north-east of Subarnapuri. It was then that the famous battle of Nong Saray took place, in which Nareshvara killed the Crown Prince of Burma in single combat. The Burmese, having lost their leader, withdrew, and in 1593 Nareshvara was able to proceed to the reconquest of the ports of Tenasserim and Tavoy on the Gulf of Bengal. No longer threatened from the west, he set about bringing people in to resettle the northern provinces. By the end of the year Siam had had its frontiers of 1549 restored. In commemoration of his victory, Nareshvara had a large stupa erected in the Vat Jayamangala (*Ch'aimongk'on*), which had been built in 1357 by Ramadhipati I for the monks who had been ordained in Ceylon. The stupa was a replica of the Ph'u Khao T'ong that Bayinnaung had had built in 1569. That same year, 1593, saw the expedition against Cambodia which ended in the taking of Lovek in January 1594.

Nareshvara then renewed the offensive against Burma. On the request of the Portuguese who resided at Moulmein, he sent an army to take Martaban. The ruler of Toungoo came to the help of Martaban, but the Siamese army pursued him as far as Thaton. Thus a large part of Pegu became attached to Siam. In 1599 Nareshvara again attacked Burma, and was imprudent enough to place confidence in the ruler of Toungoo, who fomented rebellion in the provinces of Pegu that had recently become part of Siam. Nareshvara then decided to march against Toungoo, but had to beat a retreat in 1600. Although the expedition failed in its objective, it nevertheless led to the fall of Nandabayin and the disintegration of the Burmese kingdom. In 1604 Nareshvara led a campaign in defence of the Shan States, which were peopled by T'ais, against an attempt to reconquer them on the part of the Burmese king of Ava; but after crossing the Salween in 1605 he fell ill, and died on May 16th. His brother Ekadasharatha, who was with him, gave up the campaign and brought his body back to Ayudhya.

With the accession of Ekadasharatha the third period in the history of Ayudhya begins – that of relations with foreign powers. We have seen that already in 1516 Ramadhipati II had concluded a treaty with the Portuguese. In 1598 Nareshvara had concluded one with Spain. It was with Holland that Ekadasharatha entered into relations in 1608, when he sent an embassy to Prince Maurice of Nassau. During this same period a certain number of Japanese immigrants were enlisted into the Royal Guards under the command of Yamada Nagamasa,[16] and friendly relations were entered into with the Shogun Iyeyasu. Ekadasharatha's successors followed the same policy. The attraction Siam had for European merchants was partly due to the value they attached to various products of the country such as hides, lacquer, wood for extracting dyes from, tin, etc., but even more because of the importance of the Siamese ports as markets, where they could lay in stores of Chinese and Japanese merchandise. Moreover, the complete absence of xenophobia on the part of the Siamese authorities and the alacrity with which they entered into relations with anyone from whom they stood to gain something in commercial exchanges must have encouraged foreign merchants to trade there.

Shortly before his death in 1610, Ekadasharatha had had his son executed on a charge of conspiracy, and the succession passed to Prince Indaraja (*Int'arach'a*) – probably a son of the late king – who had entered a monastery under the name of Vimaladhamma. He is known to historians under the name of P'ra Chao Song Th'am, 'the prince who observes the Law (*dhamma*)'. At the very beginning of his reign he had to suppress the rebellion of his Japanese guards, and then to repel the attack of a Laotian army which, on the pretext of coming to his aid against the Japanese, had advanced as far as Lop Buri. Relations with England were entered into in 1612, when a British ship arrived bearing a letter from King James I. The British were authorized to establish factories at Ayudhya and at Patani. After a quarrel with his Burmese neighbours over the ports of Tavoy and Tenasserim, which had been lost and then retaken by Siam in 1614, Song Th'am made peace with them. The Burmese relinquished all claims upon Chiang Mai in return for the port of Martaban (1618). In the same year Cambodia repudiated Siamese suzerainty. An expedition to quell this defection was unsuccessful, and until his death in 1628, Song Th'am tried in vain to obtain the support of the British and the Portuguese against Cambodia.

Jettharaja (*Ch'ettharat*), the son whom Song Th'am had appointed to be his successor, was fifteen years of age when his father died. His claim to the throne was supported by a cousin of his father called Shri Varavamsha (*Voravong*) or Suriyavamsha (*Surivong*) against a rival claimant – a younger brother of the late king – and his followers. Shri Varavamsha, after having got rid first of the rival claimant and then of the young king, put a ten-year-old child on the throne – a younger son of Song Th'am called Adityavamsha (*At'itatayavong*). He then got rid of Yamada Nagamasa, who had supported this new king's claim, by sending him to put down a revolt at Ligor, and then appointing him to be governor of the city. Finally, having had the young king Aditya-vamsha executed, he himself seized the throne in 1630. He is known under the name of P'ra Chao Prasat T'ong, 'the king with the Golden Palace'. European writers paint him in the darkest colours as a cruel and unscrupulous ruler. But it must be remembered that from the very beginning of his reign he was faced with opposition on all sides: from Portugal, with which country Siam had been at war since the preceding reign over the question of the seizure of some ships; from the Japanese guards, whom he only succeeded in quelling by massacring them wholesale; and from his neighbours, Cambodia, Chiang Mai, and Patani. The Dutch were his only allies. The years 1633–36 were darkened by mass executions, notably of those members of the royal family who regarded him as a usurper. The latter part of Prasat T'ong's reign was less eventful, and his name is associated with important legislative reforms, including laws on appeals (1633), inheritance

(1635), enslavement for debts (1637), marriage with foreigners (1638), and debts (1648). Lastly, Prasat T'ong seems to have succeeded, without resorting to war, in making Cambodia acknowledge his suzerainty, which it had repudiated in 1618. In order to celebrate this achievement he had a temple built on one of the branches of the river to the north-east of the capital. The temple was named Nak'on Luang (the Siamese equivalent of the Khmer Angkor Thom), and the lay-out was modelled on that of the Khmer capital. Also from his reign dates the construction of the Vat Jayavadhanarama (*Ch'aivath'anaram*) at Ayudhya, which has a large prang in imitation of the Khmer towers of the twelfth century.

The succession struggles after Prasat T'ong's death were as full of dramatic incident as his own accession had been. His eldest son Chao Fa Ch'ai seized the throne, dispossessing the heir apparent, Shri Sudhammaraja (*Suthiammarach'a*), a younger brother of the late king. But Prasat T'ong's second son, Narayana (*Naray*), sided with his uncle, and Chao Fa Ch'ai was deposed after reigning for only a few days. After Shri Sudhammaraja had become king, he fell in love with one of his nieces, a sister of Narayana. The princess complained to her brother, who with a group of followers attacked the palace and put his uncle to death. Thus it was that Narayana came to power, but the date of these events has not been established with any exactitude. All one can say is that they must have occurred around 1657.

The first thing the new king had to do was to get rid of several suspected conspirators, among whom were two of his younger brothers. Almost the only military exploits of his reign were the temporary occupation of Chiang Mai, Martaban, and Rangoon in 1662. Otherwise the reign was mainly taken up with forging closer links with the Western powers. In 1664 the Dutch, by means of their blockade of the Menam, obtained a treaty which gave them the monopoly of the trade in hides and the privilege of extraterritoriality for their nationals. Relations with the British were for the most part strained.[17] It was with France that relations were liveliest,[18] its interests being promoted by the manœuvres of the Greek adventurer Constance Phaulkon,[19] who, soon after his arrival in Siam in 1675, had secured for himself an important post as superintendant of foreign trade. French missionaries had been well received and had established themselves in Siam as early as

1662,[20] and the Jesuits had persuaded the Court of Versailles of the possibility of converting the country to Catholicism. In 1673 Louis XIV sent a letter to King Narayana thanking him for the welcome extended to the missionaries, and in 1680 the East India Company set up a factory at Ayudhya. The embassies exchanged between Ayudhya and Versailles between 1684 and 1687, the details of which are too well known for there to be any need to relate them here, ended in the signing of a treaty (10th–11th December 1686) granting certain privileges to missionaries and substantial commercial advantages to the Company.[21] But the presence of a garrison of French troops in the fort of Bangkok, where they had arrived in September 1687, and the pro-Jesuit policy of Constance Phaulkon aroused a certain amount of nationalist feeling which was focused on Bedraja (*P'et'rach'a*), a foster-brother of the king.

When Narayana fell ill in 1688, the dignitaries of State got him to appoint Bedraja as regent. Bedraja had the Greek adventurer arrested and executed on 5 June 1688, and mounted an attack against the French in the fort of Bangkok, who held out. On 11 July 1688 Narayana died, and Bedraja was immediately proclaimed king. The new reign began with a certain amount of persecution of Catholics and French nationals. The soldiers of the Bangkok garrison managed to withdraw to Pondicherry, but during the years that followed the Jesuits' efforts to negotiate a new treaty met with no success. This marked the end of French influence in Siam, and indeed the beginning of the decline of European influence as a whole, despite the conclusion of a new treaty with Holland renewing the privileges previously granted.

Largely owing to the Burmese wars, there had been an eclipse of literary activities, but the reign of Narayana is considered to be the golden age of Siamese poetry. The king – himself a poet – was surrounded by talented writers who created new forms which were much admired. Four poetical works are attributed to the king himself: the translation of the middle part of the *Samuddhaghosa* – one of the Fifty (apocryphal) Jataka – which had been begun by Maharajaguru and was completed at the beginning of the nineteenth century by Prince Paramanujita Jinorasa; and three moralistic pieces: the Instructions of Valin to his younger brother (Sugriva), the Instructions of Dasaratha to Rama, each based on an episode from the Ramayana, and lastly *Rajasvasti*. He is also supposed to have been the author of the *P'ra Lo*, one of the *chefs-d'œuvre* of Siamese literature; but this poem in varied metre (of the *lilit* type) may date back to the beginning of the seventeenth century. The theme of the poem is similar to that of *Romeo and Juliet*, with which it has been compared. It is about a young prince and two princesses who are crossed in love because of family feuds. The most celebrated among the writers of this reign are: Maharajaguru, to whom is attributed the first part of the verse translation of the *Samuddhaghosa*, and the translation of the *Gavi*, another of the Fifty Jataka, as well as a work on grammar and poetic composition entitled *Chintamani*; Shri Prajna (*Si Prat*), who was possibly the son of the foregoing – a precocious young poet who led a hectic life at Court and was finally executed as a result of amorous intrigues, and whose output, apart from his poem *Aniruddha*, consisted chiefly of very short occasional poems, madrigals, and verses with set rhymes based on a theme taken from a line of one or other of the king's poems; Shri Mahoshadha (*Si Mahosot*), who wrote artificial verse and a eulogy of the king; and Khun Devakavi (*T'ep Kavi*), author of the earliest collection of lullabies for the white elephants – a text full of Sanskrit, Khmer, and dialect words. It was during the reign of King Narayana that the first poems in the *nirasa* (*nirat*) style were composed. These are tales of travels in which is described the sadness of the poet at being parted from those he loves – a sadness made all the more poignant by the sight of certain landscapes.

During his reign, Bedraja had to suppress revolts at Nagara Nayaka (*Nakhon Nayok*, 1690), and at Korat and Ligor (1691). He died in 1703, and was succeeded first by his son Sarashakti, known by his reign-name P'ra Chao Sua, 'the tiger king' (1703–09), and then by the latter's son, Bhumindaraja, known under the name of P'ra Chao T'ai Sa, 'the king who resides (in the palace) at the end of the lake', whose reign was occupied with works of irrigation of great practical benefit, and with a campaign against Cambodia, in which Banteay Meas on the Gulf of Siam was taken in 1717. Upon his death in 1733, his younger brother disputed his son's claim to the throne, and reigned from 1733 to 1758 under the name of Mahadhammaraja, although he is now usually referred to by his posthumous title, Paramakosha (*Boromokot*), 'the king of the great funerary urn'.

His reign is considered by the Siamese to have been a particu-

larly brilliant and happy one. The country enjoyed plenty and
prosperity, and Siamese Buddhism achieved so great a prestige
that in 1750 an embassy from Ceylon came to request that a mission
of Siamese monks be sent to reform Sinhalese Buddhism, which
had declined, despite the fact that Ceylon had been the country
where it originated. In literature, dramatic works assumed a new
importance. The themes of the fourteen plays which are known to
date from this period are taken from stories of the former lives of
the Buddha, especially from the Fifty Jataka. The fact that two
princesses in Ayudhya had a Malay entourage accounted for the
vogue for the Javanese story of Raden Panji which was adapted for
the stage under the title of *Inao*. But the drama was not the only
form of literature that was cultivated. The king's eldest son,
Dhammadhipesha (*Th'ammath'ibet*), who had become a monk in
1735, wrote poems of Buddhist inspiration, the most famous of
which, *Maleyya*, describes the visit of the *thera* of this name to
heaven and hell, and treats at some length of the retribution
brought about by actions. After the prince came out of his
monastery in 1741 he composed profane poetry, especially battle
songs, and he wrote a descriptive poem in which he sings of his
beloved, using as background the beauties of nature. Other notable
writers of this period are Shri Prija, and the monk Mahanaga, who
wrote a poem on the footstep of the Buddha that was first discovered by King Song Th'am and later restored by Paramakosha.

But soon Siam was to be under threat of invasion again, after
Alaungpaya, the third unifier of Burma and the founder of a new
dynasty, came to the Burmese throne in 1752. When Paramakosha
died in 1758 after considerable legislative achievements, he left his
second son, whose apellation was Dok Madu'a 'fig blossom' (in
Pali Udumbara [*Ut'ump'on*], which has the same meaning), as his
appointed successor. As soon as his father had been cremated,
however, this second son abdicated in favour of his older brother,
Ekadasha (*Ekat'at*), known upon his accession under the name of
P'ra T'inang Suriyamarin, after the name of his residence. The new
king was unable to withstand a Burmese attack which in 1759
brought enemy forces to within thirty miles of Ayudhya, and he
had to abdicate in favour of Udumbara, who had meanwhile
retired into a monastery. The following year Burmese reinforcements set siege to the capital, but had to raise the siege because
the Burmese king fell ill. He died on his way home and was

succeeded by his son, Naungdawgyi. In 1762 Udumbara once more retired from public life, and the very next year the new Burmese king, Hsinbyushin, who had just succeeded his brother, Naungdawgyi, seized the first opportunity to renew hostilities. First came the capture of Tavoy, Mergui, and Tenasserim, and then General P'raya Tak managed to stop the Burmese advance when it reached Bejrapuri. But between June and September 1765 the Burmese succeeded in occupying most of the Menam basin, and in February 1766 once more arrived in front of Ayudhya. The siege lasted for over a year, but on 7 April 1767 the city fell and was sacked and burnt down. The king fled and met his death, and Prince Udumbara was led into captivity. The Siamese kingdom appeared to have received a fatal blow. Before recounting how it was restored again, I must first look back over the Ayudhya period and say a word or two about various aspects of Siamese civilization during that period.

There is no need to say anything further about literary activities, since the outstanding works have already been mentioned in connection with the times at which they were produced. With regard to the art and architecture of Ayudhya, the destruction of the city by the Burmese has made the study of it difficult. For four centuries Ayudhya was one of the liveliest and most prosperous cities in the whole peninsula, but it is the one that has suffered the most destruction, and those of its monuments which have not been completely destroyed, or which have escaped the damage caused by diggings conducted by local people in search of treasure buried during the siege, have been overgrown with vegetation. There still remain considerable portions of the brick wall, with its twenty-three gateways, and of the sixteen bastions that once formed the island's defences. Within the walled city lay the royal palace, of which little more than the foundations remains, and the dwellings of princes and high officials, the commercial quarters, and the various religious buildings. Some idea of the appearance of that part of the city where the merchants of the various nations doing trade with Siam had their quarters is conveyed by the plans of it published by several sixteenth-century European writers. A few of the five hundred religious buildings that finally invaded every corner of the city still stand, though partially in ruins, and show the same variety of architectural styles as the buildings of Sukhodaya and Shri Sajjanalaya. I have already referred to some of them under the reigns in which they are thought to have been built. The best preserved of them, and the most historic, is the royal temple of Shri Sarvajna (*Si Sanp'et*) in the southern part of the palace enclosure. It consists of a group of buildings, the nucleus of which consists of three large hemispherical stupas in brick faced with stucco, containing Buddhist relics and the ashes of several kings. They are placed on a terrace surrounded by a gallery that must have contained long rows of statues of the Buddha. These buildings are of different periods, from that of the large eastern stupa, which dates from the fifteenth century, to that of the large western shrine, dating from the middle of the eighteenth.

No doubt the buildings still in use in Bangkok today give a fairly accurate idea of what the ruined buildings of Ayudhya were like. The main feature of every Buddhist temple is the meeting-hall for the monks (*uposathagara*, in Siamese *bot*)[22] or that for the laity (*vihara*, in Siamese *vihan*), with a very steep and slightly concave roof covered with brightly-coloured tiles. The interior consists of a single nave or of a nave flanked by two low-roofed aisles. The statue of the Buddha is placed on a pedestal at the western end of the hall. The most elaborately ornamented parts of the hall are the ceiling, the doors, and the windows, and the internal walls often have frescoes depicting episodes in the life of the Buddha or in his earlier lives. In the more important temples the hall is surrounded by a rectangular cloister, with rows of seated Buddhas in its gallery. Among other types of building the commonest are the chetiya (*chedi*) or stupa, which can be in many forms bearing traces of Mon, Burmese, or Sinhalese influence; the mandapa (*mondop*), which has a square ground plan, the building being a cube crowned with small receding storeys and surmounted either by a spire or by a sort of shikhara in the Burmese manner; and lastly the prang, which derives directly from the Khmer tower, and consists of a slim cylinder which is the main body of the building, mounted on a high multi-terraced platform.

The statuary of Ayudhya has been very little studied on account of its alleged mediocrity. One's first impression is that it combines features of Khmer sculpture and of the school of Sukhodaya. In the eighteenth century there seems to have been a predilection for images of the Buddha decorated with regal ornaments.

The Siamese, and indeed the T'ais as a whole, arrived in

Indochina too late to be able to benefit directly from Indian influence, and their civilization cannot be regarded as an offshoot of Indian civilization in the same way as that of the Khmers, the Mons, and the Burmese. The direct parentage of Siamese civilization must be sought in the territories where the Syam first settled and where they received their cultural heritage – namely, the territories in the Menam valley that had been, both politically and culturally, dependencies of the Khmers.

In Sukhodaya, which was on the periphery of the Khmer cultural zone, there had been a tendency to react against what might be called a colonialist government, liberation from which enabled specifically T'ai characteristics to emerge. But after the foundation of the kingdom of Ayudhya, which was situated in a region that had been an integral part of Cambodia for four centuries, the capacity for assimilation so typical of the T'ai peoples asserted itself.

Ayudhya may be regarded as the heir of Khmer civilization, and, as we have seen, Khmer influence is apparent in almost every sphere: in that of institutions (divine kingship adapted to Buddhism), of art (the transformation of the Khmer tower into the prang, and the U Thong school of sculpture), and of language and literature (many Khmer words borrowed by the Siamese language, and the entire Khmer vocabulary of kingship). Later, political circumstances enabled Burma to make its influence felt in the domain of art (the mandapa surmounted by a prang, recalling the shikhara of Pagan architecture), and even more in that of legislation.[23] Since the Ayudhya period, Europe has exercised a certain amount of influence on Siam, as instanced by the use of bricks in the construction of the royal palace where formerly wood had been used.

Now we must return to the events that followed the fall of Ayudhya. Before the city fell into the hands of the Burmese, P'raya Tak, the general who four years earlier had halted the enemy advance before Bejrapuri, managed to escape with a body of 500 men who formed the nucleus of the forces with which he was to perform the miracle of saving the country from its ruins. From the base he established in the region of Rayong-Jalapuri, he occupied Chandapuri, and having gathered together an army of 5,000 men, he advanced up the Menam valley and took Dhanapuri (*Thonburi*), where he had himself crowned at the end of 1767. He was still only in control of the southern part of Siam, and the three years after he seized power were taken up in eliminating his rivals – four in number – who between them controlled the rest of the country. At the same time he had to prevent any further attack by the Burmese, who had almost completely withdrawn from Siam in order to meet a Chinese invasion of their country. In 1770, after having restored the former kingdom of Ayudhya, he attempted to incorporate within it the kingdom of Lan Na, but did not succeed in doing so until five years later. His general, P'raya Chakri, was meanwhile forcing Cambodia to recognize the suzerainty of Siam. During the ensuing years, the Burmese showed signs of returning to the attack, but the accession in 1776 of a new king who was opposed to Siamese adventures put an end to the Burmese threat. In 1778 a disagreement with Vieng Chan gave rise to an expedition against Laos led by P'raya Chakri, which ended in the occupation of the capital and the annexation of the country, lasting until 1782. In 1781 P'raya Chakri was in Cambodia when he heard alarming news about the king's health. Since 1777 the king had shown signs of mental derangement, claiming to have attained the highest degree of sainthood, and to have been given supernatural powers which entitled him to marks of respect on the part of the leading clergy. On 20 April 1782 P'raya Chakri arrived in front of Bangkok, and soon put an end to the troubles fomented by various rivals for the throne. He was enthusiastically received by the people, and was proclaimed king upon the execution of P'raya Tak. Thus was founded the Bangkok, or Chakri, dynasty, which still reigns today.

P'raya Tak's reign is known as the Dhanapuri period, from the name of the royal residence situated on the opposite side of the river from Bangkok. The first known Siamese version of the Ramayana, the *Ramakirti* (*Ramakien*), dates from this period. It is incomplete, and was composed between 1770 and 1780 by the king himself. The first complete version dates from the reign that followed.[24]

P'raya Chakri (Rama I), known under the name of P'ra P'utth'a Yot Fa Chulalok (the name of the statue to his memory in the royal temple Vat P'ra Keo), built his residence on the left bank of the river, opposite the residence of his predecessor. It formed the nucleus round which the present city of Bangkok was built. His reign lasted from 1782 until 1809, and as regards internal affairs, was occupied with the task of restoring the damage caused by the destruction of Ayudhya.[25] Religious, legal, and literary texts had to be restored. A synod was called for the purpose of collating the canonical writings, and a commission appointed to revise the ancient law codes (1805).[26] As far as literature, properly speaking, is concerned, the personal contribution of the king and his entourage was a complete version of the *Ramakirti*, a dramatic adaptation of the Javanese Raden Panji entitled *Dalang*, and the play *Aniruddha (Unarut)*, drawn from the cycle of Krishna legends. There was a new flowering of prose literature, of which there had been little since the Sukhodaya period. It took the form of translations of a number of foreign works, such as the Sinhalese *Mahavamsa*, a collection of Persian tales in the Malay language, and the *San Kuo Chih Yen-i* (in Siamese, *Sam Kok*), a Chinese historical romance set in the period of the Three Kingdoms. The translation of the latter (1802) was chiefly the work of Chao P'raya P'ra K'lang, who died in 1805. He is also the author of the *Rajadhiraja (Rach'ath'irat)*, written in 1785. It is a historical novel set in Lower Burma at the end of the fourteenth century.

The following are the oldest of Bangkok's architectural monuments:[27] the Tusita Mahaprasada palace (*Dusit Mahaprasat*), where the first king was crowned and the gold urn containing his ashes exhibited; the temple Vat Mahadhatu (*Mahath'at*), built in 1782;[28] the royal temple Shri Ratnashastarama (*Si Ratanasatsadaram*), usually called Vat P'ra Keo, 'Temple of the Precious Stone Buddha' (supposed to be of emerald, but in fact of jasper), built in 1785 to hold the famous image of the Buddha brought back from Vieng Chan in 1778; the temple of Jetavana (*Ch'etup'on*), usually known as Vat P'o, built in 1793 on the site of an older building to enshrine the statues from the ruins of Ayudhya; the temple of Sudassana (*Sut'at*), begun in the first and continued and completed in the second and third reigns. These temples and buildings bear witness to the vitality of Siamese artistic traditions during the last years of the eighteenth century.

As regards external affairs, Rama I still had to defend his country against the Burmese, who had not yet lost all hope of reconquering it. The operations he carried out in the Malay Peninsula provided him with the opportunity for re-establishing Siamese suzerainty over the sultanates of Kedah and Patani, and extending it to those of Kelantan and Trengganu. This was when the Sultan of Kedah ceded Penang, and the territory facing the island that was later to become Wellesley province, to the English East India Company. Siam repelled the Burmese attacks of 1786–87 against Kanchanaburi and the north. Tavoy, which Siam had occupied since 1791 owing to the treachery of the governor, was recaptured by the Burmese in 1793; but their advance in the north, which had reached Chiang Mai, was halted, and they were finally driven out of Chiang Saen in 1802.

Rama I died on 7 December 1809, and was succeeded by his son, Prince Isara Sundara (*Isara Sunt'on*), known under the name of P'ra P'utth'a Lot La Nop'alai (after the name of his statue) or Rama II. No sooner had he come to the throne than he had to counter a Burmese attack in the Malay Peninsula in which Puket had been taken and the enemy forces had advanced as far as Chumphon. An expedition against Cambodia led to the flight of King Ang Chan to the Mekong delta area. In 1821 the Siamese army invaded Kedah, where the sultan had two years previously gone over to the Burmese, who were once more preparing to attack Siam. In 1822 Rama II received the mission sent by the East India Company, led by the Englishman John Crawfurd, and trade relations with England were renewed.

The second reign of the Bangkok dynasty is regarded as one of the best periods of Siamese literature. The king, himself gifted with a marked talent for poetry, gathered round him a group of poets of whom the most famous was Sunt'on Ph'u (1786–1855). The poetic forms most cultivated were love poems, accounts of travels of the genre known as *nirat*, and narrative songs or *seph'a*. The last category includes a masterpiece – the story of Khun Ch'ang and Khun P'en. Several writers collaborated in it, and it was not completed until the following reign. It is based on a dramatic incident which actually took place during the Ayudhya period in the time of Ramadhipati II (1491–1529), and paints, in very fine language, a sort of panorama of life in Siam at the beginning of the nineteenth century.[29] The drama, too, was enriched by a number of works at the hand of the king and his circle, in particular, a new version of the *Ramakirti* dealing with the events that occurred between the departure of Hanumat for Lanka and the return of Sita; a new version of the *Inao*; and half a dozen other pieces inspired by the most popular of the Fifty Jataka stories. Sunt'on Ph'u, the outstanding poet among the members of the king's circle, collaborated in most of the works attributed to the king, and was responsible for a large part of the story of Khun Ch'ang and Khun P'en. He is the author of several poetic romances of which *Aph'aimani* is the best known, as well as of several accounts of travels (*nirat*). Prince Paramanujita Jinorasa (1790–1853), a son of Rama I and a high dignitary of the Buddhist church, was a contemporary of Sunt'on Ph'u, but adopted a more learned style. He has left a number of works, both in prose and in poetry. Among the latter, the best known are the *Lilit Taleng P'ay*, which tells of one of the most famous episodes in the history of Ayudhya – the victory of P'ra Naret over the King of Burma in 1592; and the part of the *Samuddhaghosa* which had not been completed by King Narayana.

When Rama II died on 20 July 1824, the rightful heir to the throne was his son by the queen, Prince Maha Mongkut, who was twenty years of age. But an older son, by a concubine, was brought to power. He is known under the name of Rama III or P'ra Nang Klao, and reigned for twenty-seven years.[30] In 1826 he signed a trade treaty with the East India Company after receiving the mission of Captain Burney, and another in 1833 with the United States of America.

From the reign of Rama III (1824–51) onwards, an entirely new atmosphere was created owing to the growing influence of the West, and also to the spread of literature following upon the introduction of printing in 1835, and this had a profound effect on Siamese literary activities. The process of change was a gradual one, but it led to the development of a prose literature and to an enrichment and increasing flexibility of language under the influence of writers steeped in Western culture. But traditional poetry was still cultivated under Rama III and his successors. Apart from the king himself, other poets could be mentioned, such as the brothers Bhuvanesha (*Ph'uvanet*, 1781–1856) and Tejatisara (*Dech'adison*, 1793–1859), and P'um, a poetess who wrote satirical poetry.

Thus Siam was gradually opened up for foreign trade and the introduction of new ideas. Rama III could scarcely have had the far-sightedness and breadth of outlook required for a full realization of the danger his country was likely to be in as a result of European colonial expansion in Asia. Siam's position became a precarious one, with Burma being nibbled away by the British on one side, and Viet-nam and Cambodia coming under French protection on the other; and the credit for having saved his country's independence must go to King Mongkut, or Rama IV, who, when nearly fifty, gave up his life in a monastery to succeed his brother, who died on 2 April 1851.

The new king realized that England's defeat of China in the 1840–42 war marked the beginning of a new era for the Asiatic nations. A learned historian and theologian,[31] this enlightened monarch instigated the monastic reform known as Dhammayuttika (*Th'ammayut*), which was designed to combat the lax practices and the wave of popular superstition from which Buddhism had suffered during the troubled period since the destruction of Ayudhya. What it aimed to do was to enforce upon the clergy a stricter observance of the rules of monastic discipline as revealed by a study of the canonical texts, and to bring about a return to Sinhalese orthodoxy. The rational attitude behind the reform was largely due to the repeated contacts the king had had with Catholic missionaries – particularly with Bishop Pallegoix[32] who had arrived in Siam in 1830 – and with American Protestant missionaries who had been there since 1828. The ideas of the reform had greatest effect among the Siamese *élite*, and among other enlightened sections of Siamese society; and later they spread among aristocratic circles in Cambodia which were strongly influenced by Siam at this time.

King Mongkut, himself sufficiently acquainted with the English language as to be able to use it in his correspondence with Europeans,[33] was of the opinion that the Siamese must learn about the Western nations which now were at the height of their colonial expansion. In marked contrast to the last kings of Burma, who, as we shall see, were completely ignorant of the outside world, King Mongkut was clever enough to grant the necessary economic and commercial concessions to the European powers. He pursued a policy of balance of power towards the two Western nations that had become Siam's neighbours – England and France; and this policy was continued by his successors. Following upon the mission of Sir John Bowring,[34] he signed a treaty with Great Britain on 18 April 1855 which granted freedom of trade, the appointment of a consul at Bangkok, and the privilege of extra-territoriality. A similar treaty was signed with France on 15 August 1856, following upon the mission of M. de Montigny.[35]

Similar arrangements were then made with the United States in 1856, with Denmark and the Hanseatic Towns in 1858, with Portugal in 1859, with the Netherlands in 1860, with Prussia in 1862, and finally with Belgium, Italy, Sweden, and Norway in 1868. Thus the open-door policy was established in Siam. Although its independence was to some extent curtailed by the extraterritorial rights granted to foreign powers, it had nevertheless been preserved.

King Mongkut died on 1 October 1868, and found a worthy successor in the person of his son, King Chulalongkorn, or Rama V, during whose long reign (1868–1910) Siam became progressively more and more modernized in every sphere, including that of government, the army, the system of justice, railways, postal and telegraph services, and so on. Even social matters were affected, and the abolition of slavery in 1905 was, among many other important reforms, the one that does most credit to the foresight and the sense of justice of the reigning monarch. It was during the reign of Rama V that the frontiers of Siam were finally fixed – first those with French Indochina by the treaties of 3 October 1893 (when Siam relinquished the territories on the left bank of the Mekong that became the protectorate of Laos), and of 23 March 1907 (granting the retrocession of the Cambodian provinces of Battambang, Siem Reap, and Sisophon, in exchange for France's abandonment of extraterritorial rights for her Asiatic nationals); and then with Great Britain, by the treaty of 15 July 1909 (when Siam relinquished her rights over the sultanates of Kelantan, Trengganu, and Perlis in exchange for the renunciation by Great Britain of extraterritorial rights for both her European and Asiatic nationals).

King Vajiravudh (Rama VI), who succeeded his father on 24 October 1910, had been educated in England, and his Western education made him a modern-minded ruler. But he remained very attached to the traditional ceremonies of the Court, and continued, like his predecessors, to contribute to Siamese literature. The intervention of Siam on the side of the allies in the First World War (2 July 1917) enabled her to abolish in whole or in part the extraterritorial rights enjoyed by nationals of the European powers. Great Britain and Denmark had already abolished theirs, in 1909 and 1913 respectively; the United States followed in 1920 and France on 14 February 1925. King Vajiravudh died on November

25th of the same year. He was succeeded by his brother Prajadhi-
pok, who was the last absolute monarch in Siam. After the *coup
d'état* of June 1932, the king bestowed upon his people a new
constitution inaugurating a parliamentary régime.

Thanks to the wisdom and foresight of her kings, Siam, without
resorting either to wars or to bloody revolution, succeeded in
leaping the vast gap that separates an Asiatic kingdom with a
medieval structure from a modern constitutional monarchy.

2

Laos[1]

AT THE END of the twelfth century Cambodian rule extended up the Mekong valley as far as Vieng Chan, where a stele belonging to one of the hospitals founded by Jayavarman VII has been found. This was the time when the T'ais who had settled in this region first came into contact with the Khmers and acquired their Indianized culture. Vieng Chan was part of the territory conquered by the Siamese kingdom of Sukhodaya during the last years of the thirteenth century, but the Khmers still retained the territory downstream from there for another half century, and only abandoned it after the kingdom of Lan Ch'ang was founded.

The decline of Sukhodaya and its final submission to the kingdom of Ayudhya produced the circumstances that led to the founding of Lan Ch'ang. Its founder was Fa Ngum, the son of an exiled T'ai chief who had found refuge at the Court of Angkor. The young prince had been brought up there by a Buddhist monk, and on reaching the age of sixteen, the king gave him one of his daughters in marriage. Between 1340 and 1350 Fa Ngum took command of an army put at his disposal by the Khmer king for the purpose of reconquering the territories of his ancestors on the upper Mekong. After marching his army along a route which is difficult to make out according to the information given by the Laotian chronicles, he had himself proclaimed king at Ch'ieng Dong Ch'ieng T'ong (now known as Luang Prabang). He then occupied Vieng Chan, and after restoring order to the reconquered territories, he was solemnly consecrated at Ch'ieng Dong

Ch'ieng T'ong in 1353 as sovereign of the kingdom of Lan Ch'ang, 'country of a million elephants'.

This event, which sanctioned the founding of a State that was destined to play an important political role in central Indochina, had a further consequence: it resulted in the introduction of Khmer civilization, which had hitherto reached little farther than Vieng Chan, into the upper Mekong valley, and in the spread of Sinhalese Buddhism over this area due to the teachings of the young king's former master, who had been brought by him from Angkor.

The history of Laos can be divided into three periods. First came the period of inauguration and organization, which lasted roughly from the middle of the fourteenth century until the middle of the sixteenth. The next period is that of the Burmese wars, lasting from the middle of the sixteenth until the middle of the seventeenth century. Lastly, after half a century of peace, there is the period when Laos was divided into two separate kingdoms, covering the whole of the eighteenth century and lasting well into the nineteenth.

Fa Ngum died in 1373. His son carried out a census of the population in 1376, and the resulting figure of 300,000 males of T'ai race led to his being known under the name of P'raya Sam Sen T'ai, 'chief of 300,000 T'ais'. The census also gave him the opportunity of reorganizing the army, and thus of providing his country with a military force strong enough to make him respected by his neighbours. From his reign there survives the head and torso of a colossal Buddha in bronze which was placed in the temple of Vat Manorom, built in 1372, and now completely in ruins.

His second son, Lan K'am Deng, who succeeded him in 1416, was a contemporary of Le Loi, the founder of the Vietnamese Le dynasty, to whom he offered support in his struggle against China. But the Laotian contingent went over to the Chinese, and this treachery provided an excuse for Viet-nam's intervention in Laotian affairs fifty years later. King Sai Chakrap'at, Sam Sen T'ai's youngest son, who had by then come to the throne, chose prudence as his policy, but was unable to ward off the danger with which his country was threatened owing to Viet-nam's expansionist policy and desire for revenge. The first opportunity for attacking Lan Ch'ang came in 1478, and Emperor Le

Thanh-tong seized it. In 1479 Luang Prabang was taken and the king was obliged to take flight. He died shortly after this, and his two sons, Then K'am (1480–86) and La Sen T'ai (1486–96), had the task of restoring the damage caused by the invasions. Another son, Visun (1501–20), married a princess of Chiang Mai, and his reign is noted for its many architectural monuments, the most outstanding of which is the temple which bears his name (Vat Visun), built in 1503 to house a relic. It is a very fine building, with delicately carved wooden walls widening outwards towards the roof, giving it a form which recalls that of Laotian coffins.

Visun's son, who succeeded him under the name of P'oth'isarat, moved the capital from Luang Prabang to Vieng Chan, which was better situated from the point of view of trade. His mother was a princess of Lan Na, so when the throne at Ch'ieng Mai fell vacant in 1545 he felt entitled to lay claim to it. He arranged for his eldest son to be accepted as king, and had him crowned at Chiang Mai in 1548. In the same year he himself met with an accidental death.

The newly crowned King of Chiang Mai now had to return to Luang Prabang to claim his right to succeed his father, and had himself crowned there under the name of Jetthadhiraja (*Setthath'irat*). His absence from Lan Na provided the Burmese king, Bayinnaung, who had just annexed the Shan States and wished to extend his authority over all the T'ais, with an opportunity to further his plans. Chiang Mai fell in 1556, and Jetthadhiraja allowed it to remain in the hands of a T'ai puppet ruler under Burmese protection. He concluded a treaty of alliance with Ayudhya in 1560, and definitively moved the capital from Luang Prabang to Vieng Chan, which he fortified. He also built a palace there, with a temple that held the P'ra Keo or Precious Stone Buddha that had been brought from Chiang Mai. Nothing now remains of this temple except the shrine, which has recently been restored. It stands upon a foundation of three terraces, and at the back of the hall there is a huge altar where the statue of the Buddha once stood, until removed by the Siamese in 1778, since when it has stood in the temple of the royal palace at Bangkok. A mile away from Vieng Chan the king had the Th'at Luang, the 'great shrine', built, which is supposed to have contained a relic of the Buddha.[2] This *chef-d'œuvre* of Laotian architecture, built in 1566, represents the cosmic mountain marking the centre of the world, like the temple-mountain of Khmer architecture. In the centre there rises an oblate stupa with four ribs, surmounted by a spire, the central part of which is bulbous in form and rests upon a three-tiered plinth with a decoration of large lotus-petals round its base. The lower part of the stupa is surrounded by thirty small shrines, and the whole is enclosed by a square gallery with a main gateway in the centre of each side, which again is surrounded by an enclosure consisting of a single terrace with four axial chapels, and finally by a cloister measuring 278 feet on each side, with an entrance pavilion in the centre of each side.

Twice – in 1554 and 1570 – the Burmese tried to take Vieng Chan, but without success. When Jetthadhiraja died in 1571, General Sen Surint'a proclaimed himself regent in the name of Prince No Keo Kuman, who was still a child. But in 1574 the Burmese at last succeeded in entering the city, and the King of Burma had another Laotian prince, whom he had taken as hostage ten years earlier, crowned king. The child-king was taken away as captive, and was soon after joined by the regent.

Laos remained under Burmese rule for several years, but after a period of internal unrest in Burma (1583–91), Nandabayin came to the throne there and released the young Prince No Keo Kuman from captivity when he found himself in difficulties with Siam. No Keo Kuman was crowned king at Vieng Chan in 1591 (or 1594). Luang Prabang was regained, and Laotian suzerainty re-established over the province of Xieng Khouang (Tran-ninh), which had had to accept that of Burma.

No Keo Kuman died in 1596 without leaving an heir, and was succeeded by his nephew, Dhammikaraja (*Th'ammikarat*, 1596–1622), whose reign was marked by an expedition against Siam in 1612. He died by assassination at the hand of his son, and this was the signal for the outbreak of revolts that lasted for fifteen years. Then in 1637 a great-grandnephew of Dhammikaraja had himself proclaimed king under the name of Suriyavamsa. He had a long reign of fifty-seven years, during which he came to terms over the delimitation of frontiers with the Emperor of Viet-nam, Le Than-tong, whose daughter he had married. It was during his reign that Laos received the visit of the Dutchman Gerrit van Wusthoff (1641)[3] and of the Jesuit J. M. Leria (1641–47), both of whom have left valuable accounts of their travels.[4]

On the death of Suriyavamsa in 1694 there was a struggle for the succession which ended in the partition of Lan Ch'ang into two rival States, Vieng Chan and Luang Prabang. In 1696 a nephew of Suriyavamsa who had been born in Viet-nam came, supported by a Vietnamese army, to stake his claim to the succession, and succeeded in establishing himself at Vieng Chan. He is known under the name of Sai Ong Hue. On becoming king in 1700 he sent an army to take possession of Luang Prabang, which was occupied by two grandsons of Suriyavamsa in the direct line, Kingkitsarat and Int'asom. They had to withdraw to the Sip Song Phan Na, which is where their mother had come from. There they obtained the aid of a small army with which they were able to recapture Luang Prabang. Kingkitsarat had himself proclaimed king there, and in 1707 he announced to Sai Ong Hue that he was now ruler over the northern provinces, but that he abandoned his claims over the provinces in the south. The partition of Lan Ch'ang into two kingdoms was now a *fait accompli*.

The rulers of Vieng Chan during the eighteenth century were Sai Ong Hue (1707–35), his grandson Ong Long (1735–60), followed by another grandson, Ong Bun (1760–78) and by descendants of the last. It was during Ong Bun's reign that Siam waged its victorious campaign against Burma which ended with the taking of Ayudhya in 1767. When Siam had recovered from this, it mounted a campaign against Vieng Chan, which seems to have been on the side of the Burmese. The campaign was led by the Siamese general P'raya Chakri, who took the city in 1778 after a siege lasting four months, annexed the territory, and removed the statues of the P'ra Keo and the P'ra Bang and took them back to Bangkok. Vieng Chan was under Siamese rule for four years, but after P'raya Chakri had founded the Bangkok dynasty in 1782 he handed it back to Ong Bun's eldest son, Chao Nan, at the same time returning the P'ra Bang statue (but not the P'ra Keo one). In 1791 Chao Nan was deposed by the Siamese and replaced by his brother Chao In, who, upon his death in 1805, was succeeded by another brother, Chao Anu. In 1820 Chao Anu built the Vat Si Saket at Vieng Chan, with its sanctuary, in imitation of the large temples at Bangkok, surrounded by a double cloister containing a hundred and twenty statues of the Buddha. In 1826 he suddenly declared war on Siam, after having remained loyal for twenty years; and a lightning advance brought him to within three days' march of Bangkok. But the counter-attack mounted by General

P'raya Bodin led to the capture of Vieng Chan in 1828. The city was destroyed and there was a mass transfer of its inhabitants to Siam.

In Luang Prabang the two brothers Kingkitsarat and Int'asom quarrelled after their joint victory in 1707. The former reigned at first, until 1726. Then Int'asom, after removing a rival, seized power and kept it until 1776. His long reign was marked by a number of events, the most serious of which was the Burmese invasion of 1752. The Burmese penetrated as far as Luang Prabang and imposed their protection over the territory. Int'asom had to wait until their power declined under the blows of a re-awakened Siam, but in 1774 he was able to conclude a treaty of alliance with P'raya Tak, which was renewed in 1776 upon the accession of Jotikakumara (*Sotikakuman*), son and successor of Int'asom. But when P'raya Chakri took Vieng Chan in 1778, Luang Prabang had to recognize the suzerainty of Siam.

In 1781 the king had to abdicate in favour of his brother, Chao Vong, who died in 1787 without an heir. Vieng Chan took advantage of the fact that the country was without a king, and occupied Luang Prabang in 1791; but in 1793 Anurut, who had taken refuge at Bangkok, returned to Luang Prabang and became king. He restored the city, and in 1796 built the Vat Mai on the site of an older building, in which to enshrine the P'ra Bang statue which Chao Nan had brought back from Bangkok in 1791. It is a vast sanctuary consisting of three naves with seven bays; at each end there is a porch with a double row of columns.

Mant'at'urat, who became king in 1817, refrained from intervening in the war which King Anu of Vieng Chan had declared against Siam. His son, Suk Som, whom the Siamese put on the throne in 1839, reigned until 1850. His reign was comparatively peaceful, owing to the rivalry that then existed between Siam and Viet-nam. His brother, Chandakumara (*Chant'akuman*, 1852–68) received a visit from the French naturalist Henri Mouhot in 1861, and also the mission for the exploration of the Mekong, led by Doudart de Lagrée and Francis Garnier,[5] which arrived in Luang Prabang on 20 April 1867. In 1864 he had to repel the first invasion of the Ho, a tribe from South China that had been forced to flee their country owing to wars and famine.

His brother, Un K'am, became king in 1868, but did not obtain recognition from Siam until 1872. Siam was at this time awaiting the first opportunity to transform its nominal suzerainty over the country into effective occupation. A new invasion of the Ho into Tran-ninh provided that opportunity. The Siamese first sent an expedition of intervention in 1872, but following upon the signature of the treaty establishing the French protectorate of Tongking in 1883, the Court of Bangkok put the whole region to the north and east of Luang Prabang under military occupation (1885). Protests from the government of Viet-nam led to a French vice-consulate being established in the city of Luang Prabang – a post to which Auguste Pavie was appointed.[6] With his intimate knowledge of the country, every corner of which he had traversed during his geographical missions, and the great prestige he enjoyed among its people, he had no difficulty in rallying the Laotians and their king to his side when he asserted the rights of France's protégé, Viet-nam, to the left back of the Mekong. A number of incidents between France and Siam led to the French staging a demonstration of naval strength off Bangkok, which brought about the signing of the Franco-Siamese treaty on 3 October 1893, by which Siam agreed to withdraw from the left bank of the Mekong and to recognize Laos as a French protectorate.

Laos did not inherit its civilization direct from India any more than Siam had done. The T'ais of the Mekong showed the same capacity for assimilation as their brothers of the Menam. At first they acquired much of the Khmer civilization which, before their arrival, had already spread all over the southern part of the territory that later formed part of Lan Ch'ang. Their language and religion give proof of this, and so no doubt would their art, except that unfortunately no trace of it is left. Later, owing to the sequence of political events summarized above, it was Lan Na and Burma that exercised influence on their literature and art, and on the script used for religious texts. Later again, the main influence was that of Siam, especially in Vieng Chan, where the art of the eighteenth and nineteenth centuries in particular draws its inspiration from Siamese art.

Nothing but a few statues remain from the period of the foundation of the kingdom and the centuries immediately following. Apart from the few buildings which have been mentioned in connection with the times when they were built, all the early architecture was built of perishable materials and did not withstand the ravages of time. But more recent buildings modelled on early prototypes enable us to assume that the style of buildings constructed of perishable materials was perhaps imported from India via Burma; and this style was probably the departure point for the architecture of all the various regions of South East Asia. What gives Laotian architecture its own particular character is the widespread use of double-tiered roofs. This is a type of roofing found all over the Far East and South East Asia. It is sometimes termed 'telescopic', because it consists of successive layers which span the various sections of the building to form a covering for the building as a whole.

Three separate artistic centres existed in Laos: Vieng Chan, Luang Prabang, and Xieng Khouang. Of these, Xieng Khouang is the one where the early architectural features have been best preserved, particularly the type of roofing in which the roof of the main body of the building covers the roofs of the porches and descends low over the low side walls to form a wide hood, which has been compared to the drooping wings of a hen hatching eggs; whereas at Luang Prabang the side walls of buildings are higher and the roof does not descend so far, and at Vieng Chan this tendency is still further accentuated.

The characteristic type of building of Laotian architecture is the *th'at* (*dhatu*) or reliquary. This is the counterpart, in Laotian terms, of the Indian, Sinhalese, and Burmese stupa, combined with the Khmer and Siamese chetiya. Its origin is perhaps to be found in the type of shrine characteristic of the art of Sukhodaya. It appears in the widest variety of forms and betrays the widest variety of influence. Indeed, the essential spirit of Laotian architecture is perhaps best expressed in buildings which combine a number of styles of different origin. In the *th'at* there is always a difference in proportions, sometimes greater and sometimes less, between the lower part of the building and the spire which surmounts it – a feature which is clearly derived from the stupa, either in its original hemispherical form, or in the later bell-shaped, bulbous, or bottle-shaped versions.

Laotian sculpture is on the whole of mediocre quality. From the end of the fourteenth century the face of the Buddha seems to have become fixed in type (as in the statue of the Vat Manorom), with highly stylized treatment – as unrealistic as could be – of the hair and ears, and with an aquiline nose obviously inspired by the style of Sukhodaya.

Both the sculpture and the architectural style of the *th'at* convey an impression of an art that developed in a border region far removed from the main artistic trends. The same applies to Laotian literature. To some extent, it can be regarded as a dialectal branch of Siamese literature. Siamese literature was primarily the expression of a cultured aristocracy, and its surviving works can be dated and ascribed to individual authors. Laotian literature, on the other hand, is anonymous, and no dates have been established for the works produced. It gives a fairly accurate idea of the folk literature of the T'ais of the Mekong, and includes edifying religious works, the most popular of which are the apocryphal Fifty Jataka (originally composed at Chiang Mai), the lives of monks – especially monks such as P'ra Malai, who penetrated the secrets of the other world – and the history of relics. Among the outstanding works of profane literature, a special place must be reserved for what is called the Laotian Panchatantra,[7] consisting of four collections of tales, most of which are to be found in the famous Sanskrit collection, and which also exist in Siamese under the title of *Nang Tantrai*. The greatest number of works are in the style of the poetic romance, the most popular poems being the *Kalaket, Lin T'ong, Surivong, Chambang,* and *Usabarot*. In the words of Louis Finot, 'the plot is almost always the same: a gallop on horseback, a rendezvous, kidnappings, separations, fights against yakshas or against enraged fathers, ladies lost and found, deaths and resurrections, a final meeting together again and a happy ending – this is more or less the entire content of these poems. . . . The romances in prose scarcely differ from those in verse except in form. They are all based on endless repetitions of the themes of popular tales. But here the compilers have often followed the form of the jataka, which gives a certain Buddhist flavour to these tales.' It may be added that the Fifty Jatakas are the most common source of inspiration of these romances.

Other Laotian texts known to us include inscriptions concerning religious foundations, historical and legal texts, pietistic religious works, and short treatises or manuals on astrology, medicine, etc., none of which come within the domain of literature proper. On the other hand, Laotian folk-songs, like those of neighbouring countries, although they are naïve in form, show a genuine freshness of inspiration.

3

Burma

THROUGHOUT THE WHOLE LENGTH of its history, the kingdom of Burma has suffered from one chronic drawback: the heterogeneous nature of its population. The Burmese people consist of a number of very different ethnic groups at very different stages of advance, and it has always been difficult to weld them into a unified whole. Several times Burmese leaders have unified the country by force, but they have always shown themselves incapable of going on from there to organize the country in an effective manner.

Less than two and a half centuries after the country had been unified by Aniruddha, the fall of Pagan in 1287 had once more plunged it into a state of anarchy, and it shortly became divided into three. In the south, the Mon inhabitants of the delta found themselves under the rule of a T'ai named Wareru (T'ai: Chao Fa Rua), who established himself at Martaban in 1281. In the north, Upper Burma – the future kingdom of Ava – remained in the hands of the descendants of the dynasty of Pagan, who continued to reign under the surveillance of three brothers of T'ai origin. In the south-east, the principality of Toungoo on the river Sittang, founded in 1280, became the refuge for Burmese who wanted to escape from T'ai domination.

In the delta, Wareru, the T'ai ruler of Martaban, formed an alliance with Tarabya, the governor of Pegu, where the two allies had succeeded in getting rid of the Burmese governor and in occupying the region. Subsequently Wareru got rid of Tarabya and remained in sole charge. He is credited with having drawn up the first Dharmashastra (*Dhammathat*) or law-code of Burma. He died in 1313, assassinated by the sons of Tarabya. This murder was the signal for the outbreak of a series of conflicts with the Siamese kingdom of Sukhodaya, which was endeavouring to obtain possession of the ports of Tenasserim and Tavoy on the Gulf of Bengal. The only descendants of Wareru that need be mentioned are: Binnya U (1353–85), who moved the capital to Hamsavati (= Pegu) in 1369; his son Rajadhiraja (*Razadarit*), who succeeded in defending his kingdom against the repeated attacks of Ava and of Ayudhya, and who divided it into thirty-two districts (he died in 1423); Dhammachetiya (*Dhammazedi*, 1472–92), chiefly known for the embassy he sent to Ceylon in 1475, on the return of which the rites for the ordination of monks regarded as orthodox by the Mahavihara sect became the only valid ones. This led to a religious unification which went far beyond the frontiers of Pegu.[1] His grandson, Takayutpi (1526–39), fell before the victorious advance of the ruler of Toungoo, and thus became the last ruler of the kingdom of Pegu, which had been the most civilized of the three States into which Burma was at that time divided, and the first to enter into close relations with Europeans.

In the north, Kyoswa, a son of the last king of Pagan, remained in favour with the three T'ai brothers who governed the three districts of Kyaukse. A sister of their's married Kyoswa's elder brother, Sihasura (*Thihathu*), who died in an attack on Pegu. The eldest of the three brothers then put an end to Kyoswa, and the city of Pagan was destroyed. The renewed Sino-Mongol attack in 1300 did not get beyond Myinsaing, the city where the three T'ai brothers had been born and bred, and they remained masters of the situation.[2] After the death of the two older brothers, the youngest established his capital at Pinya, where his descendants continued to reign until 1364. One of his sons established himself at Sagaing in 1315, and it was a scion of this northern branch named Thadominbya who in 1364 founded the city of Ava,[3] situated on the Irrawaddy at the lower end of the Kyaukse plain. The history of Ava is nothing but a confused sequence of wars, sometimes with Pegu, sometimes with the T'ais in the northeast, until in the middle of the sixteenth century it was conquered by the second king of the Toungoo dynasty.

The fortified city of Toungoo, founded in 1280, became the

capital of a new State when Thinhkaba took the title of king in 1347. The capture of Ava by the T'ais in 1525 and again in 1527 brought many Burmese refugees to Toungoo during the reign of Minkyinyo (1486–1531). He was the father of Tabinshweti, who, for the second time in Burma's history, was to achieve its unification.

This unification was carried out by force, following upon a series of victorious campaigns in the course of which Tabinshweti was constantly aided by his brother-in-law, Bayinnaung. He began in 1535 by attacking the delta, which had grown prosperous through foreign trade. After having got possession of Bassein and Myaungmya without any difficulty, he attacked Pegu and entered it in 1539. He then marched on Prome, but had to fall back when faced with troops from Ava. The death of Takayutpi, the last king of Pegu, brought many Mons to his side, and in addition he succeeded in enlisting a corps of Portuguese troops. In 1541 he took Martaban, where he procured an enormous amount of booty, and then Moulmein, and proceeded to occupy the coast as far as Tavoy. Tabinshweti then had himself crowned at Pegu as king of Lower Burma. In 1542 he once again marched on Prome, which he at last brought down after a five months' siege. In 1544 the whole of central Burma was in his power, and he had himself crowned at Pagan as king of Upper Burma. His solemn consecration as sovereign of a united Burma took place at Pegu in 1546, and he kept Pegu as his capital.

In 1546–47 Tabinshweti invaded Arakan, but had to come to terms with its king because Siam had taken advantage of his absence to mount an attack against Tavoy. The reply was not long in coming, and the winter of 1547–48 was spent in preparing a Burmese expeditionary force which included a certain number of Portuguese. It reached Ayudhya via the Three Pagodas pass and Kanchanaburi, but had to withdraw after a siege that lasted for a month. In order to safeguard their retreat by the Rahaeng route, the Burmese were even obliged to release several distinguished prisoners. During the last years of his reign Tabinshweti gave himself up to drink, and his brother-in-law, Bayinnaung, had to take charge of affairs. Bayinnaung's chief task was to take measures against the rebellion of one of the descendants of the former Mon kings, who was occupying the mouths of the Irrawaddy. In 1551 Tabinshweti was assassinated as the result of a plot hatched by his

Mon guards, one of whom was proclaimed king at Pegu. This was the signal for a general rising.

Bayinnaung then found himself obliged to reconquer from the Mons, and from his own relatives who had now become independent rulers at Prome and at Toungoo, the kingdom which his brother-in-law had unified less than ten years before. Aided at first by the Portuguese De Mello, he began by recapturing Toungoo from one of his brothers and having himself crowned there. Then, having put the leader of the Mon rebels to flight, he took Pegu. The fall of Pegu put an end to the rebellion, and having reconquered the kingdom won by his predecessor, Bayinnaung now proceeded to enlarge it. In 1555 he marched on Ava, which fell without a blow being struck; and between 1556 and 1559 he reduced all the T'ai principalities as far as Mogaung and Bhamo in the north, and Chiang Mai and Luang Prabang in the east. It was during this period that the Shan States became part of Burma.

The hostilities with Siam that began in 1563 arose over the refusal of King Mahachakrabarti to send his neighbour a white elephant. After Kamphaeng Phet and Sukhodaya had been taken, the capital, Ayudhya, was attacked in 1564, and the king was forced to accept the conqueror's terms. Another campaign in 1568 was in reply to an affront inflicted upon the leader of the pro-Burmese party by Mahachakrabarti, who died soon after. Ayudhya was taken on 30 August 1569, and the new king, Mahindra, was led away into captivity.

The reign of Bayinnaung, which marks the apogee of the Toungoo dynasty, came to an end in 1581, just as preparations were in train for the conquest of Arakan, with Sandoway already taken. Although Bayinnaung's sway extended over the whole of Burma and the Shan States as far as Chiang Mai, it was only Mon country that he ruled over directly, and he resided at Pegu, surrounded by Mon counsellors. At his capital he built a large temple known as the Mahachetiya (*Mahazedi*), in which he placed a replica of the tooth-relic from Ceylon in 1576.

Bayinnaung's son, Nandabayin, began his reign by having to suppress a revolt led by his uncle, the viceroy of Ava, and few years passed without his having to deal with a rebellion of some kind in an empire that lacked a strong centralized government. The revival of Siam under its king, Nareshvara (1590–1605), proved fatal for him. Nareshvara, before coming to power, had laid siege to Pegu as early as 1584, and in 1587 he had victoriously defended the capital of his own country against a Burmese attack. In the Burmese campaign against Siam in 1592–93, Nandabayin's son, the Crown Prince, was killed in single combat by Nareshvara in the region of Subarnapuri. The viceroys, most of whom were close relatives of Nandabayin, betrayed him instead of uniting behind him and supporting him against the Siamese threat. One of them – the viceroy of Toungoo – offered to share his spoils with Arakan. Arakanese troops came and laid siege to Pegu, and succeeded in taking and sacking the city. The king died shortly after, in 1599.

The country again fell into a state of anarchy, which lasted for sixteen years. In 1605 Anaukpetlun, a grandson of Nandabayin, was already master of the city of Ava, of Upper Burma, and of several of the Shan States in the north, and he had no great trouble in reconquering Lower Burma: in 1607 Prome, in 1610 Toungoo in 1613 Syriam (from the Portuguese De Brito), and in 1614 Tavoy. In 1613 the Court moved from Ava, and Pegu once again became the capital. In 1619 Anaukpetlun received envoys from the English East India Company, which set up factories at Syriam, Ava, and Bhamo.[4] The Dutch, for their part, had factories at Syriam, Pegu, and Ava.

Anaukpetlun died in 1628 at the hand of his son Minredeippa, who succeeded him, but who only reigned for one year, killed in his turn by his uncle Thalun. Thalun, after being crowned at Pegu in 1629, moved to Ava in 1635. He was crowned there for the second time, and made Ava his capital, thus moving the centre of the kingdom from the delta area and from Pegu, which was gradually becoming silted up. This decision had far-reaching consequences. With their capital removed from the coast, the Burmese kings became shut off from foreign influences and remained in dangerous ignorance about what was going on in the world; and their departure from that part of the country that was peopled by Mons made it impossible for them to weld together the two main population groups, and left the people of the delta under the constant temptation to make themselves independent of a government that no longer ruled them directly, but from a distance.

Pindale, who succeeded his father Thalun in 1648, was incapable of dealing with the situation brought about by the arrival in Burma of Chinese armies of Ming loyalists that had been formed after the fall of the Ming dynasty in 1644. These armies occupied the plain of Kyaukse and even got the length of pillaging Pagan. Pindale's inability to cope with the situation led to his being deposed, and finally to his being killed in 1661 by his brother Pye, whose reign (1661–72) was much disturbed by Siamese raids in the delta area and by the ravages caused by the Chinese armies.

The decline of the Toungoo dynasty, which was already evident towards the end of Nandabayin's reign, became more and more rapid under its last kings. Its fall was in part caused by the attacks of the State of Manipur, which had been a vassal State under Bayinnaung, but which had since declared its independence, and had carried out frequent raids between 1724 and 1749 which created a permanent sense of insecurity; and in part by quarrels with Pegu, where Smim Htaw Buddhaketi (1740–47) and his successor Binnya Dala (1747–57) obtained domination over the lower part of Burma up to Prome and Toungoo. The fatal blow came in 1751 with the occupation of the plain of Kyaukse by the Mons, and Ava was finally taken in 1752. But the Mons were unable to take full advantage of their success, and they withdrew to Pegu, leaving Ava weakly garrisoned.

But now, for the third time in Burma's history, a powerful leader of Burmese stock arose to unite the country by force, just in time to save it from anarchy. This leader was Alaungpaya (or Alompra as he is called by European writers). He was born in 1714 at Shwebo, to the north of Ava. After the fall of the capital he refused to swear the oath of loyalty to the Mons, who had failed in their attempt to capture his village. Having gathered together a large enough number of followers, Alaungpaya marched on Ava, which the Mon garrison was not strong enough to defend, and which he occupied in December 1753. A month later the Mons withdrew from Upper Burma, and their attempt to recapture Ava in March 1754 ended in their defeat. The following year Alaungpaya took Prome, and then, in May 1755, Dagon, which he renamed Rangoon and proceeded to develop in preference to Syriam, which he occupied in July 1756. In May 1757 Pegu fell, after some dramatic incidents, and was completely destroyed. In 1758–59 Alaungpaya turned his forces westwards and invaded Manipur, reaching and entering its capital, Imphal.

Alaungpaya then seized the first opportunity that offered, which happened to be the detention by the Siamese of the captain of a Burmese boat, to attack his neighbour to the east in the hope of bringing back a large number of prisoners with which to repeople Burma. In 1760 he led his troops via Martaban, Tavoy, and Tenasserim, and then across to Bejrapuri on the east coast of the Malay Peninsula. But by the time he reached Ayudhya it was too late in the season to attack, and he had to withdraw. He died on the way back after a reign of eight well-spent years.

His eldest son, Naungdawgyi, who only reigned for three years (1760–63), had to put down a rebellion led by one of his generals who had occupied Ava, and then another led by his uncle, who was governor of Toungoo, and who submitted in 1762. His brother Hsinbyushin succeeded him, and moved the capital, which since Alaungpaya's time had been transferred to Shwebo, the dynasty's place of origin, back to Ava. He restored its buildings and summoned Brahmans from Benares who, with the help of Burmese scholars, translated a large number of Sanskrit works, especially collections of laws. The years 1764 to 1767 were occupied with the last phase of the age-long conflict with Siam. A Burmese army approaching from the north via Chiang Mai and another advancing from the south via Tavoy and Bejrapuri ended, after various adventures, by joining forces in front of Ayudhya. The siege of the city lasted for fourteen months, but on 7 April 1767 the Siamese capital was taken and completely destroyed by pillage and fire.

The Burmese army was ordered to return home to face Chinese attacks incited by trivial frontier incidents in which the northern Shan States supported the Chinese. After advancing as far as Ava, the Chinese were turned back in 1769. The last years of Hsinbyushin's reign were darkened by trouble with the Mons (1773) and by reverses in Siam (1775). He died in 1776 and was succeeded by his son Singu, who put an end to the incessant wars of the preceding reigns, but who was assassinated in 1782.

The conspirators failed in their attempt to put a cousin of the assassinated king on the throne, and it was one of his brothers, the oldest of the surviving sons of Alaungpaya, who came to power. Bodawpaya (1782–1819) moved the capital to Amarapura, near present-day Mandalay, a year after his accession. In this same year of 1783 Rangoon had to be recaptured from a small force of Mons who had seized it. The following year Bodawpaya completed the conquest of Arakan, and brought back from there a famous statue, the Mahamuni, for which he had a temple built in which copies of the six hundred ancient inscriptions concerning monastic estates were also placed. An attempt in 1785–86 to reconquer Siam proved unsuccessful, but this defeat by no means spelt the end to hostilities between the two countries. Bodawpaya built a large number of temples, and found time before his death to embark upon the conquest of Assam in 1816.

His son Bagyidaw (1819–37) moved the capital back to Ava again. As soon as he came to the throne he had to continue with the conquest of Assam, but Burmese entry into territory belonging to the British in the Brahmaputra valley resulted in the first Anglo-Burmese war, which was declared on 5 March 1824.[5] By May 11th the British expeditionary force had disembarked at Rangoon. Its commander, Sir Archibald Campbell, confined himself at first to occupying the ports of Syriam, Tavoy, Mergui, and Martaban. The following year operations were extended inland: Prome was occupied on 25 April 1825, and Arakan at the end of the spring of that year. Proposals for an armistice were then made, the British offering to agree to a cease-fire on the cession of Arakan, Tavoy, and Mergui, together with the payment of a heavy indemnity. King Bagyidaw at first refused the offer, and fighting started up again; but when the British had advanced beyond Pagan and had come within twenty-five miles of the capital, he capitulated, and signed a treaty on 24 February 1826. Assam, Arakan, and the Tenasserim coast, including the part consisting of the province of Martaban to the east of the Salween, were ceded to England. King Bagyidaw was deeply humiliated by his defeat, and in 1832 began to show signs of insanity.

In 1837 he was deposed by his elder brother, Prince Tharawadi, whose reign of nine years was not marked by any important events. He was succeeded in 1846 by his son, the Prince of Pagan, whose incapacity as a ruler resulted in a second war over the seizure of two British ships at Rangoon. Fighting began on 1 April 1852; Martaban was occupied on the 5th, Rangoon on the 12th – not without losses on the part of the British – and Bassein on May 19th, Pegu on June 3rd, and Prome during the course of the summer. After Prome and Pegu had been won again and then recaptured, the king was informed that the province of Pegu would thenceforth form part of British territory, and its annexation was proclaimed on 20 January 1853. The fighting came to an end although no formal peace treaty had been concluded, because on January 1st Prince Mindon, a younger brother of the Prince of Pagan, occupied the suburbs of Amarapura, the capital, and on February 18th entered the city and the palace and had himself proclaimed king.

The new king hastened to put an end to the war, and on 30 June 1853 peace was concluded without any treaty actually being signed. The first British commissioner at Pegu was Arthur Phayre, who accompanied Henry Yule's mission to Ava in 1855.[6] In 1856 King Mindon began to build a new capital, with a new palace, at Mandalay, slightly to the north of Amarapura. He took up residence there in June 1857, and the whole population of Amarapura was transferred to the new capital. In 1871 he sent an embassy to England. He died in 1878.

A palace intrigue brought his son Thibaw to power on 8 October 1878. His reign began with the execution of seventy to eighty members of the royal family whom Queen Supayalat and her mother had decided to get rid of (February 1879). The third Anglo-Burmese war was now brewing over questions of piracy and of maltreatment of British subjects, and also over King Thibaw's refusal to submit a matter concerning a fine of £230,000 imposed on a British commercial company to arbitration. The British delivered an ultimatum on 22 October 1885, and on November 7th the king ordered the mobilization of his forces. But by November 14th the Indian army had crossed the frontier and in a rapid advance reached Pagan on November 22nd, Myingyan on the 25th, and finally arrived before Ava on the 26th. The next day the king ordered his troops to cease fighting. On the 28th Mandalay was occupied and the king made prisoner and sent to India with his family. The British pushed north from Mandalay until they reached Bhamo, and by December 28th the whole of the Irrawaddy valley was in their hands, although piracy and guerrilla fighting continued for some time after this. Britain's official annexation of Upper Burma dates from 1 January 1886, that of the Shan States from the following year, and that of the Chin Hills from 1889. Thus it was that the British colony of Burma came into being. Its frontiers with Siam were settled in 1893, those with the French Protectorate in Indochina in 1895, and those with China in 1900.

Burma had been one of the first regions of the Indochinese peninsula, or perhaps the very first, to be affected by the spread of Indian culture, and both the Mons of the delta and the Pyus of Shrikshetra had benefited directly from Indian influence. But since the time when the Burmese, after their conquest of the delta, assimilated the Indianized civilizations of the Mons and the Pyus, Burma had probably been less influenced by neighbouring countries and foreign powers than any other of the Indochinese States. During the brilliant Pagan period the Burmese evolved their own distinct type of civilization, and by their adoption of the doctrines of the Sinhalese reform, established the form of Buddhism that has since prevailed all over their own country and has spread eastwards as well; but later, during the periods following upon the unification of Burma by the founders of the Toungoo and Shwebo dynasties, the Burmese seem to have spent all their energies in trying to unite a divided country and in embarking upon military adventures and territorial expansion; and by the late nineteenth century they were totally unaware of the great events that were taking place in the world. The ignorance of the last Burmese kings and their failure to understand the implications of British colonial expansion were in marked contrast to the foresight displayed by the Siamese kings of the Bangkok dynasty, and betrayed a complete lack of response to foreign influences. This was paralleled, in the cultural field, by a state of stagnation that was inimical to the rise and development of new ideas, and which amounted, in effect, to a kind of cultural vacuum.

There had been plenty of cultural vitality during the two and a half centuries when the kingdom of Pagan was in existence. Its material prosperity had favoured the rise of a style of art and architecture which has left many surviving monuments. But during the centuries that followed, Burma was torn with internal conflicts and preoccupied with external wars which, even when victorious, led to no lasting settlement; and the times were not propitious for the production of works of art. This is borne out by the fact that Burma never gave rise to new architectural forms – unless perhaps one were to regard the exaggeration of the concave profile of the conical stupa as a new form. Its architecture displays, rather, a degeneration of the old forms, together with a profusion of ornamentation that is sometimes reminiscent of the Gothic flamboyant style. It is true that the successive capitals of later times[7] – Sagaing, Ava, Pegu, and Amarapura – suffered much more serious damage through destruction or abandonment than was the case with Pagan. But then Pagan's architectural monuments were built of solid materials, and they survived not only the capture of the city by the Mongols (who do not seem to have carried out any systematic destruction of the city), but also the ravages of time. In the later capitals many of the buildings were constructed of wood, and we can only form some idea of what they were like from those that survive in Mandalay.[8] The surviving buildings in non-perishable materials consist mainly of conical stupas with a concave profile and a wide flaring base, such as the famous Shwe Dagon pagoda in Rangoon.

As regards literature written in the Burmese language,[9] the earliest surviving works date from the second half of the fifteenth century when Owen was the capital. They consist of ballads concerning historical events, poems composed in praise of kings, short verses inspired by nature or by amorous sentiments, and above all, tales of the early lives of the Buddha, directly based on the Jataka of the Buddhist canon. In the last category, the outstanding writers were Thilawuntha – who is also the author of the oldest extant prose texts, consisting of stories of monks, and a summary of the chronicle of Ceylon (the *Yazawingyaw*, 1520) – and his rival, a Mon named Ratathara, who produced two versions in verse of the *Bhuridattajataka*, one in 1484, and the other in 1494; and also Aggathamadai, whose adaptations of the *Nemijataka* appeared in 1535, 1538, and 1542. The military exploits of the first kings of the Toungoo dynasty gave rise to a number of poems glorifying their mighty deeds. The soldier-poet Nawade wrote many poems of this kind. His contemporary, the Mon Binnya Dala, composed a Burmese version of the historical romance *Razadarit*. But the most celebrated poet of this period was Padethayaza (1684–1754), author of the oldest extant play, and of the first examples of pastoral poetry deriving its inspiration from peasant life. So many works survive from the period since the accession of Alaungpaya in 1752 – many of them modelled on Siamese prototypes or showing Siamese influence – that it would be impossible to single out either poets or prosewriters for individual mention. Both continued to cultivate the same forms as before, the favourite still being early lives of the Buddha. There was also a considerable output of historical works of a more or less fictitious character. The best known is the *Hmannan Yazawin* or 'The Glass Palace Chronicle' (1826). One of its authors, Monywe Sayadaw (1766–*c.* 1837), was also outstanding as a writer of stories concerning the early lives of the Buddha.

4
Cambodia

IN 1283 a small Mongol army had entered Cambodia from the direction of Champa. This raid had no sequel, except that in 1285 Jayavarman VIII sent tribute to Emperor Kublai acknowledging his vassalage. In 1295 he abdicated in favour of his son-in-law, Shrindravarman (1295–1327). It was during the latter's reign that Cambodia received the visit of the Chinese envoy Chou Ta-kuan, whose celebrated report on the customs of Cambodia[1] gives a description of the state of the country in 1296–97 which, in conjunction with epigraphic material, enables us to form a fairly complete picture of what the civilization of Angkor was like on the eve of its decline.

After mentioning the various stages of his journey, Chou Ta-kuan gives an extraordinarily accurate description of the capital, and then discusses various types of dwelling, beginning with the royal palace, in which 'there is a golden tower (Phimeanakas) at the top of which the king has his sleeping apartments. All the natives believe that in the tower there is a spirit in the form of a nine-headed snake who is lord of the soil of the whole kingdom. It appears every night in the form of a woman. She it is with whom the king first sleeps and unites himself.' This would seem to be a folk memory of the far-off time when the Brahman who founded Fu-nan married the daughter of the local chief who was lord of the soil. As regards clothing, the Chinese envoy notes that Western materials (apparently from India) were much in use, and describes the king's costume in a manner which corresponds fairly accurately with the costume worn by the king in the bas-reliefs of the twelfth century. In his section on officials – 'ministers, generals, astronomers' and minor functionaries – Chou Ta-kuan correctly conveys the aristocratic and oligarchical nature of Khmer government. 'Most of the time, princes are chosen for office; if others are chosen, they offer their daughters as royal concubines.' He confirms the information given by inscriptions about insignia of rank: palanquins with a gold or a silver shaft, and parasols with gold or silver handles. He points out the existence of three distinct religious sects: *pandits* – that is, Brahmans – 'who dress like other men, except for the white cord they wear around the neck, which is the distinctive mark of the lettered class'; *chao ku* (a term of Siamese origin) – that is, Buddhist monks – 'who shave the head, wear yellow robes that leave the right shoulder bare and a cloth skirt knotted round the lower part of their bodies, go barefoot, worship an image exactly like Buddha Shakyamuni, eat only one meal a day, and recite many texts, all of them written on palm leaves'; and *tapasvin*, or ascetics who worship the linga, 'a block of stone like the altar-stone of the god of the soil in China'. In a long paragraph based on information which Chou Ta-kuan could not guarantee to be accurate ('since no Chinese is allowed to witness these things, it is impossible to know whether they are true or not'), he describes the rite of the deflowering of girls who had reached the age of puberty, to which he gives the unexplained name of *chen-t'an*. An interesting chapter is devoted to the various annual festivals. Among those mentioned are the Feast of Lanterns which must have been connected with the Festival of the Dead; the 'throwing of the ball' that still accompanies the alternating songs of boys and girls at the New Year; the washing of the statues of the Buddha that also takes place at New Year; the review of the population – a kind of census that used also to be a Siamese custom; and the burning of rice, an agricultural festival held at harvest time. With regard to the administration of justice, Chou Ta-kuan records that 'the disputes of the people, however insignificant, always go before the soverign', but for the rest, he speaks only of tortures and trials by ordeal. Leprosy is one of the illnesses he mentions. 'One of the kings', he says, 'caught this illness.' In his treatment of funeral rites, he scarcely mentions any other means of disposal of the dead except exposure to wild beasts. 'Nowadays,' he adds, 'there is a gradually increasing number of people who burn their dead; but these are mostly descendants of Chinese. . . . The king is buried in a tower, but I do not know whether his body is buried or only his bones.' This last is evidence of capital importance in explaining why so many sarcophagi have been found in most of the temples of Angkor. Chou Ta-kuan also speaks of agriculture, of the physical geography of the country, of its products, its trade, the Chinese merchandise in demand there, and of its plants and animals. He describes the furniture and table-ware of the Khmers, which always have been, and still are, of a very simple kind, as well as their palanquins, boats, junks, and canoes. Very few of the provinces he singles out for mention among the ninety that existed are identifiable. 'Each village,' he says, 'has a temple or a stupa. . . . On the main roads there are rest-houses similar to our postal relay stations' (these being the staging posts or 'houses with fire' of Jayavarman VII). After giving some details about the annual collection of human gall (a custom still practised when the French Protectorate was established), and about baths and weapons, Chou Ta-kuan winds up his account by describing how the king rode forth in full pomp and ceremony, and how he held audience in the palace.

In 1307 Shrindravarman, in whose favour his brother-in-law had abdicated, abdicated in his turn and became a Buddhist monk. The new king on mounting the throne took the name of Shrindrajayavarman, and reigned for twenty years. He made gifts to the temple built at Angkor by Jayavarman VIII in honour of the Brahman Jayamangalartha, who had died during the latter's reign at the age of 104. No other event in Shrindrajayavarman's reign is recorded, except the arrival in 1320 of a Chinese embassy. He was succeeded in 1327 by Jayavarmaparameshvara, best known in connection with the great Sanskrit inscription said to be from Angkor Vat,[2] but which actually comes from a site that used to be called Kapilapura, to the north-east of the temple. The inscription, which is the work of the Brahman savant Vidyeshadhimant, is the last Sanskrit inscription of Cambodia. It shows that, although Hinayana Buddhism, with Pali as its language, must have been gaining ground in the country as a whole (the earliest Pali inscription dates from 1309 and was composed by Shrindravarman after his abdication),[3] Hinduism still survived at the Court. An embassy to China in 1330 may have been sent by Jayavarmaparameshvara, as may also a mission sent to the Cua Rao pass to pay respects to Tran Hien-tong, the Emperor of Viet-nam, which must have encountered the mission sent from Sukhodaya.

No link has yet been found between Jayavarmaparameshvara and the first kings mentioned in the Cambodian chronicles,[4] which begin around the year 1350 with a name that is presumably posthumous: Nirvanapada (*Nippean Bat*). Not only is there a complete break between the kings formerly mentioned in inscriptions and the kings later listed in the chronicles, but there are no reliable dates for these later kings except those of embassies and changes of reign recorded in the Chinese history of the Ming dynasty. Unfortunately this history refers to the Cambodian kings by their reign titles (Samdach, Chao Ponhea), never by their personal or posthumous names, so that it is difficult to identify them with the kings mentioned in either the Cambodian or the Siamese chronicles, which in any case rarely tally.

Apparently between 1350 and 1430 there was an almost permanent state of war between Angkor and Ayudhya. According to the chronicles, the Siamese succeeded at least twice in taking Angkor, the first time in 1352, the second in 1394; but these are sources of dubious reliability.[5] After a period of about thirty years of which nothing certain is known, history only becomes once more firmly based on fact with the reign of the Khmer king, Dhammashokaraja (*Thommeasokareach*), who came under attack from the king of Siam, Paramaraja II (*Boromorach'a*). This resulted in the capture of Angkor – indubitable, this time – in 1431. The Khmer king was killed, and his son Ponhea Yat succeeded him. An immediate decision was made to abandon the capital as being too vulnerable and too difficult to defend. After a brief sojourn at Basan (Srei Santhor) in 1433, the Court, driven away by floods, moved in 1434 to the site where the city of Phnom Penh now stands.[6] There a royal palace was built and a bell-shaped stupa which overlooked the city from an artificial hill in the manner of the temple-mountain of the former capital. Ponhea Yat was crowned in 1441 under the glorious name of Suryavarman (*Soriyopear*), and restored not only peace, but some of its former power to Cambodia. He abdicated in 1459, transmitting the throne first to his eldest, and then to his second son. In 1473 the latter was taken prisoner by the Siamese during a campaign in which Cambodia temporarily lost the provinces of Chandapuri (*Chanthaburi*), Korat, and Angkor. After three years' fighting, Ponhea Yat's third son drove the Siamese out of the country, and was crowned king under the name of Dhammaraja (*Thommoreachea*). He died in 1504. A nephew of his, Ang Chan, after putting down the rebellion of the usurper Kan, established a new capital at Lovek, half-way between the Phnom Penh site and the lower end of the Great Lake. By 1540 the army had been reformed and the country sufficiently reorganized to enable him to repel another Siamese attack. He had a palace built in the new capital, where he was crowned in 1553. Two years later he withstood the attack of a Siamese army near Pursat, after which peace was maintained until the end of his reign, in 1566. He is remembered as one of the greatest of the post-Angkor kings of Cambodia. Possibly it was he who, while on a hunting expedition sometime around 1550–51, so to speak 'discovered' the ancient city of Yashodharapura which had been abandoned for over a century. His successor, Paramaraja (*Boromoreachea*), who died in 1576, settled a few inhabitants there. Paramaraja's son, Satha I, moved the Court to a place near Angkor, and it was then that Angkor was seen for the first time by Europeans – Portuguese missionaries whose accounts are of the greatest interest.[7]

These successors of Ang Chan won some victories against Siam, which at that time was prey to attacks from its neighbour to the west. But in 1590 Nareshvara came to power in Ayudhya and put the Burmese to flight in 1592. The following year he returned to the fight against Cambodia, and marched on Lovek, which he took in January 1594, procuring a large amount of booty. Satha I took refuge in Laos with his two elder sons, and died there. Meanwhile a usurper had superseded him in Cambodia, and it required the intervention of two Europeans, the Portuguese Diogo Veloso and the Spaniard Blas Ruiz de Hernan Gonzalez, and two expeditions sent from Manilla, one in 1596 and the other in 1598, to place a son of the late king named Ponhea Tan on the throne (Paramaraja II). In 1599 Ponhea Tan met his end through assassination at the hands of some Malays who several months before had taken advantage of an incident that had arisen to massacre the Spaniards stationed in a camp near Phnom Penh. He was succeeded by his uncle, Ponhea An, second son of Paramaraja I and brother of Satha. But he in turn was assassinated, after reigning as Paramaraja III for a year. The high dignitaries of the kingdom then obtained the consent of Siam for the release of Prince Suryavarman (*Soriyopear*), who had been kept in captivity since the capture of

Lovek; and they proclaimed him king sometime around 1603. In the interim Ponhea Nhom, Satha's third son, had acted as regent.

In 1618 Suryavarman, or Paramaraja IV, abdicated in favour of his son Jayajettha (*Chei Chettha*), who built himself a palace at Oudong, which is situated between Lovek and Phnom Penh, and who in 1620 married a Vietnamese princess, the daughter of King Sai Vuong of the Nguyen dynasty. The marriage was celebrated with great pomp and ceremony, and had far-reaching consequences, because thanks to the princess, an embassy from southern Viet-nam was able, in 1623, to obtain the Cambodian king's authorization for the establishment of a custom-house at Prei Kor, the site of the present city of Saigon, and this was one of the things leading to Vietnamese settlement in the Mekong delta. It was during Jayajettha's reign that the Dutch established a factory at Phnom Penh, despite Portuguese opposition. Jayajettha died about 1625.

After several intervening reigns, there was a palace revolt in January 1642, and Prince Chan, a son of Jayajettha whose mother was a Laotian, proclaimed himself king under the name of Ramadhipati (*Reameathipdei*). A short time afterwards he became converted to Islam and surrounded himself with Malay and Javanese immigrants. It was apparently at their instigation that in 1364 he ordered the massacre of all the Dutch residing at Phnom Penh, including their warehouse manager, Pierre de Regemortes. But faced with the threat of an alliance between the Dutch and the Siamese, the 'apostate king' agreed, in 1646–47, to hand back some of the prisoners and merchandise that had been seized. The peace treaty concluded in 1655 granted an indemnity to the Dutch East India Company, but did not give it the trade monopoly it had sought to obtain. These events more or less marked the end of European commercial dealings with Cambodia.

Meanwhile, those Cambodians who were opposed to the apostate king and his Malay entourage had formed a group round two princes who were the sons of the former king, Jayajettha, and the Vietnamese princess. They sought support from their cousin, Hien Vuong, the second successor of Sai Vuong; and in 1658 an army was sent which captured the apostate king and replaced him with Padumaraja (*Batumreachea*), the elder of the two princes.

Padumaraja reigned from 1660 until 1672, and upon his death, a struggle for the succession ensued between a son of Ang Non and a son of Ang Sor. The former was supported by the southern Vietnamese, but was finally defeated, and died at Saigon in 1691. This fratricidal struggle was the prelude to a series of civil wars which cannot be described in detail here. They provided an excuse for both southern Viet-nam and Siam to intervene in Cambodian internal affairs, greatly to the detriment of Cambodia's territorial integrity, since the aid supplied by either neighbour was never given free. These struggles filled the whole of the eighteenth century. We shall see in the following chapter how the southern Vietnamese took advantage of Cambodia's weakness and ended by occupying most of the Mekong delta through a process of slow but steady infiltration.

Finally, during the very last years of the eighteenth century Cambodia suffered the amputation – *de facto* if not *de jure* – of its western provinces (Battambang and Siem Reap) in the following manner. Because of internal troubles in Cambodia, the newly proclaimed king, Ang Eng, had to take refuge in Siam, where the first king of the Bangkok dynasty was reigning. He was crowned at Bangkok in 1794, and then returned to his own country accompanied by a Siamese army for his protection. The army was in the command of a Cambodian high official named Ben, who had been appointed as governor of Battambang by the King of Siam, and who, after restoring Ang Eng as king, withdrew there with his Siamese army. Battambang, together with the province of Siem Reap, thereafter became his family fief; for although in theory the two provinces remained Cambodian soil, their governor received his orders from the King of Siam, by whom he had been appointed and to whom the army of occupation belonged; and after the army returned to Siam, Ben continued to collect the revenue for his own use. But he made regular presents to the King of Siam which came to be regarded as a tribute of vassalage which his descendants continued to pay after his death. This was the way in which these provinces were annexed by Siam, without any written treaty of ratification.

Ang Eng died in 1796 and was succeeded by his son, Ang Chan, who was crowned at Bangkok in 1806. On his return to Cambodia, he immediately sent tribute to Viet-nam, a custom which had started during the reign of Ang Non. Thus by the beginning of the nineteenth century the descendants of the kings of Angkor received their crown at the hands of the kings of Siam and paid tribute to the emperors of Viet-nam.

In 1811 Ang Chan sought Vietnamese aid against Siam, which was giving support to one of his brothers. He had to take refuge in Saigon in 1812, but was finally restored to his throne in 1813 by Emperor Gia-long. In retaliation, the Siamese occupied the northern provinces of Cambodia, and in 1832 Ang Chan again had to flee the Siamese and take refuge in southern Viet-nam. The Siamese army was under the command of General P'raya Bodin, the general who four years earlier had ravaged Vieng Chan; it advanced as far as Chaudoc and Vinh-long, but had to withdraw when faced by the Vietnamese forces. Ang Chan returned to Oudong in 1833; but the southern Vietnamese general, Truong Minh Giang, remained there to keep an eye on things.

When Ang Chan died in 1834, Truong Minh Giang managed to prevent both his brothers, who were vassals of Siam, from coming to power, and placed a daughter of the late king, the Princess Ang Mei, on the throne as nominal ruler under the suzerainty of Viet-nam. Her reign lasted from 1835 to 1841, when she went into exile at Hué; for meanwhile the Cambodian ministers, anxious to loosen the hold of Viet-nam, had obtained permission from the Court at Bangkok for the release of Ang Chan's younger brother, Prince Ang Duong. The Siamese army that brought Ang Duong to Cambodia was again commanded by General P'raya Bodin. At first it met with defeat at the hands of the Vietnamese in 1842, but finally it got the upper hand, and in December 1845 a treaty (ratified in 1846) was concluded between the three interested parties, whereby Ang Duong became king of Cambodia and Ang Mei was set at liberty. Delegates from both Bangkok and Hué attended the coronation of Ang Duong at the end of 1847, and in 1848 P'raya Bodin returned to Siam.

Cambodia continued, however, to have inroads made on her territory by Siam in the north and Viet-nam in the south; so in 1854 Ang Duong decided to send an emissary to the French consul in Singapore to ask for French aid. France sent a mission in 1855, but it failed owing to the mismanagement of its leader, the consul de Montigny; and the following year Ang Duong, who felt that his strength was failing, asked the Court at Bangkok to send his eldest son to him, who succeeded him in 1859 under the name of Norodom.

In March 1861 Admiral Charner, who was in command of the French forces occupying Saigon, sent the new king a message of friendship; and in September of the following year Norodom, on his return from Bangkok, where he had taken refuge and sollicited aid to counter the rebellion led by his brother, Si Votha, received a visit from Admiral Bonard, who had been charged with the task of establishing Viet-nam's ancient rights of suzerainty over Cambodia in order to counteract Siamese claims. Negotiations carried out by Captain Doudart de Lagrée enabled Admiral La Grandière, the governor of Cochin-china, to sign a treaty at Oudong in July 1863 establishing a French protectorate over Cambodia. But before France could ratify the treaty, Siamese delegates had forced Norodom to sign another treaty accepting Siamese suzerainty. Doudart de Legrée had the presence of mind to prevent Norodom from going to Bangkok, where the royal insignia were kept, to be crowned there; and immediately upon receipt of ratification for the protectorate from France, the coronation took place at Oudong on 3 July 1864, when the crown, which had been brought from Bangkok, was received from the hands of the French representative. Soon after this, however, a Franco-Siamese treaty, ratified in 1867 by Napoleon III, ceded to Siam the provinces of Battambang, Siem Reap, and Sisiphon; and it was not until 1907, under the reign of King Sisovath (1904–27), that Cambodia recovered possession of these provinces.

Ever since its decline in the thirteenth century, Cambodia had ceased to play the political role it had formerly played in Indochina; yet it continued to exercise a great deal of cultural influence on the two States – the Siamese kingdom of Ayudhya, and the Laotian kingdom of Lan Ch'ang – which were founded in the middle of the fourteenth century in territories which had belonged to, or were dependencies of, Cambodia. Later, however, Cambodian civilization in its turn came under the influence of Siam in a number of spheres, particularly those of religion, literature, and art.

With regard to religion, it has been mentioned above how King Mongkut of Siam introduced religious reforms in order to counteract superstition and enforce a stricter discipline among his Buddhist clergy, and how these reforms spread in aristocratic circles in Cambodia. In architecture, later styles in Cambodia differ little from those in Siam. It is true that both descend from the same prototypes of buildings in perishable materials represented in the bas-reliefs of Angkor, which give some idea of what the earliest prototypes must have been like; but late Cambodian architecture must undoubtedly have come under direct Siamese influence.

In a more specialized field – that of vocabulary – a curious phenomenon is to be observed: the Cambodian language reborrowed from Siamese certain Khmer loan-words which had been borrowed by Siamese when it first evolved as a language, but which were no longer recognized as being of Khmer origin after they had undergone the changes of pronunciation inflicted upon them when used by a T'ai-speaking people.

As regards literature, the oldest poem in Cambodian that can be dated with certainty is an inscription of 1702.[8] It is one of a number of seventeenth and eighteenth-century inscriptions found on the walls of Angkor Vat, describing, with fervent piety, the ceremonies performed in the Buddhist shrine that had formerly been a Vaishnavite temple. Otherwise all that remains of the ancient literature based on Indian models are a few cosmological fragments rather grandly known as the *Traiveda* (*Traipet*), and the *Ramakirti* (*Ream Ker*), a piece for the theatre of uncertain date drawing upon the most frequently performed episodes of the Ramayana. All later Cambodian literature is so to speak divorced from the ancient civilization of the country. Sinhalese Buddhism, which did little to foster art and literature, had a disintegrating effect on the civilization of Angkor.

There is a great difference between spoken or written Cambodian prose and the language used in poetry, which is full of archaic words and loan-words from Pali and Sanskrit. As a result, the Cambodians themselves often have difficulty in understanding the classical poems of their literature. These poems are for the most part anonymous and undated. The best known of them are the collections of gnomic stanzas – some of which may indeed date from quite early times – such as the *Chbap Kram* or code of etiquette, the *Chbap Pros* ('Morals for Boys'), the *Chbap Srei* ('Morals for Girls', attributed to King Ang Duong), the *Ker Kal*, *Kon Chau*, etc. These combine the precepts of Buddhism with the traditional codes of formal behaviour, and they provide the Cambodians, who are brought up from childhood on them, with rules of conduct for all the occasions they are likely to meet with in their lives.

A large part of Cambodian prose literature consists of religious texts: translations of canonical texts or treatises of exegesis in which the discussion of merits acquired by the faithful as a result of good works holds an important place. Adaptations of the early lives of the Buddha – especially the last ten – have enjoyed great popularity, the most popular of all being the Vessantarajataka; and as in Siam and Laos, the apocryphal Fifty Jataka have supplied the themes for a number of novels.

The spoken language – and folk humour too – finds its best expression in tales and fables,[9] the study of which invites comparison with the Indian Panchatantra collections and Tales of the Vampire. But the figure of Thmenh Chei (the Cambodian version of Dhananjaya, as he is known in Siam and Laos), who is a sort of Till Eulenspiegel, and also those of the Hare Judge and the Four Bald Men, are typically Cambodian in character.

Most Cambodian verse consists of romances based on the legends of the Rama cycle or those of the Fifty Jataka. Cambodian drama, closely linked with these romances, draws from the same sources, and has been strongly influenced by Siamese dramatic works.

It was in its songs[10] that Cambodia found fullest and most spontaneous expression for its own particular genius.

5

Viet-nam

AS MENTIONED in an earlier chapter, the Tran dynasty of Viet-nam set up the Cham prince, Che Nang, as puppet ruler of Champa; but when, in 1314, the emperor, Tran Anh-tong, followed the usual procedure and abdicated in favour of his son, Tran Minh-tong, Che Nang seized the opportunity to make an attempt to reconquer the Cham provinces north of the Col des Nuages. The attempt failed, and in 1318 Tran Minh-tong removed Che Nang and put in his place a military commander named Che A-nan. But he in turn made a determined effort to become inde-pendent, and called upon Mongol aid. After a victory over Vietnamese troops in 1326 he did in fact free himself from Tran domination, and ceased to pay tribute. It was during his reign that Champa was visited by the Franciscan monk Oderic de Pordonone.[1]

Tran Minh-tong was followed by two of his sons – first by Tran Hien-tong, in favour of whom he abdicated in 1329, and who remained in power until 1341; and then by Tran Du-tong (1341–69), who in 1353 had to repel a Cham attempt to reconquer the region of Hué, and then had to counter the first attacks of King Che Bong Nga of Champa in 1361 and 1368.

Nothing is known about the origins of Che Bong Nga, whose reign must have begun about 1360. Profiting at first from the fall from power of the Mongols, and then by coming to terms with the first ruler of the Ming dynasty in China, who recognized him as King of Champa in 1369, Che Bong Nga conducted an uninterrupted series of victorious campaigns against his northern neighbour between 1361 and 1390.

In 1369 Tran Du-tong died without an heir, and was succeeded by another son of Tran Minh-tong, who reigned from 1370 to 1372 under the name of Tran Nghe-tong. The queen-mother, who had hoped to bring another prince to the throne, fled to Champa and urged Che Bong Nga, who had meanwhile received Chinese recognition, to attack Viet-nam from the sea. In 1371 the Chams reached the capital, which they set fire to and sacked. Emperor Tran Nghe-tong abdicated in 1372 in favour of his brother Tran Due-tong, who conceived the bold plan of carrying the war into Cham territory. His campaign ended in disaster, and he himself met his death in 1377. Che Bong Nga lost no time in setting sail for Viet-nam, and arrived before the capital just as the retired emperor, Tran Nghe-tong, was about to crown his nephew Tran De Nghien (a son of Tran Due-tong). The city was sacked once again.

The new emperor had to face further Cham raids between 1378 and 1384. Che Bong Nga seemed bent on gaining control of the delta; but a successful defence was put up by a high official of Chinese origin named Le Quy Ly, who was connected with the imperial family. He was greatly trusted by the former emperor, Tran Nghe-tong, who, in his retirement, continued to direct affairs; hence he was able to bring about the abdication, and finally the assassination, of Tran De Nghien. In 1388 one of the old emperor's sons, Tran Thuan-tong, was put on the throne. The following year the Chams conducted another victorious campaign which brought them into the delta; but in February 1390 Che Bong Nga was assassinated, and his armies fell back. His successor, La Khai (1390–1400), had to hand back the provinces to the north of the Col des Nuages.

Viet-nam had been saved; but the dynasty only lasted for another ten years. Emperor Tran Nghe-tong died at last in 1394 at the age of seventy-four. Shortly after his death, Le Quy Ly forced the reigning emperor, Tran Thuan-tong, to abdicate, and placed one of his sons, who was barely three years old, on the throne. The new emperor happened to be a grandson of Le Quy Ly himself through the maternal line. He reigned nominally from 1398 to 1400 under the regency of his all-powerful grandfather. Le Quy Ly then forced him to abdicate in his own favour, which meant that the Tran dynasty had virtually ceased to exist.

The attacks which this dynasty had had to face, both from the Mongols and from the Chams, had not prevented it from continuing the work of its predecessors as far as internal affairs were concerned. Its chief innovations had been the classification of rice-fields into various categories and the payment of a land-tax in kind reckoned according to the amount of land owned; the introduction of a poll-tax applying only to landowners; and the construction of embankments along the Red River right down to the sea. The country had been divided into twelve provinces, and was administered by a fully-staffed hierarchical system of scholar-officials, whose prestige had been heightened by the increased emphasis placed on the examination system of recruitment, and by the greater impressiveness of their titles.

The Tran dynasty promoted the rise of literature using the Chinese language as its medium, but much of the work produced during the Tran dynasty period has perished. A bibliographical list was drawn up last century by the great historian Phan Huy Chu and includes manuals of ritual, legal codes, and military treatises. Poetry is represented by poems composed by several of the emperors as well as works by Nguyen Trung Ngan, Chu An, and Nguyen Phi Khanh, to mention only the names that are best known. Two historical works also date from this period: the *Dai Viet su-ky* or 'Historical records of Dai Viet', by Le Van Huu, and the *Viet su cuong muc* by Ho Ton Thoc.

Tran dynasty art was primarily Buddhist art. The style of the few buildings that have survived is heavier and bulkier than that of earlier periods. It is typified by a tower built in 1310 in front of the Tuc-mac pagoda in Mam-dinh province.

When Le Quy Ly proclaimed himself emperor he reassumed the surname Ho, which had been that of his Chinese ancestors, and under the name of Ho Quy Ly he founded the short-lived Ho dynasty. He renamed the country Ta Yü (*Dai Ngu*) after the legendary Chinese emperor, Yü the Great, from whom he claimed to be descended; and he founded a new imperial capital in Than-hoa province. The new capital was built in the form of a square measuring over 500 yards on each side, and was strongly fortified by an earthen rampart faced with freestone and pierced on each side by a huge stone gateway, the gate on the south side having three entrances. No surface traces of the buildings inside remain, but their ground-plan – particularly that of the palace situated in the centre of the citadel – can be clearly seen on aerial photographs. The entry stairway to the palace has been identified by means of the remains of two balustrades in the form of dragons. The city gateways are built of huge blocks of limestone, which according to calculations must weigh sixteen tons. They are extremely well built, and a notable feature is that they have keystone arches.

After reigning for eight months, Ho Quy Ly abdicated in favour of his son, Ho Han Thuong (1400-07). But in Ming China the enfeeblement of Viet-nam had been followed with close interest and attention, and at the combined request of the Chams and of Tran dynasty loyalists, Chinese armies were sent to Viet-nam in 1405 and again in 1407, when Ho Quy Ly and his son were taken prisoner and led away to China, where they died. The country was annexed and placed under the authority of a Chinese governor, who tried to restore the former régime. Champa was handed back the province corresponding to present Quang-nam, which it had had to relinquish in 1402.

China's annexation of the country provoked a Vietnamese resistance movement led by a younger son of the emperor, Tran Nghe-tong, and after 1409 by a nephew. Chinese reprisals were ferocious, and the country remained under Ming domination until 1418, when Le Loi, the head of a peasant family in Than-hoa province and the great hero of Vietnamese history, rallied and reorganized the nationalist forces.

In 1418, at the head of an army recruited from his native district, he embarked upon a struggle against the Chinese that was to last for ten years. He gradually occupied the low country and forced the Chinese to fall back on positions in fortified strongholds. In 1424–25 he took Tay-do, the Ho dynasty capital, and in 1426 he seized Dong-do (Hanoi). At the beginning of 1428 the former Court dignitaries offered him the throne of Dai Viet, and the Ming recognized his accession in exchange for acceptance of their suzerainty.

Le Loi, known by his posthumous name Le Thai-to, died in 1433, and was succeeded by his son, Le Thai-tong, who, during his reign of nine years, undertook the heavy task of reorganizing the finances of the country after the impoverishment caused by the wars. His successors, Le Nhan-tong (1442–59), and Le

Thanh-tong (1460–97) – the greatest king of the dynasty – continued his work and finally brought Champa under their control. During the time of the Chinese occupation Jaya Simhavarman V had eagerly grasped the opportunity to retake the northern provinces. He died in 1441, and five years later Le Nhan-tong sent an army to Champa which took the capital and made the new king prisoner. In 1471 it was Le Thanh-tong's turn to seize the first occasion for invading Champa; the capital was taken once again, and the whole of the northern part of the country occupied, as far as Cape Varella. On his western borders, Le Thanh-tong made the Laotian kingdom of Lan Ch'ang recognize his suzerainty.

The following reigns were all very short. That of Le Hien-tong, the son of Le Thanh-tong, lasted from 1497 to 1504; his son, Le Tuc-tong, had a reign lasting only for the year 1504; while that of the latter's brother, Le Uy Muc, lasted from 1504 to 1509. A revolt then brought to power another grandson of Le Thanh-tong, Le Tuong Duc (1509–16), who was assassinated by the high official Trinh Duy San, and replaced, after an interim when there was no ruler, by a great grandson of Le Thanh-tong who was crowned under the name of Le Chieu-tong (1516–26). Internal dissensions were threatening to ruin the country. The Le dynasty continued in theory to be the sole legitimate power, but from the beginning of Le Chieu-tong's reign there was in fact an open struggle for power between three families – the Mac, the Trinh, and the Nguyen – which continued throughout the first half of the sixteenth century and finally led to the partition of Viet-nam into two distinct political entities.[2]

In 1524 General Mac Dang Dung took advantage of his success in putting down a rebellion that had forced Le Chieu-tong to leave the capital, and seized power for himself. He obtained recognition from China in 1527. Meanwhile Nguyen Kim, a high official who remained loyal to the Le dynasty, had fled to Laos and raised an army there, and in 1533 he set up another emperor – Le Trang-tong, the son of Le Chieu-tong. In the southern part of the now divided empire one legitimate emperor after another was restored during the years 1539 to 1541. In 1545 Nguyen Kim was assassinated; but this did not improve the position of the Mac family, for they now found themselves opposed both by Nguyen Hoang, the second son of Nguyen Kim, and by Trinh Kiem, Nguyen Kim's son-in-law and successor. In 1591 Trinh Tung, the son of

Trinh Kiem, put up a successful resistance to the Mac in the Red River delta, and restored the Le dynasty in its capital, Thang-long (Hanoi), in 1592. The Mac withdrew to the region of Cao-bang, which remained a centre of revolt until they were finally eliminated in 1677.

Meanwhile Nguyen Hoang, thoroughly distrustful of his brother-in-law Trinh Kiem, had had himself appointed governor of the southern provinces (from Quang-binh to Quang-nam), and in 1558 he left the capital to take over his administrative duties. This is an important date in Vietnamese history, because while Nguyen Hoang proceeded to pacify the south and to carve out a fief for himself there after getting it under his control, Trinh Kiem and his family gradually acquired all the important posts at the Court of the Le. Conflict soon arose between the Nguyen, who regarded the Trinh as usurpers and refused to pay taxes, and the Trinh, who professed to be trying to establish the rightful rule of the Le emperors over the southern provinces; but it did not become acute until after the end of the century.[3] By 1660 the country was in fact divided into two: the Red River delta area in the north, ruled over by the Trinh, and the south, under Nguyen rule. The Le emperors continued to be regarded as the legitimate rulers by both sides, each of whom accused the other of rebellion. The river Song Gianh, which runs through the northern part of the present province of Quang-binh, marked the frontier between the two rival States.

Fighting broke out between them after 1620 and continued until 1673, with successive changes of fortune on both sides. Finally the Nguyen won recognition from the Trinh as independent rulers with a kingdom stretching from the Song Gianh to Cape Varella. The Nguyen had had the advantage of very effective aid from the Portuguese and the Dutch, to whom they had given a good reception and who had established themselves in the country; whereas the Trinh had not succeeded in attracting foreigners to their country and were therefore reduced to relying entirely upon their own resources.

This fifty-year war was followed by a century of peace (1674–1774), during which the Trinh managed to take all effective power out of the hands of the Le emperors, while the Nguyen little by little extended their territory towards the south. This was an important period in the history of Viet-nam, both because of the many administrative measures carried through by the Trinh in the name of the Le in the north, and because of the consequences of Nguyen expansion into the Cambodian provinces in the Mekong delta in the south.

The Nguyen reached Qui-nhon in 1602, Phu-yen and Song-cau in 1611, and the provinces of Nha-trang and Phan-rang in 1653. During the reign of Nguyen Phuoc Tan (Hien Vuong, 1648–87), the son of Nguyen Phuoc Lan (Cong Thuong Vuong, 1635–48), and grandson of Nguyen Phuoc Nguyen (Sai Vuong, 1613–35), they seized the first opportunity that offered of getting rid of the petty Cham kings, who were still vegetating in the region of Phan-ri.

During the last centuries of their existence as a political entity, the Chams erected one or two buildings, but in a style that betrays the drying-up of their sources of inspiration, as instanced by the seventeenth-century Po Romé. Their late sculptural style shows signs of degeneracy. Statues tend to be reduced to a torso, or to a head emerging from a block of stone, until finally only the stone is left in the form of a simple stele.

Farther south, Cambodia was gradually being infiltrated. The first immigrants consisted of vagabonds, deserters, and other undesirables who had been banished from their villages. Once they had settled down, they were joined by settlers sent by the Nguyen government from the poorer provinces; and these in turn were followed by soldiers freed from military service to whom the Nguyen had granted land. We have seen that in 1623 the King of Cambodia, after marrying a southern Vietnamese princess, authorized the setting up of a custom-house on the site of the present city of Saigon. In 1658 the Nguyen took Mo-xoai (present Baria), and after that intervened openly in Cambodian affairs, and occupied Saigon, Kampot, and Phnom Penh. In 1679 Hien Vuong sent Chinese refugees to colonize the region of Gia-dinh, but upon their arrival by sea at the mouths of the Mekong some of them settled at My-tho, and the rest went up the river Dong-nai and settled in the region of Bien-hoa. Later they annexed the whole of the Dong-nai valley, after the death of the Cambodian king, Ang Non, who was a vassal of the Nguyen. In 1698 this region was divided into three districts, corresponding to the present provinces of Gia-dinh, Bien-hoa, and Saigon.[4]

In the north, during the first three-quarters of the century of peace between the Trinh and the Nguyen, Trinh Cuong (1709–29) and his son Trinh Giang (1729–40) governed well, continuing the work of their predecessors. When the latter was in power several rebellions broke out, the most serious of which was that fomented by the princes of the Le imperial family in 1737. One of the rebels, Le Duy Mat by name, succeeded in gathering a large following in the south-west of the country, and on receiving news of the death of Trinh Giang's son, Trinh Dinh, who had succeeded his father in 1767, he marched on the capital. But Trinh Sam, the new mayor of the palace (1767–82), forced Le Duy Mat to retreat to his residence, where he committed suicide.

After this success, Trinh Sam considered that the time had come to go into the attack against the Nguyen. On the excuse of providing support against the Tay-son rebellion (discussed below) which had just broken out in the region of Qui-nhon, he launched an expedition against the south. Nguyen Phuoc Thuan (Hue Vuong, 1765–78) was unable to halt the northern armies at the wall of Dong-hoi, built by Sai Vuong to defend his northern frontier. The wall was razed to the ground, and Hue Vuong had to flee his capital (Hué), which was entered by Trinh Sam's army in 1775 and remained under occupation for twelve years. Meanwhile the Tay-son rebellion continued in full swing in the south, and the last two of the Trinh family, Trinh Khai (1782–86) and Trinh Phung (1786–87), met their end in the general turmoil.

Something should be said here about the cultural aspects of the Le dynasty period in Viet-nam (1418–1786).

Once external affairs had been set in order, the first emperors were able to concentrate on the reorganization of the internal administrative system. Whilst preserving everything that had been borrowed from China – the language used by the educated, literature, art, religion, and the system of administration by officials – they nevertheless made an effort to free themselves from their intellectual ties of vassalage to that country. This effort is nowhere more clearly illustrated than by the Code of Hong-duc, compiled in 1483, which, far from slavishly copying Chinese legislation of the time, attempts to codify all the laws and regulations promulgated by emperors of previous dynasties within one traditional framework. This task in the field of national jurisprudence had been preceded by the carring out of a similar task in the religious field in 1472, consisting of a revision of all the legends concerning the local gods which played the role of patron for each and every village. In addition, a large number of administrative, fiscal, and agrarian measures provided the country with institutions which had hitherto been lacking.

The Le period is the golden age of Sino-Vietnamese literature, in which the outstanding names are Nguyen Trai (the first half of the fifteenth century), who, inspired by nationalist sentiments, wrote a proclamation to the people;[5] the emperor, Le Thanh-tong, who wrote the 'Nine Songs of the Garden of the Immortals'; Nguyen Binh Khiem (died in 1585); and Dang Tran Con (second half of the eighteenth century), who wrote the 'Song of the soldier's wife'. The *Dai Viet su-ky* or 'Historical Records of the Great Viet', begun in 1479 by Ngo Si Lien, and the 'General Mirror of Dai Viet' completed in 1511 by Vu Quynh, demonstrate the interest evinced by writers of this period in historical studies. Le Quy Don (1726–84) is regarded as the most notable all-round talent of the period. He was the son of a minister, and himself an official, and he was sent on a mission to China in 1759. He is the author of a 'History of Dai Viet', of an account of the embassy to China, and of collections of poems, literary and philosophical essays, an explanation of the Chinese classic, the *Shu-ching*, and other works.

As regards art, the whole country was covered with buildings dating from the first quarter of the fifteenth century to the end of the eighteenth, many of which still survive and still preserve their original appearance despite numerous repairs and restorations. The Le dynasty period was the great period of Vietnamese art, the prime examples of which are the tombs of the early Le emperors at Lam-son in Than-hoa province. These tombs now lie buried in a thick forest, with the ceremonial alleyways leading to them marked out by fallen bricks and tiles which are all that remains of the halls and gateways that once stood there. A magnificent stairway flanked with dragons is still intact, and the commemorative steles are large, handsome limestone slabs, rounded at the top, and placed on top of tortoises. The similarity with the tombs of the Ming emperors is obvious. But the buildings erected by the Le at Hoa-lu, the former capital of the Dinh, show how Vietnamese artists were able to give an individual and original interpretation of Chinese themes. Also dating from the Le period are the remains of the ancient palace within the citadel of Hanoi, including the outstandingly magnificent dragon balustrades of the stairway.

The history of the Nguyen in the eighteenth century is closely linked with that of Cambodia, where incessant internal dissensions enabled them to continue expanding their territory ever farther at the expense of that unfortunate country. We have seen how in the previous century they had established their dominion over the Dong-nai valley. At the beginning of the eighteenth century, under the reign of Nguyen Phuoc Chu (Minh Vuong, 1691–1725), they gained protection over the Cambodian province of Banteay Meas, on the Gulf of Siam. The governor of this province, a Chinese named Mac Cuu,[6] began by administering it on behalf of the King of Cambodia, but later found it more opportune to seek the protection of the Nguyen of southern Viet-nam.

In 1731 Nguyen Phuoc Tru (Ninh Vuong, 1725–38), who had succeeded his father, Minh Vuong, annexed the Cambodian provinces of Vinh-long and My-tho; and sixteen years later Nguyen Phuoc Khoat (Vo Vuong, 1738–65) put troops at the disposal of some rebel Cambodian princes, who took Basak (present Soc-trang) and then marched on Oudong, where King Ang Tong had just been crowned. Ang Tong requested aid from Mac Thien Tu, the son of Mac Cuu, and Mac Thien Tu arranged a truce with Vo Vuong in exchange for the cession of the districts of Go-cong and Tan-an. In 1757 a rival of Ang Tong, known under the name of Utei, succeeded, with the help of Vo Vuong and Mac Thien Tu, in seizing the Cambodian crown, and repaid their services first by handing over five other districts, including Kampot and Kompong Som, and then by finally ceding the provinces of Basak and Prah Trapeang (Soc-trang and Tra-vinh), which had in effect been occupied since 1683. In 1765, the year of Vo Vuong's death, the territory belonging to the Nguyen of southern Viet-nam extended from the Song Gianh to the present frontiers of Cambodia; and that of Mac Thien Tu, who was a vassal of the Nguyen, extended from Kampot to Ca-mau.

When Vo Vuong died, the irregular succession of his sixteenth son, Nguyen Phuoc Thuan (Hue Vuong), and the exactions of the regent gave rise to a troubled situation which was exploited by three brothers whose native district was Tay-son, on the An-khe plateau in Binhdinh province. With their capture in 1773 of Qui-nhon, they gained control over the whole central area of southern Viet-nam. As we have seen, this was the moment chosen by Trinh Sam for his attack against the south. The capital fell in 1775 and Hue Vuong fled to the south, taking his family with him, including his nephew, Nguyen Anh, the son of the prince who had been dispossessed in favour of Hue Vuong.

Nguyen Anh was the only Nguyen to survive the massacre carried out by the victorious rebels of Tay-son, now masters of Saigon. He found refuge among the Christians of Ha-tien, in the house of a French missionary named Pigneau de Béhaine, who was Bishop of Adran. After his short-lived reconquest of Saigon (1780–82), Nguyen Anh asked his former benefactor to procure the aid of the French. The Bishop of Adran went to Versailles, where he pleaded the cause of the Nguyen; and on 28 November 1787 he obtained a treaty by which France promised to send an expeditionary force to southern Viet-nam in exchange for the port of Tourane (Danang), the island of Poulo Condo, and complete freedom of trade. But the treaty was never fulfilled, and the reconquest on behalf of the Nguyen of what was later to be Cochinchina was the work of a handful of officers and volunteers from the French Navy whose enthusiasm had been aroused by the Bishop of Adran.[7] Nguyen Anh once again became master of southern Viet-nam in 1789; but it was not until 1801 that he finally got the better of the Tay-son rebels in the course of a naval engagement off Qui-nhon. The following year northern Viet-nam, formerly the territory of the Trinh, submitted, and in 1802 Nguyen Anh was able to have himself crowned as sole monarch of a united empire which included the former domains of the Nguyen, the lower part of the Mekong delta, and the whole of northern Viet-nam. In 1803 China gave its recognition to Nguyen Anh, thereafter known as Gia-long, by bestowing the official name of Viet-nam on the whole of his united empire.

His son Minh-mang, who succeeded him in 1820, adopted quite a different policy towards the West, which resulted in religious persecution. This reached an acute stage during the reigns of Thieu-tri (1841–47) and Tu-duc (1848–83); and when two missionaries were put to death in 1851–52, and a Spanish bishop tortured in 1857, France decided to intervene, and was supported by Spanish forces. An expedition arrived off Tourane (Danang) on 31 August 1858 and destroyed its forts; but when Admiral Rigault de Genouilly found it impossible to complete the operation, he decided to occupy the port of Saigon (18 February 1859).

Soon the garrison of Saigon had to be reduced to eight hundred men on account of the second French campaign against China, and a Vietnamese army laid siege to the city. In 1861 Admiral Charner, returning from his victorious campaign in China, came to its relief. The battle of Chi-hoa (25 February 1861) gave him control over the provinces of Gia-dinh, My-tho, Thu-dau-mot, and parts of Bien-hoa and Go-cong. It was not long before the Court at Hué asked to come to terms, and on June 5th its plenipotentiaries signed a treaty with Admiral Bonard ceding to France the three eastern provinces in the Mekong delta. The Marquis de Chasseloup-Laubat obtained its ratification from Napoleon III, who was at that time involved in the expedition to Mexico. In 1867 the three western provinces were occupied without resistance, and thus the French colony of Cochin-china came into being.

During the Nguyen period Sino-Vietnamese literature, which is written in Chinese characters and can be read by anyone who knows Chinese, continued to be produced. Much of the poetry was written by the emperors themselves. History is represented by three important works: the *Institutions of all the Dynasties* by Phan Huy Chu (1821), the *Description of Gia-dinh* by Trinh Hoai Duc, and the *Description of Dai Nam* by Cao Xuan Duc. But the outstanding feature of the period was the rise of a literature in the Vietnamese language.

To write their own language, the Vietnamese either had recourse to *chu-nom* – the use of Chinese characters modified according to principles which varied with each individual author – or later to *quoc-ngu*, a romanization invented by Catholic missionaries, the chief inventor being Father Alexandre de Rhodes, whose version dates from 1651. Quoc-ngu or 'national script' is the only system in use today.

Few works in Vietnamese exist dating from earlier than the end of the eighteenth century, and the best known are those written during the nineteenth century.[8] Of the oldest works, mention might be made of the *Family Instructions* by Nguyen Trai (first half of the fifteenth century), and Doan Thi Diem's translation, the 'Complaints of the soldier's wife', from the poem by Dang Tran Con already referred to in the remarks concerning the literature of the Le period. Most of the extant works consist of poems, proverbs, couplets, and songs. The best known of the nineteenth-century poets writing in the national language are Ho Xuan Huong, Nguyen Cong Tru, Chu Manh Trinh, and Tran Ke Xuong.

The most interesting works, however, are the moral tales in verse. The most famous of these is the *Thuy Kieu* or *Kim Van Kieu*,[9] written in a learned, literary style, but enjoyed nevertheless by the common people just as much as by the cultured *élite*. It was composed in 1813 by Nguyen Du (1765–1820) who was appointed by the emperor, Gia-long, to various official posts. He is also the author of poems in Chinese, and of an 'Address to the Dead' in the national language (1792). The *Kim Van Kieu*, with its 3,253 lines of verse, was the first work to make the literati feel that the Vietnamese language was worthy of their attention, and that raised it to the dignity of a literary language. The theme of the poem is taken from a Chinese novel of the end of the eighteenth century. It is based on the Buddhist idea of the retribution that follows upon acts committed in former lives, and on the Confucian idea of filial piety and loyalty to the prince. Some passages are simply translated from the Chinese; but the author has introduced his own additions and omissions, and produced a work of incomparable harmoniousness of style and perfection of form.

After the *Kim Van Kieu*, the best known of these verse tales is the *Luc Van Tien*,[10] of which the first edition, in *chu-nom*, dates from 1865. It was written by Nguyen Dinh Chieu (1822–88), who belonged to a family of southern Vietnamese officials. He was the author of a number of other poetical works, some of them of considerable length, and all full of Confucian moralizing.

Along with the verse tale, the drama was greatly cultivated by Vietnamese authors writing in their own language. Most of the plays are taken from the Chinese repertory, the main source being those based on the historical romance called *San Kuo Chih yen-i* or 'Romance of the Three Kingdoms'. The characters are those of the Chinese theatre, and wear the traditional costumes, headdresses, and masks. Among the published plays may be mentioned the *Kim Thach Ky-duyen* or 'Miraculous union of Kim and Thach', [11] written in *chu-nom* script shortly before 1860 by Bui Quang Nghia (1807–72). The theme is taken from a Chinese semihistorical work probably dating from the end of the eighteenth century, and the action takes place during the Sung dynasty, and has absolutely no unity of either time or place. The lines are in different metres according to the nature of the passage in question.

In the poetry written in Vietnamese, poetic form may be based on Chinese models, such as the five or seven syllable line in groups of four or eight (great variety being introduced by the use of rhyme or the placing of tones), or may be indigenous, as in the *Kim Van Kieu* and the *Luc Van Tien*.

The art of the Nguyen period only begins with the reign of the emperor Gia-long, at the beginning of the nineteenth century, and is found chiefly at Hué. The architectural style of the imperial palaces, which have recently been in large part destroyed, shows traces of the great influence of the Chinese style of building in Peking.

Conclusion

IN THE FOREGOING PAGES I have tried to show how each of the States that arose in Indochina developed a civilization of its own. In most parts of the peninsula these civilizations were of Indian parentage. Viet-nam alone came under Chinese cultural influence from the very beginning of its history, and borrowed so many cultural traits from China that even when it achieved political independence it still remained an offshoot of Chinese civilization. One might expect to find that when the Vietnamese expanded southwards they became influenced by the Indianized culture of the peoples at whose expense their frontiers were enlarged; but nothing of the sort happened, because such was the dynamic force of the process of expansion they had embarked upon, that the already sinicized Vietnamese destroyed rather than assimilated cultures that differed from theirs. It is true that they have some cultural traits that seem to be of indigenous, non-Chinese origin. For instance, the *dinh* or temple of the village tutelary deity which serves as meeting place for the worthies who look after the affairs of the district is always built on piles – even if sometimes the piles are rudimentary – in the manner of the dwellings of South East Asian peoples.[1] Again, in the legislation of the Le period provision is made for co-ownership of belongings between spouses; and there are many indications in Vietnamese customary law[2] of the importance of woman's role in the household, although this is something that is not mentioned in the code of Gia-long which is modelled on Chinese legislation. But repeated contacts with China, the temporary reconquest of the country by the Ming at the beginning of the fifteenth century, and the tendency to imitate the Court of Peking at the beginning of the nineteenth century, have all contributed towards keeping Viet-nam within the Chinese cultural zone.

As regards the other Indochinese States, their civilizations differ widely from each other, and each seems to have an entirely individual character; yet they all owe so much to India that it is worth discussing the question in some detail in these concluding remarks.[3]

Indian influence on Indochina was deepest in those areas where it operated most continuously, and where there was a strong centralized government run by an oligarchy of princes and dignitaries who, whether laymen or clerics, were impregnated with Indian culture, and who by means of an administrative system directly under the central government were able to exercise control over the provinces and even down to village level.

Because of the historical consequences involved, the most important result of the spread of Indian cultural influence in Indochina was the rise of monarchies which ruled over vast territories where hitherto the social group had not extended beyond the village or the tribe. There were several contributory factors leading to the breaking down of barriers between self-contained groups and the welding of such groups into a more or less centralized organization. In the first place, public works such as drainage, irrigation, and the construction of highways could not be carried out at the local level and required the existence of a central government for the allocation of tasks. Secondly, indigenous peoples who were accustomed to look upon their chief as the embodiment of the god of the soil, and were thus prepared to accept him as their spiritual leader, were readily persuaded to recognize the spiritual authority of a king who, according to the Indian conception of kingship, was the earthly equivalent of the king of the gods and a mediator between earth and heaven. Furthermore, indigenous social groups, each with its own particular form of customary law, found in Indian law, with its concept of *dharma*, a general framework within which their own institutions could be included in a way that did not necessitate uniformity being imposed upon them, yet that overrode particularism.

Again, where occupational groups or age grades formed part of the social structure of indigenous peoples, these found an echo in the castes and age grades of Indian social organization. Thus indigenous peoples who came under Indian influence, unlike those who were subjected to Chinese domination, were never forced to conform to norms imposed upon them, but needed only to allow themselves to be penetrated by a civilization which, with its pre-Aryan substratum, was at root little different from their own culture and which provided them with a general framework within which their own particular variety of culture could be integrated without losing its own individual characteristics. This is why Indian civilization showed a marked tendency to become differentiated as soon as it was transplanted overseas, yet retained a basic cultural unity through the use of Sanskrit as a common language.

The Indian conception of divine kingship was adopted by the Indochinese peoples who came within the orbit of Indian culture, and indeed found exceptionally fertile soil there in which to flourish. The king was regarded as a god on earth, uniting in his person the guardian spirits of the cardinal points, and escaping the cycle of rebirth after death. In the brief sketch of Khmer civilization during the Angkor period given above we saw the remarkable results of this notion when developed as it was in ancient Cambodia: the role played by the king in the State, the institution of the cult of the divine king, and the posthumous names given to the kings. The adoption of Sinhalese Buddhism as the official religion by kingdoms where Hinduism had formerly predominated did not deprive the king of his divine nature; on the contrary, it made of him a sort of living Buddha. The coronation rites were – and still are – designed precisely to confer this divine character upon the monarch, as many of the terms make clear. In Siam the Crown Prince used to be called 'Bud of the Buddha', and the king, who at death was thought to enter nirvana, is still known as 'Our Lord Holy Buddha'. In Burma the throne in the main hall of audience in the royal palace of Mandalay was placed exactly under the tall spire that surmounts the roof and seems to pierce the heavens, and it was thought to occupy the 'centre of the world',[4] like the cosmic mountain on which Indra, the king of the gods, is seated.

Once the Indianized peoples of Indochina had taken the step from their original tribal society to a monarchy on the Indian pattern, the kingdoms thus formed were able to develop and to extend their sway over adjacent territories by following the principles of Indian rule. All they had to do was to apply the theory of universal monarchy and form a kind of federation under the sceptre of a sovereign who had achieved the conquest of the four directions and taken the significant title of *chakravartin* or *sarvabhauma*. The second title, which means 'possessing all the earth', was indeed that borne by the king of Fu-nan in the sixth century. When Cambodia was partitioned in the eighth century, it returned for a time to the rulerless state it had known before the introduction of Indian ideas, and the foundation of the Angkor dynasty with the accession of Jayavarman II at the beginning of the ninth century was primarily a move to break down local particularism and create once more a centralized State 'in which there would be only one king who would be universal monarch'. This political move was accompanied on the spiritual level by a religious unification taking the form of the institution of an official cult centred on the person of the king which transcended all local cults, since the king was the temporal exemplar of the eternal principle of kingship whereby the king was Lord of the Soil. The symbol of divine kingship was the royal linga, which was the object of the cult; and the cult, according to the tradition mentioned earlier, was instituted upon a hill bearing the significant name of Mahendraparvata or 'Great Indra's Mountain'. We have seen what importance was attached to the raising of a temple-mountain in the centre of the capital. The temple-mountain sometimes was, and sometimes was not placed on top of a natural or an artificial hill; but always it represented Mount Meru, the cosmic mountain.[5] There is little doubt that the Phnom of Phnom Penh and the Ph'u Khao T'ong or 'mountain of gold' (= Meru) in Bangkok, on top of which rise Buddhist temples, are the equivalent of the temple-mountain that formerly marked the centre of the royal city.

Below the king, the oligarchy of high officials who held all the important posts was recruited from members of the royal family and members of several great families holding hereditary office. We have seen that in Cambodia some posts were held by Brahmans who had either come from India and settled in the country, or were indigenes who had been to India. Brahmans in Cambodia, however, and also in Champa, do not seem to have held so high a rank as in India. Their position came below that of the king, who, as 'guru (that is, spiritual lord) of the whole world', was supposed to unite in his person the two highest castes. The spiritual power of the Brahman paralleled the temporal power of the king and legitimized it. Brahmans occasionally exercised considerable power, as for instance when the king was a minor, or when there was a change of dynasty; and it was they who helped to maintain Indian traditions and Sanskrit culture, and who instigated the building of large architectural monuments – all of which, it must be remembered, were buildings for religious purposes. In the kingdoms where Buddhism was adopted, all that remains of the ancient traditions of the Court Brahmans is the cord which they wear, the manner of tying their hair in a knot, and a few Sanskrit ritual formulae which they recite without any longer understanding their meaning. They only preside at certain rites in the royal ceremonial,[6] and the great spiritual authority they formerly wielded has passed over to the high dignitaries of Buddhism.

There is no evidence whatsoever to indicate that a government run by Indians was ever imposed upon any part of ancient Indochina. The earliest documentation provided by epigraphy records that officials of all grades, with very rare exceptions, were native born. All that was imported from India was the administrative system that had been evolved there through long experience with taxation, corvées, and public works; the carrying out of the system was done by natives. Clear evidence for this lies in the fact that in all the Indianized countries of Indochina the grades of the official hierarchy, like the ranks within the royal family, have vernacular names which probably go back to the pre-Indianized past, whereas the offices held have Sanskrit names. There was a very large number of these offices, indicating a large body of officials. The names are still in use today. Sanskrit names were also given to the large territorial divisions – and some of these, too, are still in use. The basic unit, the village, was administered by a kind of council of elders and worthies, just as in India. Most of the population – in Cambodia, at any rate – were divided into classes rather than castes (although the word for class is the same as the Indian word for caste: *varna*). These classes seem to have consisted of corporations of persons following the same hereditary occupation. The abolition of this system as a form of social organization must have been largely due to the introduction of Buddhism.

Slaves,[7] who formed a very large class, were recruited from mountain-dwellers who had not been integrated into the Indianized societies, prisoners of war, and insolvent debtors, and their status was apparently hereditary. Both free men and slaves had many prestations and corvées imposed upon them, many of which were exacted by the religious foundations. These in turn enjoyed many exemptions both for the foundation and for its personnel. That is why the typical feature of their charters, especially in Cambodia, is the anxiety displayed by the founders to have the rights of ownership guaranteed by the king and perpetuated for their families and descendants.

All the epigraphic and literary evidence shows that the Indianized countries of ancient Indochina had a knowledge of Indian law.[8] For, despite the fact that India never exercised any suzerainty over these countries, it provided them with 'the concepts, the methods, and the terminology which formed the necessary apparatus for the creation of a legal system that could be applied to already existing institutions. . . . Local customary law found in [Indian legal works] a model on which to pattern itself and a means whereby it could be improved.'[9]

Apart from a code written in Pali in twelfth-century Burma, and known only in the Burmese translation made in the eighteenth century, inscriptions are the only source of information about the laws in use in ancient Indochina. Both Cambodian and Cham inscriptions contain many references to Indian legal treatises. It was the *dharma* codified in these treatises that the kings had the duty to maintain and protect, and if necessary they carried out their duty by themselves giving sentence and ensuring that it was carried out. Cambodian epigraphy gives some idea as to how court cases were conducted. Usually they resulted from the filing of a petition by the plaintiff. At the Court of Justice there was a 'reciter of the dharmashastra' (treatise of Indian jurisprudence), whose duty it apparently was to cite the Sanskrit text appropriate to the case being judged. Some indications are given about the scale of punishments, which, as in India, became more severe the higher the social status of the accused. It is interesting to note that in the epigraphic records of court cases a Sanskrit terminology is used for all the legal aspects, while the factual aspects are described in the vernacular. This is clear confirmation of how Indian law provided the framework within which legal procedures were conducted.

Cham and Khmer epigraphy gives the impression that the kings, as in India, had no legislative powers as such. 'The kings confined themselves to performing acts which did not go beyond the statutory regulations . . . their edicts, despite their detailed nature, were not in the nature of laws. . . . They were no more than commands. The king who issued them of course saw to it that they were carried out. But his commands were not binding on his successors.'[10] Thus there are instances of kings who, upon their accession, commanded that the edicts of their predecessor be recorded, or brought into force again. Apparently the law of the Chams and the Khmers was never formulated in a written code, for no trace of one from early times survives, and inscriptions only refer to Indian law. All the later codes of the Indianized Indo-chinese kingdoms bear the imprint of Indian law, in form if not in substance; and this holds good until modern times, when new codes on Western models were drawn up.

While there is good reason to suppose that any knowledge or deep understanding of the dogmas of Hinduism and Buddhism was confined to the circles of a small *élite*, there is no doubt at all that the ritual and the outward manifestations of the Indian religions constituted the most enduring and firmly established element in the process of Indianization. Moreover, the original animistic beliefs of the masses, their ancestral rites, and the worship of local gods and chthonian deities were easily integrated within an Indian framework, especially when the religion in question was Shivaism, as can be seen throughout the process of Aryanization of the various regions of India. The gods of the Hindu and Buddhist pantheons could without difficulty be worshipped alongside indigenous gods, or even merged with them, without the indigenous peoples realizing that they were worshipping strange gods.[11]

Relations between India and South East Asia were continuous during the ten centuries following upon the initial spread of Indian cultural influence, and this explains the parallel development of Hinduism in India and overseas. At first the Shivaite cults predominated; but during the eleventh and twelfth centuries the worship of Vishnu came into favour overseas at the same time as it flourished in India. As for Buddhism, all the main sects – Theravada, Mahayana, Tantrism, and Sinhalese reform – played their part in Indochina. References in inscriptions to religious rites and ceremonies are confined to mention of the morning, midday, and evening rites, New Year ceremonies, the Feast of Lanterns and the

Festival of the Dead, and other annual festivals which are still celebrated today. But a systematic study of the vernacular inscriptions ought to yield information about ritual furnishings and all the various accessories used in the Indian cults.

The history of religion in the Indianized parts of Indochina reveals certain features which, while originating from India and occurring there also, found particularly fertile soil in which to flourish. The feature of commonest occurrence is the close association of a deceased person, or even of a person still living, with the image of an Indian god. The oldest form of this is the identification of the king with the linga, the phallic emblem of Shiva, which the king set up in a temple. In Champa King Bhadravarman gave his name to the linga Bhadreshvara in the fourth century, while in Cambodia the earliest example is the foundation of the linga Pushkaresha by King Pushkaraksha in 716. But identification with a divinity was no mere royal privilege, for both in Champa and in Cambodia there arose cults of individuals in which the image worshipped was that of a Hindu or Buddhist divine being which, however, bore a name combining the name of the individual human being for whom the cult was inaugurated with that of the god.[12] Another feature of Indian religions in South East Asia, which is also typical of India, is the tolerance they showed towards each other, often amounting to a tendency towards syncretism. Everywhere, Hindu and Buddhist cults coexisted peacefully. At the most, a movement of protest might arise such as the Shivaite protest in thirteenth-century Cambodia against the Buddhism introduced by Jayavarman VII, which led to the systematic scratching out of Buddhist images on the walls of the temples of his reign and their replacement by lingas and representations of Shivaite ascetics.

When Theravada Buddhism in Ceylon underwent the reform introduced by King Parakramabahu I (1153–86) after he had adopted the tenets of the Mahavihara sect, a number of monks from Indochina were drawn towards it and visited the island. We have seen how the return of one of them, the Mon Chapata, led in 1190 to a schism in Burmese Buddhism, and finally resulted in the adoption of the Sinhalese reform as the orthodox form of Buddhism throughout the peninsula. It passed from Burma to the T'ai countries, and from there to Cambodia, where, at the end of the thirteenth century, Chou Ta-kuan mentions it as being one of the three religions of the country, and refers to the Buddhist monks by the term *Chao Ku*, 'Monseigneur', borrowed from Siamese. From Cambodia it was introduced into Laos in 1353 at the latest – the date at which the kingdom of Lan Ch'ang was founded by a T'ai prince who was the king of Cambodia's son-in-law.

Sinhalese Buddhism was the last direct cultural contribution made by India to Indochina, and the one which has had the deepest influence. While doubts may be entertained as to whether Indian culture ever reached the lower strata of society during the Hindu period, it cannot be denied that in the Buddhist States of Indochina the entire population is steeped in Buddhism. This means that ever since the fourteenth century the Burmese, the Siamese, the Cambodians, and the Laotians have shared the fundamental ideas of Indian thought. The cosmogony, the belief in transmigration and in the retribution brought about by actions, and all the other basically Indian concepts contained in Buddhism are inculcated into them from childhood on, whatever their social status may be; and thus it is that they continue to belong to the Indian cultural zone.

The overseas manifestations of India's philosophic doctrines and scientific disciplines is an aspect that has so far been little studied. Sanskrit epigraphy, both in Cambodia and Champa, shows by the quotations and allusions that occur that the authors of the inscriptions, and no doubt other members of the cultural *élite*, were acquainted with the great Indian philosophical systems. But it is difficult to know whether they underwent any adaptations or transformations in Indochina. This is, however, an unlikely occurrence, because the very nature of these systems places them above local variations.

The same is true of scientific disciplines, for the same reason. Although Indian medicine could incorporate indigenous anatomical and physiological speculations and each country's recipes for cures, mathematics and other sciences of a universal nature did not lend themselves to local variation. What can be observed, however, is that in one and the same country the Indian way of doing things is found in juxtaposition with the older way used before the introduction of Indian cultural influence. For instance, in Khmer epigraphy the Indian decimal system and the use of nine digits together with zero as a positional value occur when dates

226

are given, whereas in the counting of objects and the expression of measurements use is made of an indigenous system of enumeration based on the numbers four and five.[13] But while the figures of the decimal system are in part identical with the Indian figures known to have been in use since the end of the sixth century, the figures of the indigenous system are written differently. They, too, were borrowed from an Indian script, but one which was in earlier use, from the first centuries of the Christian era.

Astronomy as it was known in ancient Indochina was purely Indian, except possibly for astronomical data found in Cambodian inscriptions[14] which are related to a Cambodian meridian. As regards the calendar, the Indian lunisolar year was adopted and is still used – if not officially, at least in popular practice – in all the Indianized countries of Indochina.[15] The use of the Indian sixty-year cycle is attested in inscriptions in Mon after the end of the ninth century. At the end of the tenth another cycle of twelve years, in which each year is given the name of an animal (these names being borrowed for some unexplained reason from a dialect related to Vietnamese),[16] begins to appear sporadically in Cambodian epigraphy. When, as in China, it is combined with a ten year cycle (in which, in Indochina, the years are referred to by Indian ordinal numbers), a system is produced – not found in Cambodia until after the fourteenth century – in which, at the end of every sixty years, the same combination of animal name and ordinal number as was used for the first year re-occurs, thus forming a sexagenary cycle which has no connection with the so-called 'Jupiter' cycle of sixty years except that it comprises the same number of years. As regards eras, the only era in common use in ancient times was the Indian era beginning in A.D. 78 (the Shaka era). The era beginning in the year 638 was thought to be a Burmese invention because the first known reference to it was found in Burma; but in fact it originated from the observation of an eclipse of the sun in India on 24 March 638 which led to a correction of the meridian corresponding to the discrepancy between the Indian meridian of Ujjaiyini and that of the lower Irrawaddy. Its use in Burma as early as the seventh century seems to be attested by the funerary urns of the Pyu kings. No doubt its adoption there was due to some historical event about which nothing so far is known. It does not appear in Burmese epigraphy until after the eleventh century, but then there are no Burmese inscriptions of earlier date. Its use passed from Burma to Siam, where it is found after the beginning of the fifteenth century, although the A.D. 78 era also continued in use. It is still used in Indochina today, concurrently with the Buddhist era of Parinirvana, the starting point of which was fixed by Sinhalese orthodoxy at 544 B.C. This era has been in use in Burma since the eleventh century.

I have already said that Sanskrit was the vehicle for the spread of Indian ideas overseas, and it is almost the sole language used in epigraphy, apart from the local vernaculars. As the inscriptions show, the cultural *élite* were well acquainted with Sanskrit language and literature; but there is not a single instance of a country abandoning its own language and adopting Sanskrit, as happened in India. But although the indigenous peoples retained their own form of speech, and although the inflectional morphology of Sanskrit did not affect the structure of the isolating languages spoken by them, their vocabulary was considerably enriched; and even today, Sanskrit and Pali remain the chief sources of enrichment. Not only were abstract terms relating to religion and philosophy borrowed from Sanskrit, but also words concerning material culture, and even grammatical particles were borrowed in order to facilitate the expression of ideas, habitually expressed in an inflected language in terms of an isolating language. Lastly, the use of Indian script enabled a permanent record to be made of the vernacular languages, and this is by no means the least important of the civilizing effects of Indian cultural influence.

The only surviving Indochinese texts relating to the period treated in the second and third parts of this book are the inscriptions. It must again be emphasized that the Sanskrit inscriptions are the only ones with any pretensions to literary merit. Those of Cambodia in particular are always in verse, and many are genuine little poems of the *kavya* type. Thirteenth-century Pali inscriptions from Pagan, which have survived owing to the many successive copies made of them, are more in the nature of religious or grammatical treatises than of literary works. They are directly inspired by Pali literature from Ceylon. As for the vernacular inscriptions, hardly any of them, with a few rare exceptions, can be regarded as having any literary merit. Only in later centuries do the first true works of literature – especially of poetic literature –

in the Indochinese languages begin to appear, and it should be noted how indebted the authors are to India both for their choice of subjects, which are drawn from Indian epics and Buddhist legends, and for their prosody, for as well as using metres suitable for the phonetics and rhythm of indigenous speech, they also make great use of metres which are simply copied from Indian models. So this is another sphere in which India supplied Indochina with a framework within which a certain amount of originality could be displayed.

The origins and development of the plastic arts, the surviving monuments of which provide the best known aspects of the ancient civilizations of Indochina, have been discussed in earlier chapters. Until further research has been undertaken, little can be said about the other arts. Almost nothing is so far known, for example, about early music apart from what is conveyed by the musical instruments portrayed in the bas-reliefs, which are mostly of Indian origin. Of the music itself, nothing, of course, remains. Some survivals of early dance forms of Indian origin, some attitudes of which are familiar to us through the bas-reliefs, are still preserved; and because of their common origin, Burmese, Siamese, and Cambodian dances, despite their individual characteristics, are all in the nature of a pantomime in which the attitudes, the movements of the arms and legs, and the gestures of the hands form a dumb language capable of suggesting an object or an action, or of expressing a feeling. Furthermore, most of the classical ballets have themes taken from the Indian epics or based on legends which sometimes seem to be an Indian version of a local folk-tale translated into Buddhist terms.

I have referred here only to the most obvious features indicative of the deep influence India has had on Indochina. Such indications could be multiplied indefinitely, and provide ample justification for maintaining that the civilizations of the Indianized countries of Indochina are simply overseas extensions of Indian civilization. Certainly great changes occurred when Sinhalese Buddhism replaced both Hinduism with its accompanying social system, and the earlier forms of Buddhism. Nevertheless, if one travels through the Indianized countries of the peninsula in the company of an Indian and watches his reactions, it is easy to see how at home he feels and how familiar are the traits which he finds there, from the most banal outward forms of Indochinese behaviour (such as the gesture of greeting, with joined hands held in front of the face or breast) to the most deeply held moral or cosmological beliefs.

Although the civilization of Viet-nam seems to be patterned more closely on that of China than the Indianized civilizations are on that of India, this does not, in my opinion, argue any fundamental differences in the natural characteristics or social organization of the early Vietnamese as compared with the Mon-Khmers or the Tibeto-Burmans; and from prehistoric times, all of these peoples seem to have shared the same lack of inventiveness (see above, p. 13), and to have been receptive rather than creative when brought into contact with foreign civilizations. As mentioned at the beginning of this book, the real difference between the sinicized and Indianized areas of Indochina lies in the different way in which Chinese and Indian cultural influence was introduced – the first by conquest and political integration, the second by a process of cultural osmosis which allowed the individual characteristics of each of the Indianized countries to be expressed and manifested within an Indian framework.

Despite the difference in the manner of their diffusion, future research may show that Indian civilization exercised fully as deep an influence as did that of China. In short, the difference in Indochinese acculturation to the two great civilizations of Asia is perhaps qualitative rather than quantitative. The contributions of India and China have been equally important in forming the region which is so aptly named Indochina.

Notes

N.B. The titles of some periodicals are given in abridged form. The only initials used are *B.E.F.E.O.* for the *Bulletin de l'École française d'Extrême-Orient*. Publ. E.F.E.O. indicates publications of the École française d'Extrême-Orient. Volume numbers of periodicals are given in Roman figures, and the arabic numerals that follow refer to page numbers, unless otherwise indicated.

INTRODUCTION

[1] André Masson, *Histoire de l'Indochine* (Que sais-je? No. 398), Paris, 1950.

Brian Harrison, *South-East Asia, a short history*, 1955.

D. G. E. Hall, *A History of South-East Asia*, 1955.

Lê Thành Khôi, *Histoire de l'Asie du Sud-Est* (Que sais-je? No. 804), Paris, 1959.

[2] In the Histoire du Monde series, ed. E. Cavaignac, Vol. VIII, 2, Paris, 1948. A third edition, thoroughly revised and partly rewritten, has been published by Editions de Boccard, 1964.

[3] This expression is used by M. E. Gaspardone in 'L'histoire et la philologie indochinoise', *Revue historique*, July/September 1947, p. 13.

[4] Lê Thành Khôi; see note 1 above.

[5] Cf. G. Cœdès, 'L'avenir des études khmères' (a public lecture given at the Academie des Inscriptions et Belles-Lettres on 26 November 1960).

[6] The most important are:

H. Cordier, *Bibliotheca Indosinica* (Publ. E.F.E.O., XV–XVIII), 4 Vol. and Index, Paris, 1912–32.

J. F. Embree and L. O. Dotson, *A bibliography of the people and cultures of mainland South-East Asia*, New Haven, 1950.

Notes

Cecil C. Hobbs, *South-East Asia: an annotated bibliography of selected references*, Washington, 1952. 2nd edition 1964.

American Institute of Pacific Relations, *South-East Asia, a selected bibliography*, New York, 1955.

PART I: THE PATTERN OF SETTLEMENT IN INDOCHINA

1. THE GEOGRAPHICAL FRAMEWORK

[1] J. Sion, *L'Asie des moussons*, Part IV, Paris, 1928.

P. Gourou, *L'Asie*, Part IV, Ch. 17–19, Paris, 1953.

C. Robequain, *L'Indochine française*, Paris, 1935.

[2] P. Gourou, *Les pays tropicaux*, Paris, 1947.

[3] P. Gourou, *Les paysans du delta tonkinois* (Publ. E.F.E.O., XXVII), Paris, 1936.

[4] J. Delvert, *Le paysan cambodgien*, Paris, 1961.

2. PREHISTORY

[1] H. Mansuy, 'Le préhistoire en Indochine', in *Indochine*, ed. G. Maspero, Vol. I, p. 83.

M. Colani. 'Recherches sur le préhistorique indochinois', *B.E.F.E.O.*, XXX, 299.

E. Patte, 'L'Indochine préhistorique', *Rev. anthropologique* (1936), p. 277.

J. Fromaget and E. Saurin, in *Bull. Serv. Géol. Indochine*, XXII (1936), No. 3; and *Proc. 3rd Congress prehist. of the Far East* (1938), p. 51.

[2] *In Siam:*

F. Sarasin, 'Prehistorical researches in Siam', *J. Siam Soc.* XXVI (1933), 171.

Teilhard de Chardin, 'Le paléolithisme du Siam', *L'Anthropologie* LIV, 547.

H. R. van Heekeren, 'Prehistoric discoveries in Siam', *Proc. Prehist. Soc., Cambridge* II, 24; 'A preliminary note on the excavation of the Sai-yok shelter', *J. Siam Soc.*, XLIX (1961), 99.

Wilhelm G. Solheim II, 'Thailand and prehistory', *Silpakara*, VIII, 3 (Sept. 1964), 42.

In Burma:

J. Coggin Brown, 'Relics of the stone age in Burma', *J. Burma Research Soc.*, XXI (1935), 33.

T. C. Morris, 'The prehistoric stone implements of Burma', *Ibid.*, XXV (1935), 1; 'Copper and bronze antiquities from Burma', *Ibid.*, XXVIII (1938), 95.

H. L. Movius, 'The stone age of Burma', *Trans. Amer. Philos. Soc.* XXXII, 341; 'The lower palaeolithic cultures of South and East Asia', *Ibid.*, XXXVIII, No. 4 (1949); 'Palaeolithic archaeology in South and East Asia', *Cahiers d'histoire mondiale* II (1954).

[3] A synthesis of this kind has recently been successfully attempted by J. Naudou in *L'Homme avant l'écriture*, ed. André Varagnac, pp. 153 and 315.

[4] H. Mansuy, *Stations préhistoriques de Samrong-Seng et de Longprao*, Hanoi, 1902; 'Résultats de nouvelles recherches . . .', *Mém. Serv. Géol. Indochine* X, 1.

[5] V. Goloubew, 'L'âge du bronze au Tonkin et dans le Nord-Annam', *B.E.F.E.O.*, XXIX, 1.

O. Janse, *Archaeological research in Indo-China*, 3 vol., Cambridge (Mass.), 1947, 1951; Bruges, 1958.

A. Christie, *The bronze age in South East Asia*, 1961.

[6] F. Heger, *Alte Metalltrommeln aus Südostasien*, Leipzig, 1902.

[7] V. Goloubew, 'Sur l'origine et la diffusion des tambours métalliques', *Praehistorica Asiae Orientalis* (Hanoi, 1932), I, 137.

[8] V. Goloubew, 'L'âge du bronze . . .' *loc. cit.*

[9] E. Patte, *op. cit.*, p. 303.

[10] R. von Heine-Geldern, 'Vorgeschichtliche Grundlagen der kolonial-indischen Kunst', *Wiener Beitr. zur Kunst- und Kulturgesch. Asiens*, VIII (1934); 'Das Tocharerproblem und die pontische Wanderung' *Saeculum*, II (1951), 225.

C. Schuster, 'An ancient cultural movement . . . dated by the Dongson culture of N. Indo-China', *Actes du IVe Congrés int. des Sciences anthropol. et ethnol., Vienne, 1952*, II. *Ethnologica*, Part I, p. 285.

[11] B. Karlgren, 'The date of the early Dong-son culture', *Bull. Mus. Far-Eastern Antiq.*, XIV (1942), 1.

[12] M. Colani, 'Emploi de la pierre en des temps reculés', *Bull. Amis Vieux Hué*, 1940.

[13], [14] M. Colani, *Mégalithes du Haut-Laos*, Paris, 1935.

[15] H. Parmentier, 'Vestiges mégalithiques à Xuân-lôc', *B.E.F.E.O.*, XXVIII, 479.

E. Gaspardone, 'The tomb of Xuân-lôc', *J. Greater India Soc.*, IV (1937), 26.

[16] P. Rivet, 'Le groupe océanien', *Bull. Soc. Linguist.*, XXVII, 152; 'Les Océaniens', *Praehistorica Asiae Orientalis*, I, 35.

[17] P. V. van Stein Callenfels, 'The Melanesoid civilizations of Eastern Asia', *Bull. Raffles Mus.*, Series B, I (1936), 41.

[18] R. von Heine-Geldern, 'Urheimat und früheste Wanderungen des Austronesier', *Anthropos*, XXVII (1932).

[19] L. Finot, 'L'Indochine préhistorique', *Bull. Comité Asie française*, Feb./July, 1919.

[20] These views correspond in part to those expressed by Sylvain Lévi in 'Préaryen et pré-dravidien dans l'Inde', *Journal Asiatique*, 1923, No. 2, p. 55, and by J. Przyluski in *Ibid.*, 1926, No. 1, p. 1 and 1929, No. 1, p. 311, and by several others, according to whom 'the Dravidians and the Aryans, when they entered India from the north-west, probably pushed before them, as they spread into eastern and southern India, the aboriginal inhabitants, who must have migrated to Indochina and Indonesia and brought about there a kind of pre-Aryan Indianization, causing in turn a migration of the peoples who from there went to settle in the islands.' (G. Coedès, *États hindouisés*, p. 24.)

[21] J. Przyluski, 'Les populations de l'Indochine', in *Indochine*, ed. S. Lévi, Vol. I, p. 54.

[22] G. Montandon, *Traité d'ethnologie culturelle*, Paris, 1934.

[23] W. Schmidt, 'Les peuples Mon-Khmer, trait d'union entre les peuples de l'Asie centrale et de l'Austronésie', *B.E.F.E.O.*, VII, 213; VIII, 1.

[24] A. Conrady, *Eine indochinesische Causativ-Denominativ Bildung*, Leipzig, 1896.
K. Wulff, 'Chinesisch und Tai', *Mélanges histor. philol. Acad. Sciences* (Copenhagen), XX, No. 3.

[25] K. Wulff, 'Über das Verhältnis des Malayo-polynesischen zum Indochinesischen', *Ibid.*, XXVII, No. 2.

[26] Paul K. Benedict, 'Thai, Kadai and Indonesian: a new alignment in Southeastern Asia', *Amer. Anthropologist*, 1942.

[27] H. Maspero, 'Études sur la phonétique historique de la langue annamite', *B.E.F.E.O.*, XII, No. 1.

[28] J. Przyluski, 'Langues austroasiatiques' in *Les langues du monde* (1st ed., 1924), p. 395.

[29] A. G. Haudricourt, 'De l'origine des tons en vietnamien', *Journal Asiatique* (1954), p. 69; 'La place du vietnamien dans les langues austroasiatiques', *Bull. Soc. Ling.*, XLIX (1953), 122.

[30] H. Maspero, 'Études sur la phonétique . . .', *loc. cit.* p. 116.

[31] G. Cœdès, 'Les langues de l'Indochine', *Conférence Inst. Ling. Univ. Paris, 1940–1948*, p. 63.

[32] C. Robequain, *L'Indochine française* (Paris, 1935), p. 40; *Le Thanh-hoa* (Pub. E.F.E.O., XXIII–XXIV), Paris, 1929.

[33] H. Maspero, 'Mœurs et coutumes des populations sauvages', in *Indochine*, ed. G. Maspero, Vol. I, p. 233.

PART II: THE FOUNDING OF THE FIRST
INDOCHINESE STATES

1. THE CHINESE CONQUEST OF THE RED RIVER DELTA
AND THE BIRTH OF VIET-NAM

[1] Wang Gungwu, 'The Nanhai trade, a study of the early history of Chinese trade in the South China sea', *Journal Malayan Branch Roy. Asiat. Soc.*, XXXI (1958), No. 2.

L. Aurousseau, 'La première conquête chinoise des pays annamites', *B.E.F.E.O.*, XXIII, 137.

H. Maspero, 'Études d'histoire d'Annam', *B.E.F.E.O.*, XVI, No. 1; XVIII, No. 3.

[2] C. Madrolle, 'Le Tonkin ancien', *B.E.F.E.O.*, XXXVII, No. 1.

[3] C. Robequain, *Le Than-hoa*, p. 104 (see note 32, Part I, ch. 2).

[4] H. Parmentier, 'Anciens tombeaux au Tonkin', *B.E.F.E.O.*, XXVII, No. 1.

O. Janse, 'Rapport préliminaire d'une mission archéologique en Indochine, II. Sépultures chinoises au Tonkin', *Arts Asiatiques*, IX (1935), 209.

[5] H. Maspero, 'L'expédition de Ma Yuan', in 'Études d'histoire d'Annam', *B.E.F.E.O.*, XVIII, No. 3, pp. 11–28.

[6] Trân van Giap, 'Le bouddhisme en Annam des origines au XIIIe siècle', *B.E.F.E.O.*, XXXII, 191.

[7] Nguyên van Huyên, *La civilisation annamite* (Hanoi, 1941), p. 10.

[8] H. Maspero, 'L'expédition de Ma Yuan', *loc. cit.* p. 27.

[9] H. Maspero, 'La dynastie des Li antérieurs', *B.E.F.E.O.*, XVI, No. 1.

M. Durand, 'La dynastie des Ly antérieurs d'après le Viêt Diên U Linh Tâp', *Ibid.*, XLIV, 437.

[10] H. Maspero, 'Le protectorat général d'Annam sous les T'ang', *B.E.F.E.O.*, X, 539.

[11] *Cahiers d'histoire mondiale*, I (1954), 836.

[12] Wang Gungwu, *loc. cit.*

2. THE INTRODUCTION OF INDIAN CULTURE INTO INDOCHINA

[1] C. C. Berg, *Hoofdlijnen der Javaansche Litteratur-Geschiedenis*, Groningen 1929.

[2] N. J. Krom, *Hindoe-Javaansche Geschiedenis*, The Hague, 1931.

[3] F. H. van Naerssen, *Culture contacts and social conflicts in Indonesia*, S. Asia Inst., 1946.

[4] F. D. K. Bosch, *Het vragstuk van de Hindoe-Kolonisatie van den Archipel*, Leyden, 1946.

G. Cœdès, *Les États hindouisés*, p. 41.

⁵ J. C. van Leur, *Indonesian trade and society*, The Hague, 1955.

⁶ *Ibid.*

⁷ P. Pelliot, 'Le Fou-nan', *B.E.F.E.O.*, III, 179.

⁸ P. Mus, 'Cultes indiens et indigènes au Champa', *B.E.F.E.O.*, XXXIII, 367.

⁹ H. G. Quaritch Wales, *The making of Greater India*, 1951; 2nd ed., 1961.

¹⁰ L. de la Vallée Poussin, *Dynasties et histoire de l'Inde* in Histoire du Monde, ed. E. Cavaignac, Vol. VI, 2, p. 287.

¹¹ F. D. K. Bosch, '*Local Genius*' *en oud-javaansche Kunst*, Amsterdam, 1952.

G. Cœdès, 'Le substrat autochtone et la superstructure indienne au Cambodge et à Java', *Cahiers d'histoire mondiale*, I (1953), No. 2.

¹² *Loc. cit.*

¹³ D. G. E. Hall, 'Looking at Southeast Asian history', *Journal of Asian Studies*, XIX (1960), 243.

¹⁴ I cannot be held entirely responsible for these misunderstandings, because the title for the article mentioned in note 11 above had been decided upon before I was asked to write on the subject.

3. THE SPREAD OF INDIAN CULTURAL INFLUENCE IN THE PENINSULA

I. *Fu-nan.*

¹ The main Chinese documentation can be found in the important article by P. Pelliot in *B.E.F.E.O.*, III.

² The word *Fan* has been used by the Chinese as a surname for a number of kings of the Indianized Indochinese kingdoms. It is written with the same character as that used for the transcription of the name of the god Brahma. It was at first considered to be a transcription of 'Brahman'; then of *varman*, 'breast-plate' (= 'protected by'), a traditional termination for the names of Indian kings; and lastly as representing a clan name of indigenous origin, without any Indian connotation; cf. R. Stein, 'Le Lin-yi', *Han Hiue*, II (1947).

³ G. Cœdès, 'The date of the sanskrit inscription of Vo-canh', *Ind. Hist. Quart.*, XVI (1940), 484. The identification of Fan (Shih)-man with Shri Mara has been contested by E. Gaspardone in 'La plus ancienne inscription d'Indochine' (*Journal Asiatique*, CCXLI (1953), 477), where he suggests that the inscription dates from the fifth century, which is palaeographically untenable. Kalyan Kumar Sarkar, in 'The earliest inscription of Indo-china' (*Sino-Indian Studies*, V (1956), No. 2, p. 77), agrees with my identification. See also K. Bhattacharya, 'Précisions sur la paléographie de l'inscription dite de Vo-canh', *Artibus Asiae*', XXIV, 1961, 219.

[4] Wang Gungwu, 'The Nan-hai trade', *loc. cit.* (See note 1, Part II, ch. 1.)

[5] The reign of this foreigner, which came after the exchange of embassies with the Murunda, may be the explanation for certain iconographic motifs found in the earliest Khmer statues, the style of which was inherited from Fu-nan. They seem to show Iranian influence, as for instance in the short tunics of the Surya images, or the cylindrical mitres of the Vishnu images, which derive from Pallava statues (the Pallava may have been descendants of the Pahlava, who were Parthians); or the cult of a god named Shaka-brahmana, 'the Scythian Brahman', which is several times mentioned in inscriptions. This Brahman may have been of Iranian origin, as was the Durgasvamin who in the seventh century married the daughter of King Ishanavarman; or he may have been one of the 'wise men' who were priests in the Temple of the Sun; or the Sun itself. These possible identifications may be of doubtful value, but they should not be entirely dismissed; for the discovery of a cabochon with a Sassanid effigy in the east of the southern delta area of Viet-nam provides tangible evidence that Fu-nan had relations with the Iranian world.

[6] G. Cœdès, 'Fouilles en Cochinchine: le site de Go Oc Eo', *Artibus Asiae*, X (1947), 193.

L. Malleret, *L'archéologie du delta du Mékong* (Publ. E.F.E.O., XLIII), Paris, 1959–63.

P. Gourou, 'Civilisations et géographie humaine en Asie des moussons', *B.E.F.E.O.*, XLIV, 469. After arguing that 'the higher civilizations seem to have arisen in places which were centres of communication', he adds: 'The civilization of Fu-nan, which gave rise to the later development of the Khmer empire, arose and was centred on the western coast of southern Viet-nam at the point of access for Indian cultural influence.'

[7, 8] G. Cœdès, 'Deux inscriptions sanskrites du Fou-nan', *B.E.F.E.O.*, XXXI, 1.

[9] H. Parmentier, 'L'art présumé du Fou-nan', *B.E.F.E.O.*, XXXII, 183.

[10] P. Dupont, 'La Statuaire préangkorienne', *Artibus Asiae*, Suppl. XV, Ascona, 1955.

[11] P. Dupont, 'La dislocation du Tchen-la et la formation du Cambodge angkorien', *B.E.F.E.O.*, XLIII, 17.

II. *Champa.*

[12] General works on Champa:

J. Leuba, *Les Chams et leur art*, Paris, 1923.

R. C. Majumdar, *Ancient colonies in the Far East. I. Champa*, Lahore, 1927.

G. Maspero, *Le royaume de Champa*, Paris, 1928.

J. Y. Claeys, *Introduction à l'étude de l'Annam et du Champa*, Hanoi, 1934.

[13] R. Stein, 'Le Lin-yi', *Han Hiue*, II (1947).

[14] A. Bergaigne, *Inscriptions sanskrites du Campa*, p. 199 (See Note 1, Part III, ch. 2).

L. Finot, 'Deux nouvelles inscriptions de Bhadravarman Ier', *B.E.F.E.O.*, II, 185.

[15] L. Finot, *Ibid.*, and 'L'inscription de Chiêm-sön', *B.E.F.E.O.*, XVIII, No. 10, p. 13.

G. Cœdès, 'La plus ancienne inscription en langue chame', *New Indian Antiquary*, extra ser. I (1939), 46.

[16] Ma Touan-lin, *Méridionaux*, trans. Hervey de Saint-Denys, p. 422.

[17] G. Cœdès, 'Nouvelles données sur les origines du royaume khmèr', *B.E.F.E.O.*, XLVIII, 209.

[18] *B.E.F.E.O.*, XI, 471.

P. Dupont, 'Les Buddhas dits d'Amaravati en Asie du Sud-Est', *Proc. XXIII Congress of Orientalists, Cambridge, 1954*, p. 269.

J. Boisselier, *La statuaire du Champa* (Publ. E.F.E.O., LIV), Paris, 1963.

III. *Shrikshetra and Dvaravati.*

[19] For a detailed bibliography, see G. Coedès, *Les États hindouisés*, pp. 107–9, notes.

[20] W. Liebenthal, 'The ancient Burma Road, a legend?', *J. Greater India Soc.*, XVI (1956), 1.

[21] L. P. Briggs, 'Dvāravatī, most ancient kingdom of Siam', *J' Amer. Or. Soc.*, LXV (1945), 98. G. Coedès, 'A la recherche du royaume de Dvāravatī', *Archéologie*, I, Nov.–Dec. 1964, 58.

[22] G. Cœdès, 'A propos de deux fragments d'inscription récemment découverts à P'ra Pathom', *C.R. Acad. Inscr. et B.–L.* (1952), p. 146.

[23] P. Dupont, *L'Archéologie mône de Dvāravatī* (Publ. E.F.E.O., XLI), Paris, 1959.

PART III: THE INDOCHINESE STATES FROM THE SIXTH TO THE THIRTEENTH CENTURY

I. VIET-NAM

[1] *General works on the history and civilization of Viet-nam:*
A. des Michels, *Annales impériales de l'Annam*, Paris, 1889–94.
P. Trüöng Vinh Ky, *Cours d'histoire annamite*, 2 Vol., 1875.

L. Cadière, 'Tableau chronologique des dynasties annamites', *B.E.F.E.O.*, V, 177.

Lê Thanh Khôi, *Le Viet-nam, Histoire et civilisation*, Paris, 1955.

A. Masson, *Histoire du Vietnam* (Que sais-je? No. 398), Paris, 1960.

J. L. Claeys, *Introduction à l'étude de l'Annam et du Champa*, Hanoi, 1934.

Nguyên Van Huyên, *La civilisation annamite*, Hanoi, 1943.

P. Huard and M. Durand, *Connaissance du Viêt-nam*, Hanoi, 1954.

L. Cadière, *Croyances et pratiques religieuses des Annamites*, 3 Vols., Hanoi, Saigon, Paris, 1944, 1955, 1957. (In the title of the last two volumes 'Viêtnamiens' replaces 'Annamites'.)

L. Bezacier, *L'art vietnamien*, Paris, 1955.

For Champa, in addition to the general works mentioned in note 1 to Chapter 3 of Part II :

L. Finot, 'Les inscriptions de Mi-sön', *B.E.F.E.O.*, IV, 897.

P. Stern, *L'art du Champa et son évolution*, Toulouse, 1942.

J. Boisselier, *La statuaire du Champa* (Publ. E.F.E.O., LIV), Paris, 1963.

2. CAMBODIA

[1] *General works on the history and civilization of Cambodia :*

A. Barth and A. Bergaigne, 'Inscriptions sanscrites de Campā et du Cambodge', *Notices et extraits des mss. de la Bibl. nat.*, XXVII, 1 (Paris, 1885, 1893).

L. Finot, *Notes d'épigraphie indochinoise*, Hanoi, 1916 (Extr. from *B.E.F.E.O.*, II, III, IV, IX, XII, No. 2, XV); 'Inscriptions d'Ankor', *B.E.F.E.O.*, XXV, 289; 'Nouvelles inscriptions du Cambodge', *Ibid.*, XXVIII, 43.

G. Cœdès, 'Études cambodgiennes' *B.E.F.E.O.*, XI, XIII, XVIII, XXIV, XXVIII, XXIX, XXXI, XXXII, XXXVI, XL, XLIII, XLIV, XLVIII, (1911–56); *Inscriptions du Cambodge* (Coll. textes et docum. sur l'Indochine, E.F.E.O., III), 7 Vol., Hanoi and Paris, 1937–64.

E. Aymonier, *Le Cambodge*, 3 Vol., Paris, 1900–3.

G. Maspero, *L'empire Khmer*, Phnom Penh, 1904.

L. P. Briggs, *The ancient Khmer Empire* (Trans. Amer. Philos. Soc. 41, 1), Philadelphia, 1951.

B. P. Groslier, *Angkor, Hommes et pierres*, Paris, 1956.

G. Groslier, *Recherches sur les Cambodgiens*, Paris, 1921.

G. Porée and E. Maspero, *Mœurs et coutumes des Khmèrs*, Paris, 1938.

H. Parmentier, *L'art khmèr primitif* (Publ. E.F.E.O., XXI–XXII), Paris, 1927.

H. Parmentier, *L'art khmèr classique* (*Ibid.*, XXIX), Paris, 1939.

G. de Coral-Rémusat, *L'art khmèr*, Paris, 1940.

J. Boisselier, *La statuaire khmère et son évolution* (Publ. E.F.E.O., XXXVII), Paris, 1955.

J. Imbert, *Histoire des institutions khméres* (Annales de la Faculté de droit de Phnom Penh, II), Phnom Penh, 1961.

K. Bhattacharya, *Les religions brahmaniques dans l'ancien Cambodge* (Publ. E.F.E.O., XLIX), Paris, 1961.

2, 3 G. Cœdès, 'Nouvelles données sur les origines du royaume khmèr', *B.E.F.E.O.*, XLVIII, 209.

4 P. Dupont, 'La dislocation du Tchen-la at la formation du Cambodge angkorien', *B.E.F.E.O.*, XLIII, 17.

5 Ma Touan-lin, *Méridionaux*, trans. Hervey de Saint-Denys, p. 477.

6 K. Bhattacharya, 'La secte des Pāçupata dans l'ancien Cambodge', *Journal Asiatique*, CCXLIII (1955), 479.

7 G. Cœdès, 'Le royaume de Çrīvijaya', *B.E.F.E.O.*, XVIII, No. 6.

  G. Ferrand, 'L'empire sumatranais de Çrīvijaya', *Journal Asiatique*, (1920), pp. 1 and 161.

8 G. Ferrand, *Voyage du marchand arabe Sulaymân* (Classiques de l'Orient, VII, Paris, 1922), p. 98.

9 P. Dupont, *B.E.F.E.O.*, XLIII, 68–70.

10 'Les études indochinoises' (Inaugural lecture at the Collège de France, 16 May 1908), *Bull. Comité Asie française*, 1908.

11 V. Goloubew, 'L'hydraulique urbaine et agricole à l'époque des rois d'Angkor', *Bull, économique Indochine*, 1941.

12 G. Cœdès, 'Le culte de la royauté divinisée, source d'inspiration des grands monuments du Cambodge ancien', *Conferenze* (1st. Ital. per il medio ed estr. Oriente), I (1951), p. 1.

13 O. W. Wolters, 'Tāmbralinga', *Bull. School Orient. Afr. Studies* (1958), p. 605.

14 G. Cœdès, 'Nouvelles données épigraphiques sur l'histoire de l'Indochine centrale', *Journal Asiatique*, CCXLVI (1958), 139.

15 G. Cœdès, 'Le portrait dans l'art Khmèr', *Arts Asiatiques*, VII (1960), 179.

3. BURMA

1 *General works on the history and civilization of Burma :*

F. N. Trager, J. N. Musgrave and J. Welsh, *Annotated Bibliography of Burma*, New Haven, 1956.

Epigraphia Birmanica, 3 Vols., Rangoon, 1919–28.

Inscriptions of Burma (5 portfolios), Rangoon, 1934–56.

Pe Maug Tin and G. H. Luce, *The Glass Palace Chronicle of the kings of Burma*, 1923.

A. P. Phayre, *History of Burma*, 1883.

G. E. Harvey, *History of Burma*, 1925.

J. G. Scott, *Burma, a handbook of practical information*, 1921.

Shway Yoe (pseudonym of foregoing), *The Burman, his life and notions*, 1910.

R. Halliday, *The Talaings*, Rangoon, 1917.

W. W. Cochrane, *The Shans*, Rangoon, 1915.

[2] C. O. Bladgen, 'The Pyu inscriptions', *Epigraphia Indica*, XII, 127; and *J. Burma Research Soc.*, VII (1917), 37.

[3] G. H. Luce, 'The ancient Pyu', *Ibid.*, XXVII (1937), 249. Wilfrid Stott, 'The expansion of the Nan-Chao Kingdom between the years A.D. 750–860', *T'oung Pao*, L (1963), 190.

[4] L. de Beylié, 'Fouilles à Prome', *Rev. Arch.*, II (1907), 193; *Prome et Samara*, Paris, 1907.

C. Duroiselle, *Excavations at Hmawza*, Annual Report Archaeol. Survey of India, 1926–30.

[5] R. S. le May, 'The development of Buddhist art in Burma', *J. Roy. Soc. of Arts*, XCVII (1949), 535.

[6] J. A. Stewart, 'Kyaukse irrigation, a side-light on Burmese history', *J. Burma Res. Soc.*, XII (1921), 1.

G. H. Luce, 'Old Kyaukse and the coming of the Burmans', *Ibid.*, XLII (1959), 75.

[7] Htin Aung, 'The Lord of the Great Mountain', *Ibid.*, XXXVIII (1955), 82.

[8] C. Duroiselle, 'The Ari of Burma and tantric buddhism', *Annual Report Archaeol. Survey of India* (1915–16), p. 79.

[9] Nihar-Ranjan Ray, *Brahmanical Gods in Burma*, Calcutta, 1932.

[10] H. G. Quaritch Wales, 'Anuruddha and the Thaton tradition', *J. Roy. As. Soc* (1947), p. 153.

[11] G. H. Luce, 'Mons of the Pagan dynasty', *J. Burma Res. Soc.*, XXXVI (1953), 1.

[12] C. Duroiselle, *The Ananda temple at Pagan* (Mem. Arch. Survey India No. 56), Delhi, 1937.

[13] M. H. Bode, *Pali literature of Burma*, 1909.

[14] G. H. Luce, 'The greater temples of Pagan', *J. Burma Res. Soc.*, VIII (1918), 189; 'The smaller temples of Pagan', *Ibid.*, X (1920), 41.

U. Lu Pe Win, *Pictorial Guide to Pagan*, Calcutta, 1955.

PART IV. THE CRISIS OF THE THIRTEENTH CENTURY AND THE DECLINE OF INDIAN CONTROL

[1] Some passages in this chapter have already appeared in 'Une période critique dans l'Asie du Sud-Est, Le XIIIᵉ siècle', *Bull. Soc. Etudes indoch.*, XXXIII (Saigon, 1958), p. 387.

2 J. Y. Claeys, 'L'archéologie du Siam', *B.E.F.E.O.*, XXXI, 398.

3 R. S. le May, *Buddhist art in Siam*, Cambridge, 1938.

4 O. W. Wolters, 'Chen-li-fu', *J. Siam Soc.*, XLVIII, No. 2 (1960), p. 1.

5 J. Y. Claeys, *loc. cit.*, p. 413.

6 G. Cœdès, 'Les origines de la dynastie de Sukhodaya', *Journal Asiatique* (1920), No. 1, p. 233.

7 G. Cœdès, 'Documents sur l'histoire politique et religieuse du Laos occidental', *B.E.F.E.O.*, XXV, 1.

8 On the Mongols, cf. the works of R. Grousset, *L'empire mongol* (Historie du Monde, ed. E. Cavaignac, VIII, 3), Paris, 1941; *L'empire des steppes*, Paris, 1952.

9 E. Huber, 'La fin de la dynastie de Pagan', *B.E.F.E.O.*, IX, 633.

10 G. H. Luce, 'The early Syām in Burma's history', *J. Siam Soc.*, XLVI (1958), 123; XLVII (1959), 59.

11 G. Cœdès, 'Documents . . .', *loc. cit.*, p. 88.

12 On the history of Lan Na, cf. C. Notton, *Annales du Siam, III. Chronique de Xieng Mai*, Paris, 1932.

13 On Chou Ta-kuan see Part V, Ch. 4.
On the T'ais in the Malay Peninsula, cf. P. Pelliot, *B.E.F.E.O.*, IV, 242.

14 G. Cœdès, *Recueil des inscriptions du Siam*, Vol. I (Bangkok, 1924), p. 77, Inscr. No. 11.

15 G. Cœdès, 'L'année du Lièvre 1219 A.D.', *India Antiqua* (Mél. Vogel, Leiden, 1947), p. 83.

16 On this point, I have altered the conclusion drawn in the article referred to in the preceding note. Cf. pp 144 ff.

PART V: THE INDOCHINESE STATES AFTER THE THIRTEENTH CENTURY

1. SIAM OR THAILAND

1 *General works on the history and civilization of Siam :*
J. B. Mason and H. Carroll Parish, *Thailand bibliography* (Univ. of Florida Bibl. Series No. 4), Gainesville, 1958.

G. Cœdès, *Recueil des inscriptions du Siam*, 2 Vols., Bangkok, 1924, 1929; 'Une recension palie des Annales d'Ayuthya', *B.E.F.E.O.*, XIV, No. 3.

O. Frankfurter, 'Events in Ayuddhya', *J. Siam Soc.*, VI (1909), 1.

W. Credner, *Siam, das Land der Tai*, Stuttgart, 1935.

W. A. Graham, *Siam, a handbook of practical, commercial and political information*, 1924.

W. A. R. Wood, *A history of Siam*, 1926.

H. G. Quaritch Wales, *Ancient Siamese government and administration*, 1934.

K. Wells, *Thai Buddhism*, Bangkok, 1939.

L. Fournereau, *Le Siam ancien* (Ann. Musée Guimet, 27 and 31), 2 Vols., Paris, 1895, 1908.

J. Y. Claeys, 'L'archéologie du Siam', *B.E.F.E.O.*, XXXI, 361.

R. S. le May, *Buddhist art in Siam*, Cambridge, 1938.

K. S. Doehring, *Buddhistische Tempelanlagen in Siam*, Berlin, 1920.

P. Schweisguth, *Étude sur la littérature siamoise*, Paris, 1951.

[2] G. Cœdès, *Recueil des inscriptions du Siam*, No. 1.

[3] P. Pelliot, *B.E.F.E.O.*, IV, 242.

[4] R. S. le May, 'The ceramic wares of North-Central Siam', *Burlington Magazine*, LXIII (1933), pp. 156 and 203.

P'raya Nak'on P'ra Ram, 'Tai Pottery', *J. Siam Soc.*, XXIX (1937), 9.

[5] G. Cœdès, *Recueil . . .*, No. 11.

[6] *Ibid.*, No. 4.

[7] G. Cœdès, 'The Traibhumikatha, Buddhist Cosmology and Treaty on Ethics', *East and West*, VII (1957), 349.

[8] R. Lingat, 'Le culte du Bouddha d'émeraude', *J. Siam Soc.*, XXVII (1934), 9.

[9] G. Cœdès, 'L'art siamois de l'époque de Sukhodaya', *Arts Asiatiques*, I (1954), 281.

[10] According to the Chinese envoy Chou Ta-kuan; cf. *B.E.F.E.O.*, II, 177.

[11] *Arts Asiatiques* (1961), Chronique.

[12] E. W. Hutchinson, 'The Seven Spires', *J. Siam Soc.*, XXXIX (1951).

[13] A. B. Griswold, *Dated Buddha images of Northern Siam* (Artibus Asiae Suppl., XVI), Ascona, 1957.

[14] G. Cœdès, 'Notes sur les ouvrages pālis composés en pays thai', *B.E.F.E.O.*, XV, No. 3, p. 39.

[15] Nai Thien, 'Intercourse between Burma and Siam', *J. Siam Soc.*, V (1908, No. 1), p. 1; VIII (1912, No. 2), p. 1; XI (1914, No. 3), p. 1; XII (1918, No. 2), p. 1; XIII (1919, No. 1), p. 1.

[16] Sakae Miki, *The exploits of Okya Senaphimocq; Yamada Nagamasa the Japanese general in Siam in the seventeenth century*, Tokyo, 1931.

Koya Nakamura, 'Yamada Nagamasa, Japanese warrior in old Siam', *Cultural Nippon*, VII, 79.

[17] J. Anderson, *English intercourse with Siam in the seventeenth century*, 1890.

[18] L. Lanier, *Étude historique sur les relations de la France et du royaume de Siam de 1662 à 1703*, Versailles, 1883.

[19] E. W. Hutchinson, *Adventurers in Siam in the seventeenth century*, 1940.

[20] A. Launay, *Histoire de la mission de Siam*, Paris, 1920.

[21] G. Cœdès, 'Siamese documents of the seventeenth century', *J. Siam Soc.*, XIV (1921, No. 2), p. 7.

[22] K. Doehring, *Der Bot (Haupttempel) in den Siamesischen Tempelanlagen*, Berlin, 1944.

[23] R. Lingat, *L'influence indoue dans l'ancien droit siamois* (Et. de sociol. et d'ethnol. jurid., 25), Paris, 1937; 'Evolution of the conception of law in Burma and Siam', *J. Siam Soc.*, XXXVIII (1950), 9.

[24] R. Nicolas, 'Le Rāmāyana siamois, Analyse', *Extrême-Asie* (1928), No. 19, p. 297; No. 21, p. 409; No. 23, p. 565; No. 25, p. 21.

[25] Prince Dhani Nivat, 'The reconstruction of Rāma I of the Chakri dynasty', *J. Siam Soc.*, XLIII (1955), 21.

[26] R. Lingat, 'Note sur la révision des lois siamoises en 1805', *J. Siam Soc.*, XXIII (1929, No. 1), p. 19.

[27] E. Seidenfaden, *Guide to Bangkok*, 1927.

[28] R. Lingat, 'History of Wat Mahādhātu', *J. Siam Soc.*, XXIV (1930), 1.

[29] Abridged trans. into French by Mme J. Kasem Sibunruang, *'Khun Chang, Khun Phèn'. La femme, le héros et le vilain*, Paris, 1960.

[30] W. F. Vella, *Siam under Rāma III (1824–1851)*, New York, 1957.

[31] R. Lingat, 'La vie religieuse du roi Mongkut', *J. Siam Soc.*, XX (1926), 129; 'La double crise de l'Église bouddhique au Siam (1767-1851)', *Cahiers d'histoire mondiale*, IV (1958), No. 2.

[32] Author of a *Description du royaume Thai ou Siam*, 2 vols. (Paris, 1854), which is still useful.

[33] G. Cœdès, 'English correspondence of King Mongkut', *J. Siam Soc.*, XXI (1927), pp. 3, 127; XXII (1928), p. 1.

[34] Author of *The Kingdom and people of Siam, with a narrative of the mission to that country in 1855*, 2 Vols., 1857.

[35] H. Cordier, *La politique coloniale de la France au début du second empire (Indochine 1852–1858)*, Leiden, 1911 (extr. from *T'oung Pao*, X–XII).

2. LAOS

[1] *General works on the history and civilization of Laos:*

Mission Pavie, Études diverses, 2. *Recherches sur l'histoire du Cambodge, du Laos et du Siam*, Paris, 1898.

Annales du Laos, Hanoi, 1926.

L. de Reinach, *Le Laos* (2nd ed.), Paris, 1911.

H. Deydier, *Introduction à la connaissance du Laos*, Paris, 1952.

P. Le Boulanger, *Histoire du Laos français*, Paris, 1931.

H. Parmentier, *L'art du Laos* (Publ. E.F.E.O., XXXV), Paris, 1954.

Mission Pavie, Études diverses, 1. *Recherches sur la littérature du Cambodge, du Laos et du Siam*, Paris, 1898.

L. Finot, 'Recherches sur la littérature laotienne', *B.E.F.E.O.*, XVII, No. 5.

² *B.E.F.E.O.*, XXXIV, 771.

³ F. Garnier, 'Voyage lointain aux royaumes de Cambodge et Laouwen par les Néerlandais et ce qui s'y est passé jusqu'en 1644', *Bull. Soc. Géogr.* (Paris, 1871), p. 249.

⁴ G. F. de Marini, 'Relation nouvelle et curieuse du royaume de Laos', *Rev. indochin.* (1910), pp. 152, 257, 358.

⁵ *Voyage d'exploration en Indochine effectué pendant les années 1866–1867 et 1868 par une commission française* . . . , Paris, 1873.

⁶ A. Pavie, *A la conquête des cœurs*, Paris, 1921.

⁷ J. Brengues, 'Une version laotienne du Pañcatantra', *Journal Asiatique* (1908), p. 357.

3. BURMA

¹ *The Kalyāni inscriptions erected by King Dhammaceti at Pegu in 1476* A.D. . . . , Text and translation, Rangoon, 1892.

² Than Tun, 'History of Burma, A.D. 1300–1400', *J. Burma Res. Soc.*, XLII (1959, No. 2), p. 119.

³ Tin Hla Thaw, 'History of Burma, A.D. 1400–1500', *Ibid.*, p. 135.

⁴ D. G. E. Hall, *Early English intercourse with Burma (1587–1743)*, 1928.

⁵ W. F. B. Laurie, *Our Burmese wars and relations with Burma, being an account of military and political operations, 1824–1825–1826 and 1852–1853*, 1885.

⁶ H. Yule, *A narrative of the mission sent by Governor-General of India to the Court of Ava in 1855, with notices of the country, government, and people*, 1858.

⁷ V. C. S. O'Connor, *Mandalay and other cities of the past in Burma*, 1907.

⁸ C. Duroiselle, *Guide to the Mandalay Palace*, Rangoon, 1925.

⁹ Hla Pe, *Letteratura birmana* (Le Civiltà dell'Oriente: Letteratura, Rome, 1957), p. 791.
Maung Htin Aung, *Burmese drama. A study with translations of Burmese plays*, Calcutta, 1957.

4. CAMBODIA

¹ Trans. by P. Pelliot (into French) in *B.E.F.E.O.*, II, 123. A revised version, followed by an uncompleted commentary, is included in *Œuvres posthumes de P. Pelliot*, Vol. III (Paris, 1951).

² Barth and Bergaigne, *Inscriptions sanscrites* . . . (see note 1 to Part III, Ch. 2), p. 560, No. 65.

³ *B.E.F.E.O.*, XXXVI, 14.

4 G. Cœdès, 'Essai de classification des documents historiques cambodgiens', *B.E.F.E.O.*, XVIII, No. 9, p. 15. (This article contains a list of the various versions of the chronicle, with references to the books that have made use of it.)

5 L. P. Briggs, 'Siamese attacks on Angkor before 1430', *Far Eastern Quarterly*, VIII (1948), 3.

6 G. Cœdès, 'La fondation de Phnom Penh au XVe siècle d'après la chronique cambodgienne', *B.E.F.E.O.*, XIII, No. 6.

7 B. P. Groslier, *Angkor et le Cambodge au XVIe siècle d'après les sources portugaises et espagnoles*, Paris, 1958.

8 E. Aymonier, *Le Cambodge*, Vol. III, p. 313.

9 A. Aymonier, *Textes khmers*, Saigon, 1878.

A. Pavie, *Contes du Cambodge*, Paris, 1921.

F. Martini and S. Nernard, *Contes populaires inédits du Cambodge*, Paris, 1946.

10 A. Tricon and C. Bellan, *Chansons cambodgiennes*, Saigon, 1921.

5. VIET-NAM

1 H. Cordier, *Les voyages en Asie au XIVe siècle du bienheureux frère Odoric de Pordenone*, Paris, 1891.

2 L. Cadière, 'Le mur de Dông-hoi, étude sur l'établissement des Nguyên en Cochinchine', *B.E.F.E.O.*, VI, 87.

3 C. B. Maybon, *Histoire moderne du pays d'Annam (1592–1820), étude sur les premiers rapports des Européens et des Annamites et sur l'établissement de la dynastie*, Paris, 1920.

4 P. Boudet, 'La conquête de la Cochinchine par les Nguyên et le rôle des émigrés chinois', *B.E.F.E.O.*, XLII, 115. Phung van Dan, 'La formation territoriale du Viet Nam', *Revue du Sud-Est asiatique* (Inst. de sociologie, Université libre de Bruxelles), 1963, 4, p. 247; 1964, 2, p. 127.

5 U'ng-Qua, 'Un texte viêtnamien du XVe siècle: le *Binh Ngô dai-cao*', *B.E.F.E.O.*, XLVI, 279.

6 E. Gaspardone, 'Un Chinois des Mers du Sud. Le fondateur de Hà-tiên', *Journal Asiatique*, CCXL (1952), 363.

7 G. Taboulet, *La geste française en Indochine*, Vol. I (Paris, 1955).

8 G. Cordier, *Littérature annamite*, Hanoi, 1914.

G. Dufresne, 'Littérature annamite', in *Indochine*, ed. S. Lévi, Vol. I, p. 157.

Pham-Quynh, 'Aperçu sur la littérature annamite', in *L'Indochine française*, (Hanoi, 1938), p. 89.

G. Meillon, 'Littérature vietnamienne', in *Encyclopédie des littératures étrangères*, Paris, 1960.

⁹ *Kim-Vân-Kiêu*, trans. into French by Nguyên-van-Vinh, 2 Vols. Hanoi, 1942, 1943.

¹⁰ *Luc-Vân-Tiên*, trans. into French by Duong-quang-Ham, Hanoi, 1944.

¹¹ P. Midan, *L'Union merveilleuse de Kim et de Thach*, Saigon, 1934.

CONCLUSION

¹ L. Bezacier, *L'art viêtnamien*, p. 21.

² R. Lingat, *Les régimes matrimoniaux du Sud-Est de l'Asie* (Publ. E.F.E.O., XXXIV), Vol. I, p. 12.

³ G. Cœdès, 'L'osmose indienne en Indochine et en Indonésie', *Cahiers d'histoire mondiale*, I, 4 (April 1954), p. 827.

R. le May, *The culture of South-East India : The heritage of India*, 1954 (2nd ed. 1956).

⁴⁻⁵ P. Stern, 'Le temple-montagne khmèr, le culte du linga et le Devarāja' *B.E.F.E.O.*, XXXIV, 611.

⁶ A. Leclère, *Cambodge, Fêtes civiles et religieuses*, Paris, 1917.

H. G. Quaritch Wales, *Siamese state ceremonies; their history and function*, 1931.

⁷ Y. Bongert, 'Note sur l'esclavage en droit khmer', in *Études d'histoire du droit privé offertes à Pierre Petot*, Paris, 1959.

⁸ R. Lingat, *loc. cit.*, p. 112.

⁹ *Ibid.*

¹⁰ R. Lingat, 'L'influence juridique de l'Inde au Champa et au Cambodge', *Journal Asiatique*, CCXXXVII (1949), 286.

¹¹ P. Mus, 'Cultes indiens et indigènes au Champa', *B.E.F.E.O.*, XXXIII, 393.

¹² G. Cœdès, 'Note sur l'apothéose au Cambodge', *Bull. Comm. arch. Indoch.* (1911), p. 38; *Pour mieux comprendre Angkor* (Paris, 1947), Ch. 3, p. 44. (English translation: *Angkor, an introduction*, Hong-kong, 1963, p. 22.)

¹³ G. Cœdès, *B.E.F.E.O.*, XXIV, 347.

¹⁴ F. G. Faraut, *Astronomie cambodgienne*, Phnom Penh. 1910.

¹⁵ Tiao Phetsarat, 'Le calendrier laotien', *Bull. Amis du Laos*, IV (1940), 107.

¹⁶ G. Cœdès. 'L'origine du cycle des douze animaux au Cambodge', *T'oung Pao*, XXXI (1935), 316.

Index

Index

Buddhism (*continued*)
yana, 61, 195; Mahavihara (Sinhalese reformed), vi, 115, 121, 132, 133, 140, 142, 149, 161, 169, 173, 182, 190, 202, 220, 224, 225–6, 229; Mahayana, 79, 106, 107, 113, 132, 133, 224; Mulasarvastivada, 110; Tantrist, 113, 224; Theravada, 70, 110, 113, 114, 224, 225; *see also under various countries*
Buddhist canon, discovery of fragments of the, 68, 69
Bui Quang Nghia (Vietnamese dramatist), 216
burial customs, 61, 63, 66, 93; *see also* funerary rites
burials, 15, 17, 20
Burma:
prehistoric, 11, 15
kingdom of Pagan, 73, 74, 111, 112–17, 121, 125, 142, 190, 191; extent of, 113–14; fall of, 129, 130, 131, 181
Mongol invasion, 129
partition, 130, 131, 181
Lower Burma, 31, 58, 111, 113; T'ai rule in Martaban, 181–2; kingdom of Pegu, 182; Tabinshweti crowned king of, 183; capital removed from, 185; Mon rule over, 186; *see also* Mon, Ramannadesa
Upper Burma, 181, 182; kingdom of Ava, 134, 153, 156, 181, 182, 183, 184; kingdom of Toungoo, 182–3; Tabinshweti crowned king of, 183; Mon occupation of, 186; *see also* Pyu, Shan States, Shrikshetra
unification, 114, 183–4, 186; difficulty of unifying, 181
Chinese invasions, 6, 165, 182, 186, 187
wars: with Siam, 152, 153–6, 157, 161–2, 165, 166, 167, 176, 183 186–7, 187, 188; with Laos, 173, 175, 177; Anglo-Burmese, 188–9, 189
conquest of Arakan, 183, 184, 187–8; and invasion of Assam, 188
British annexation of, 168, 189
Buddhism in, 70, 110–11, 112, 113, 114, 115, 121–2
Hinduism in, 70, 112, 113
other refs., 6, 17, 68, 138; *see also* architecture, law codes
Burmese: chronicles, 75, 112, 114; language, 27, 28; people, 73, 138, 181;

see also civilization, inscriptions, literature, sculpture
Burney, Captain, 168

Ca-mau (Viet-nam), 8, 213
calendar, 140, 227
Cambodia (*see also* Chen-la, Kambuja): prehistoric, 11, 15, 16
as successor state to Fu-nan, 62, 88, 90, 91
Khmer empire: (i) pre-Angkor period, 89–95; customs, 92–93; extent of territory, 90, 91, 91–92; partitioned, 92, 221; relations with Java, 95–97; (ii) the Angkor kingdom, 96–109, 122; extent of territory, 97, 100, 101, 107–8, 122; as vassal of China, 101; internal revolts, 102; political organization, 103–4; social organization, 106; and the Mongols, 124, 128; decline, 124–5, 128, 131, 133, 193–6; customs, 193–5; Sukhodaya a contrast to, 133, 144, 145–6; Ayudhya as heir to, 146–7; relations with Champa, 67, 80, 85, 86, 89, 90, 91, 99, 100, 101, 107, 121, 124; with Viet-nam, 85, 86, 100, 101; with Burma, 113–14; war with Siam, 149; fall of Angkor, 150
later period, 138, 196–203; wars with Siam, 149, 153, 155, 157, 160, 165, 167, 196–8; under Siamese suzerainty, 158; under Siamese protection, 199–200; loss of territory to s. Viet-nam, 198, 199, 199–200, 210, 213; French aid sought, 200; becomes a French protectorate, 169, 201
Buddhism in, 94, 98, 100, 104, 106, 108–9, 122, 201, 202
Hinduism in, 94, 98, 101, 104, 106, 108, 122, 195
see also administrative system, architecture
Cambodian: chronicles, 196; language 27, 202; *see also* cultural influence, inscriptions, Khmer, literature, sculpture
Campbell, Sir Archibald, 188
Cansu, *see* Jayasuru
Canton, 6, 40
Cao Bien, *see* Kao P'ien
Cao Xuan Duc (Vietnamese historian), 215

Index

Celebes, 23

Ceylon, vi, 12, 114, 125, 149, 155, 161, 182, 225; relations with Burma, 114–15; with Siam, 140, 161; *see also* cultural influence (Sinhalese)

Ch'aimongk'on, *see* Vat Jayamangala

Chainat, *see* Jayanada

Ch'airach'a, *see* Jayaraja

Ch'aivath'anaram, *see* Vat Jayavadhanarama

Chaiya, *see* Jaiya

Chakri, P'raya (Rama I, q.v.), 165, 176, 177

Chakri or Bangkok dynasty, 165 ff.

Cham: language, 27, 28, 30, 65; people, 7, 29, 31, 32–33; *see also* civilization, cultural influence, inscriptions, sculpture

Chambang (Laotian poem), 180

Champa (*see also* Chan-ch'eng, Huan-wang, Lin-i): 53, 63–68, 77–79, 80–81, 81, 82, 83–84, 84–85, 85–86, 107, 121, 123–4, 128–9, 204–5, 210; Indianization of, 64 ff.; attempts to expand northwards, 47, 64; conflict with Viet-nam, 66, 77, 79, 81, 82, 83, 84–85, 121, 123–4, 128–9, 204–5, 208; occupied by Khmers, 64, 101, 107 (*see also* under *Cambodia*); invaded by Mongols 127–8; relations with China, 204, 207; decline, 82, 133, 138; Buddhism in, 67, 79; Hinduism in, 67, 70, 90, 221–2, 225; *see also* architecture

Champasak (present Bassac, Laos), 89

Chan-ch'eng (a Chinese name for Champa), 79

Chandakumara (ruler of Luang Prabang) 177

Chandan (title of a ruler of Fu-nan), 59

Chandapuri (Chanthaburi, Thailand), 147, 149, 164, 196

Chang Po-i (governor of Chiao-chih), 78

Chant'akuman, *see* Chandakumara

Chanthaburi, *see* Chandapuri

Chao dynasty (Nan-yüeh), 42

Chao Fa Ch'ai (Siamese usurper), 158

Chao Fa Rua, *see* Wareru

Chao Ju-kua, 124

chao ku (Buddhist monks), 194, 226

Chao T'o (king of Nan-yüeh), 40–41, 42, 46

Chapata (Mon monk), 115, 225

Charner, Admiral, 201, 215

Chasseloup-Laubat, Marquis de, 214

Chbap Kram, — Pros, — Srei (Cambodian poems), 202

Che A-nan (ruler of Champa), 204

Che Bong Nga (king of Champa), 204, 205

Che Chi (Jaya Simhavarman IV of Champa), 129

Che Man (Jaya Simhavarman III of Champa), 129

Che Nang (puppet ruler of Champa under Dai Viet), 129, 204

chedi, see chetiya

Chedi Luang, *see* Mahachetiya

Chei Chettha, *see* Jayajettha

Ch'en dynasty (China), 46

Chen-la (Chinese name for Cambodia), 88, 92, 137

Chen-li-fu (a dependency of Cambodia), 124

chen-t'an (Chinese term for a Cambodian rite of deflowering of girls), 194

Cheng Ni (Vietnamese rebel leader), 45

Cheng Tse (queen of Vietnamese rebels), 45

chetiya (a form of stupa), 163, 179

Ch'ettharat, *see* Jettharaja

Ch'etup'on, *see* Jetavana

Chi-hoa, battle of, 215

Chiang Mai (Thailand; capital of Lan Na, q.v.), 130, 140, 148, 149, 150, 151, 152, 153, 155, 157, 158, 167, 174, 180, 187

Chiang Rai (Thailand), 126, 130, 148

Chiang Saen (Thailand), 126, 140, 146, 149, 167

Chiao (Viet-nam as a Chinese province), 43

Chiao-chih commandery, 41, 42, 43, 45, 46, 63, 66, 95

Ch'in dynasty (China), 39–40

Ch'in Shih-huang-ti, x, 39, 40

Chin-lin or 'Golden Frontier', 58

China, 6, 12, 13, 14, 15, 17, 23, 24, 39, 51, 58, 59, 95, 101, 112, 126, 139–40, 169, 173, 189, 227; French campaign against, 215; *see also* civilization, cultural influence, embassies, source material, *and under various countries*

Chindwin river, 5, 112

Chinese language, 28, 29; use of in Viet-nam, 43, 46, 87, 206, 211; *see also* literature (Sino-Vietnamese)

Index

Mahagiri, Min (a Burmese god), 112, 142

Mahajati, Siamese version of the, 151

Mahanaga (Siamese writer), 161

Mahaparamasaugata (posthumous title of Jayavarman VII), 108

Maharajaguru (Siamese writer), 159, 160

Mahath'ammarach'a, *see* Mahadhammaraja

Mahath'at, *see* Vat Mahadhatu

Mahavamsa, Siamese translation of the, 166

Mahazedi, *see* Mahachetiya

Mahendraparvata, 96, 221

Mahendravarman (title of Chitrasena), 90, 91

Maheshvara (Shiva), 61

Mahin, *see* Mahindra

Mahindra (king of Ayudhya), 153, 154, 184

Mai Thuc Loan (rebel against Chinese rule), 78

Makuta (Mon king), 113, 114, 116

Malacca, v, vii, 147, 152

Malai, P'ra (Buddhist monk), 180; *see also Maleyya*

Malay Peninsula, v, 5, 6, 7, 21, 24, 27, 52, 53, 58, 59, 88, 95, 101, 107, 131, 147, 166, 167, 187

Malayo-Polynesian languages, 28

Malays, 161, 197, 198

Maleyya (Siamese poem), 161

Mandalay (a Burmese capital), 187, 189, 191, 220

mandapa (a form of temple), 163, 164

mandirapala, see palace guards

Mangalachetiya temple (Pagan), 117

Mangrai (founder of Chiang Mai), 130, 140, 148

Manilla, 197

Manipur, State of (Assam), 186

Mat'at'urat (ruler of Luang Prabang), 177

Manuha temple (Pagan), 114, 116

Marajivika (Buddhist monk), 47

marriages, mixed, 52, 53, 54, 57

Martaban (Burma), 130, 153, 155, 157, 158, 181, 183, 187, 188

Maspero, Henri, 47

matriarchal system, 33

Maurice of Nassau, Prince, 156

Mebon temple, the Eastern (Khmer), 99, 105

megalithic cultures, 19–21, 24

Mekong river valley, 2, 5, 6, 7, 8, 31, 33, 63, 89, 132; French mission for the exploration of the, 177; middle valley, 27, 89, 90, 92; lower valley, 27, 57 ff.; upper valley, 172 ff.; Mekong delta, 8, 27, 31, 53, 60, 62, 73, 92, 198, 215

Melanesia, 23; art of, 18

Melanesians, 13, 14, 15, 23, 25; incursions of, 78

Menam (Mae Nam) river valley, 2, 5, 6, 7, 31, 33, 129, 131, 132; lower valley, 27, 53, 68, 69 ff., 73, 107, 140, 146 ff.; upper valley, 73, 113, 125, 130, 139 ff.

Mera (nymph married to ancestor of Khmer kings), 89

merchants, European, 137, 156, 162; *see also* Arab, Persian

Mergui (Burma), 114, 115, 152, 162, 188

migrations, 10, 22–26, 68

Mimalaungkyaung temple (Pagan), 117

Mindon (Burmese king), 189

Ming dynasty (China), 186, 196, 204, 207, 218; tombs of the, 212

Mingalazedi, *see* Mangalachetiya

Minh Vuong (Nguyen dynasty), 213

Minh-mang (emperor of re-unified Vietnam), 214

Minkyinyo (Burmese king), 183

Minredeippa (Burmese king), 185

missionaries, European, 137, 158, 159, 169, 197, 214, 215

Moluccas, 23

monasteries, 81, 98, 100, 110

Mon: language, 27, 28; people, 29, 31, 68, 69–70, 73, 100, 181, 183, 184, 185, 186, 187, 190, 191; *see also* civilization, cultural influence, Haripunjaya, inscriptions, Rammanadesa

Mon-Khmer languages, 25, 26, 28, 29, 30, 31, 33, 62; peoples, 41–42

mondrop (Siamese), *see* mandapa

Mongkut (Rama IV, q.v.), 168, 169, 201

Mongol conquests and invasions, vi, 73, 116, 124, 126, 127–9, 130, 133, 191, 193, 204

Mongoloids, 14, 21, 23, 24, 25, 31

Montigny, M. de (leader of French missions to Siam and Cambodia), 169, 200

Monywe Sayadaw (Burmese writer), 192

Mouhot, Henri, 177

Moulmein (Burma), 7, 152, 155, 183

259